for
Caroline
Robin and Jonathan and Philippa
who
sustain me
and
Roland and Ruth
who
enabled me to trust my earliest environment

in gratitude for the
friendship of patients
and the
patience of friends

STRUCTURING THE THERAPEUTIC PROCESS:
Compromise with Chaos—The Therapist's Response to the Individual and the Group

by

MURRAY COX

Consultant Psychotherapist, Broadmoor Hospital, Crowthorne, Berks.
Hon. Lecturer in Psychotherapy, The London Hospital Medical College
Hon. Consultant Psychotherapist, Inner London Probation and
After-Care Service. Formerly visiting psychotherapist, HM Prison
Pentonville and part-time lecturer in forensic psychiatry, The London
Hospital Medical College. Previously a general medical practitioner.
Member, Group-Analytic Society (London)

PERGAMON PRESS
OXFORD · NEW YORK · TORONTO
SYDNEY · PARIS · FRANKFURT

U.K.	Pergamon Press Ltd., Headington Hill Hall, Oxford 0X3 0BW, England
U.S.A.	Pergamon Press Inc., Maxwell House, Fairview Park, Elmsford, New York 10523, U.S.A.
CANADA	Pergamon of Canada Ltd., 75 The East Mall, Toronto, Ontario, Canada
AUSTRALIA	Pergamon Press (Aust.) Pty. Ltd., 19a Boundary Street, Rushcutters Bay, N.S.W. 2011, Australia
FRANCE	Pergamon Press SARL, 24 rue des Ecoles, 75240 Paris, Cedex 05, France
FEDERAL REPUBLIC OF GERMANY	Pergamon Press GmbH, 6242 Kronberg-Taunus, Pferdstrasse 1. Federal Republic of Germany

First Edition 1978

Library of Congress Cataloging in Publication Data

Cox, Murray
Structuring the therapeutic process

Bibliography: p.
Includes index
1. Psychotherapy.   2. Group psychotherapy.   I. Title
RC480.5.C64   616.8'914   77–4181

ISBN 0–08–020403–1 hardcover
ISBN 0–08–020402–3 flexicover

Printed in Great Britain by Butler & Tanner Ltd., Frome and London

Contents

Prologue

We had the experience but missed the meaning.

(from *The Dry Salvages*, T. S. Eliot, 1944)

The history of every individual, like the history of every community, is a history of receiving and being received.

(from *Medicine in Metamorphosis*, Martti Siirala, 1969)

We can't just die ... we've got to have history.   (Anon., 1976)

This remarkably enigmatic reflection came not from an academic philo-sopher. It came from a patient whose history was disturbed and dis-turbing, whose intelligence was not above average, and who would be described clinically as showing transient psychotic phases in which he was 'out of touch with reality'. Yet it raises ultimate and unavoidable issues. The medical student is always taught to 'take the history' and 'examine the patient'. The exclusion of treatable organic disease is always a clinical priority and is an assumed datum throughout this text. Never-theless, in this book, which is concerned with counselling and psycho-therapy, we meet many patients who may have no organic pathology but are overwhelmed by a sense of chaos or restricted by a circumscribed symptom. They call for the therapist to adopt the paradoxical stance of 'taking (i.e. accepting) the patient' and 'examining the history'. They demand that we examine their history and look at their life with them. Erikson (1959) says that 'we cannot lift a case history out of history'. This links two recurrent themes which permeate the text. The first is the significance of the exact details of the patient's history. Exactly what the patient says in his own words, in a particular setting and at a particular time, is infinitely more important than the reductionism of almost mono-syllabic notes ... 'tense' ... 'anxious' ... 'depressed', etc.; though such objective observations must also be noted. The second is the sense of history which acts as a backcloth to the patient's clinical history, i.e. the contextual setting in history of the case history.

'We can't just die … we've got to have history.' A paraphrase offered by a fellow-member of the group, where this disclosure was made, was 'He's saying that his life has got to amount to something.'

This book attempts to assist the therapist in his formidable task of furthering the possibilities for a patient's life 'to amount to something', more than hitherto. This complex undertaking will involve many areas of experience, ranging from symptom reduction to a greater enjoyment in giving, receiving, living and loving.

> I want to be myself in my own way … not a mirror image of someone else.
>
> (Anon., 1973)

> We're not just case-notes … we're people with lives and emotions.
>
> (Anon., 1974)

> … man's besetting virtue is curiosity, and his ultimate quest is to discover the truth about himself.
>
> (from *The Language of Music*, D. Cooke, 1959)

DISCLAIMER

The central paradox of psychotherapy is that it involves an asymmetrical relationship, in which the patient is gradually enabled to take the painful risk of exposing himself to monitored self-exploration. The therapist is seriously engaged in shared psychotherapeutic work, yet retains executive discretion to be used on his patient's behalf.

Frequent reference is made to the fact that the therapist must therefore 'be in touch with his feelings' or 'at ease with himself'. This is a counsel of perfection and he will never fully achieve this 'therapeutic presence'. It is the invitational edge of psychotherapeutic experience and he is bound to feel it is infinitely improvable. References to being 'at ease with self' therefore imply a goal to aim at, rather than the arrogant impossibility of having arrived.

One of the occupational hazards of writing about professional skills which involve a relationship with another person is that it attracts the comment 'This is defensive'. There is the implication that it detracts from the value of the person, if frames of reference and the content of disclosure are 'studied'. I am not disturbed by these strictures. Because an orientating concept, such as structuring the therapeutic process, enables the therapist to engage with his patient in therapeutic work, and risk the existential abandonment of encounter, within therapeutic space.

This book is about the intricate relationship between a conceptual frame of reference and the therapist's 'purposeful' abandonment within it.

Acknowledgements

The extent of my indebtedness calls for some attempt to structure the 'thinking process'.

So many patients, professors, partners, poets, prophets and numerous others have helped me in cultivating the emotional climate, and the theoretical orientation of the book, that a generic debt of gratitude must suffice. Nevertheless, there are certain specific debts which must be acknowledged. The first is to William Osler, whose advice to clinical students has never been bettered: 'Listen to the patient, he is telling you the diagnosis.' His phrase 'Listen to the patient' could be regarded as the 'signature tune' for *Compromise with Chaos*. The second is to my friend and colleague, Martti Siirala, of Helsinki, whose cryptic comments always make me think again! 'Is the past Freud's universal scapegoat?... Does the therapist have the delusion of having no delusions?'

It is difficult to localise the debt I owe the late Dr. Donald Winnicott. The reader will discern many places where there are 'outcroppings' of his ideas. Although I never met him, we corresponded and I always feel at home in the ambience of his writing and stimulated by its content. I suspect this may be because we each started in dynamic psychotherapy after clinical experience in the cut-and-thrust of general medicine. He worked in paediatrics before embarking upon psychoanalysis, and I worked in general practice prior to undertaking full-time psychotherapy.

Though names, clinical details and any other factors affording recognition of individual patients have been changed, the ubiquitous and timeless truth of their emotional disclosures remain. Wherever appropriate, permission has been sought and kindly granted. This book could only germinate where there was a therapeutic process to structure. To my patients, both individually and corporately, I am indebted for their readiness to share therapeutic space with me and thus to make me reflect upon the core concept of mutuality.

To those mentors and colleagues who have shared ideas and experience with me, thankfulness is the only possible attitude. Their views, especially when different from mine, have helped to crystallise my conceptualisation of the therapist's *Compromise with Chaos*, but any chaos in the presentation of the material is exclusively mine.

Acknowledgements to published sources are implicit in the detailed references found in the text and the bibliography, though in one instance a separate debt of gratitude must be made. I refer to the personal encouragement I have received from Miss Kathleen Raine and her generous permission to quote from her *Collected Poems* (published in 1956 by Hamish Hamilton, London; now in its eighth impression). I have taken up her kind offer on pages 66, 79, 176.

Diana Cookson, my secretary, who has achieved an almost impossible task of structuring a process which must have been anything but therapeutic, knows how genuine my thanks are. Considering the nature of the raw material, she has succeeded in bringing order out of chaos.

I am grateful to Dr. Jack Kahn, who kindly read the entire manuscript and made many helpful comments, and to Mrs. Peggy Ducker, senior publishing manager of Pergamon Press, for her courteous advice and patience with my procrastination.

Finally, I must thank my wife for her continuing compromise with my chaos ... although it is difficult to thank someone who is part of me!

London and Broadmoor, 1977

DILEMMA:

Every clinical consultation and every counselling/psychotherapeutic encounter is an implicit statement of a human predicament.* Symptoms are described and cognitive-affective disclosures are made in a setting of tacit 'predicamentness'. The most junior student, irrespective of his discipline (nursing, medical, social work, counsellor, etc.), finds himself inescapably engaged with those who are engaged with their predicament, from his first day on the ward (in the 'department' or the 'office'). His response will either intensify or diminish his patient's resilience in the face of that with which he has to come to terms, whether it be his environment, himself or both.

Remembering the important injunction 'Never forget to talk to the patient', a student may find himself as the recipient of such a disclosure as 'I'm blind because I see too much, so I study by a dark lamp'. Can a student, relatively early in his career, begin to learn how to turn the full-stop at the end of this disclosure into a comma; so that the patient, however 'disturbed' he may be, is able to continue? For example, the simple question 'Has it always been as dark as this?' might lead to a disclosure of darkness on a much wider scale '... only since Mum died ... everything went dark then, even the lamps'.

A second example is furnished by a psychotic patient who opened a letter with the phrase 'Yours faithfully'. Can a student, without prolonged experience and psychodynamic sophistication, be taught to 'read between the lines'? If so, it gradually becomes clear that the letter opens on the theme of faithfulness, because it is an attribute of such over-riding importance that the writer daren't risk leaving it until the capricious and uncertain 'end', which he may never reach. *Structuring the Therapeutic Process* is not primarily about psychotic patients, though they throw into sharp relief the need for structuring the therapeutic process which is an inextricable part of every psychotherapeutic encounter. The student will be taught that medication is important in 'treating' psychotics, though he will rapidly discover that the skills of serious listening and counselling have a vital impact upon his relationship with the patient, whatever drugs he may need.

---

*'Predicament' implies an unpleasant or dangerous 'state of being', but its root (*praedicare*) means to 'cry in public'. A clinical predicament carries both meanings.

My contention is that it is possible to begin to learn these basic counselling skills from the very earliest days of professional experience. There is a widespread demand from students of many disciplines for a chance to learn how to engage emotionally with the patient 'now'. Such students are not content to wait for the remote and unknown days 'after you have qualified, done basic psychiatric training, had a personal analysis, etc.'

Can these counselling and psychotherapeutic skills be taught as an intrinsic part of basic professional training? This is the dilemma.

The psychotic patient is mentioned at the outset, not because psychotherapy of the psychoses is a major theme in this book, but because the psychotic demands and, mercifully, helps to evoke, a particularly sensitive yet accurate use of self by the therapist. The psychotic represents the disorganised, almost-out-of-control, chaotic, potentially eruptive and possibly catastrophically destructive, though utterly idiosyncratic, part of each of us. The compromise with chaos which is evident with transparent intensity in the psychotic, may be less obvious in the concealed chaos and inner conflict of the neurotic. The therapist, himself, may recall moments when he was 'blind because he saw too much' and the compromise with chaos is sometimes almost tangible at certain phases in individual or group counselling/psychotherapy.

Structuring the Therapeutic Process offers a 'coping' orientation which may help the therapist to cope with the existential predicament of his patient. The therapist can find himself at an apparent *impasse*, when the predicament takes this acute form: 'What do we do, when there is nothing we can do?' However, there must be an implicit answer to such an unanswerable question, because the patient has entered therapeutic space, which is *something he can do*, even though it is to say 'There is nothing I can do'.

An equally pressing experience of trapped 'wayoutlessness' was voiced in a therapeutic group:

> The group un-buries things I thought I had cleverly concealed ... How do you cope with memories you cannot cope with?

Note to the Reader

If I had the courage of my convictions, I would place the following footnote on each page and have it invisibly 'printed' above the head of each patient:

1. Am I failing to discern what my patient is disclosing, because of my undue preoccupation with the 'there and then' of his past?
2. Am I failing to discern what my patient is disclosing, because of my undue preoccupation with the 'here and now' of his predicament?
3. Are any other treatment modalities indicated alongside, or in the place of, the current therapeutic approach?
4. Are there any treatable organic components underlying the patient's clinical presentation which are not receiving appropriate attention?

(These questions may help the therapist to monitor therapeutic policy, so that the ever-present possibility of making clinical errors is reduced to the minimum.)

Murray Cox

Synopsis

The key concept can be stated with brevity, though its elaboration and illustration necessitate an expansive approach. The fundamental tenet is that in all counselling and psychotherapeutic relationships the *counsellor's/therapist's* optimal use of himself, on behalf of his patient,* can be structured in terms of Time, Depth and Mutuality. This is irrespective of the complexity of the task and is equally applicable in an individual or a group setting. It is also independent of any particular theoretical approach.

> Chaos is in me ... I am in chaos.

Chaos may be a salient feature in the experience of the neurotic or psychotic patient or the behaviour of the psychopath; though no one is free from the risk that his experience and/or behaviour might, under stress, become chaotic. It may therefore be part of a patient's 'presentation'. It may also characterise transient phases of the therapist/patient relationship. The therapist, himself, cannot be immune from the experience. This book is about the dynamics underlying the therapist's complex, paradoxical task of structuring the therapeutic process so that, among other things, a *Compromise with Chaos* is reached.

Paradox permeates the literature on counselling and psychotherapy and may pervade the actual experience of life within a 'therapeutic alliance'. The student may be baffled and even deterred by such sentences as the following, which describe various facets of the therapist's task:

(1) He gradually discovers how to be himself in the presence of his patient/client.
(2) He learns what purposeful spontaneity means.

* Because my experience is primarily 'clinical', this introductory section uses the terms 'patient' and 'therapist', though the book has a wider application. See page 48 for a discussion of Dramatis Personae.

1

(3) He is part of the outer world of his patient at the outset of the therapeutic process, but finds that he soon becomes incorporated into the patient's inner world; where he stands vicariously for previous 'significant others' from the patient's past, in addition to remaining himself.

(4) He will be temporarily invested with many qualities which the patient has previously encountered in other people.

(5) *Training in psychotherapy should enable him to act executively on his patient's behalf*, whose inner world he is 'in', but not 'of'.

(6) His external–internal presence, as perceived by the patient, depends upon an involved-yet-detached relationship which facilitates a corrective emotional experience, so that faulty definitions of self and others can be redefined and blocks to emotional growth removed.

(7) He learns how rigorous clinical precision, which may necessitate painful incursion into the patient's inner world, can be transmuted and rendered acceptable when facilitated by empathy.

Another disclaimer must be made at the outset. This book is about those dynamic aspects of the therapeutic process which are ubiquitous in every therapeutic relationship, though they may play a major or a subsidiary part in meeting the current needs of the patient. I am aware that behavioural modification techniques, medication, environmental manipulation, surgery or physical treatment such as ECT may be indicated.

Whenever the therapist's standpoint for gaining a global appraisal of his patient, and his predicament, deviates from that of a poised eclecticism, he may run the risk of ignoring what should not be ignored. To ignore organic pathology is as serious an omission as to ignore psychopathology. Each impinges upon the other. Human experience and behaviour are always influenced, though in differing proportions, by organic factors, which may be congenital or acquired, and psychodynamic factors. Therefore, vigilant monitoring and constant reappraisal are mandatory, because the therapist must always be alert to the possibility of new factors coming into operation. Thus, a patient originally 'correctly' referred for group psychotherapy, on account of low self-esteem, or inability to tolerate her sexuality, may develop an intra-cranial tumour; whereas a patient with a demonstrable organic lesion may need psychotherapy because of concomitant anxiety. This may take the form of fearful awareness that not only does the patient *have* a disease, but also fears that he has *become* a disease: 'I am like my teeth, rotten through and through; filled artificially.'

To be eclectic is not to deny precision. Indeed, it can endorse accuracy in assessment and treatment. Roth's (1969) cautionary comment, 'eclecticism is not a feeble compromise, but is inevitable', points to the fact that no single approach, no matter whether it is predominantly 'organic and constitutional' or predominantly 'psychodynamic', can be ubiquitously and at all times successful.

However, our attention is upon those aspects of dynamic psychotherapy and counselling which, among other therapeutic modalities, enable the patient to come to terms with himself as he is, as he was and as he may yet become. More specifically, our aim is to study the use the therapist makes of his own personality in his task of structuring the therapeutic process as he engages with the patient in therapeutic space.

The perennial problem confronting the author who tries to describe the ambience of the psychotherapeutic session is to convey the impression of rigorous discernment without implying detached, harsh aloofness; and an emotional climate which nourishes self-exploration, without conveying an impression of cosy, cushioned triviality.

This is the case when writing a book which attempts to discuss the compromise with chaos, which both the therapist and the patient experience. It is uppermost in my mind, as I try to avoid the pitfalls just outlined, knowing full well that I shall not succeed! In many ways this is a particularly personal book. The value of structuring the therapeutic process in terms of time, depth and mutuality, has evolved from, and proved itself in, my personal clinical experience.

The one part of the book which I can unashamedly recommend is the second part of Chapter 8, entitled 'The Patient Speaks'. This section has nothing to do with psychodynamic theory or any particular professional skill. It is at once a poignant and remarkably honest statement of the human predicament, by 'all sorts and conditions of men'.

One of the aims of this book is to try to clarify and demystify the therapist's executive action by considering ways in which he uses his own personality on his patient's behalf. It must be stressed that it presents *one way* of construing the work of the therapist. It is certainly *not the only way*, but it has been written because others have found the concepts useful. The psychotherapeutic process is regarded as one in which the patient is enabled to do for himself what he cannot do on his own. In the words of a patient: 'I wanted to come out with it ... but how to get started?' The therapist does not do it for him, but he cannot do it without the therapist. The theme underlying the sequence of chapters, and sustaining the argument, is that the therapist's prime task is so to structure time, depth and mutuality, within the context of therapeutic space, that the patient is enabled to make progressive emotional disclosures. Such disclosures occur in two clearly demarcated sequential phases.

The first has a classical Freudian *timbre* because it refers to the disclosure whereby the Unconscious becomes Conscious, which I term Conscious-withheld (i.e. not disclosed).* The second and, in my view, equally important, occurs as the Conscious-withheld becomes Conscious-disclosed. This further step is facilitated by participation in a therapeutic group in which sharing of experience leads to fuller personal disclosure which, in turn, can evolve into a self-authenticating corporate disclosure. Freudian theory which stresses the importance of gaining insight as the Unconscious becomes Conscious is axiomatic, but it stops short of grasping the richness of corporate life implicit in growth towards the Conscious-disclosed. Attention is given to the nature of disclosure and to the therapist's task of facilitating or delaying disclosure, which depends upon the ambient circumstances. Disclosure itself is rarely the end point of therapy, but it is always a hurdle to be negotiated. Thus the therapist seeks to evoke disclosure at an optimal time, and then to catalyse the individual or group response to the disclosed material.

This book deals with the nature of therapeutic space, the therapeutic process, various aspects of the complex relationship between therapist and patient, and the quality of disclosure itself which is contingent upon appropriate structuring.

There may appear to be an inherent conflict in the ideas presented, and I wish to clarify the position in order to avoid misunderstanding. The discussion ranges from considering the sophisticated psychodynamics of, say, intensive group psychotherapy, to a setting such as a psychiatric ward, in which junior nurses are in close and prolonged contact with their patients. It is certainly not my intention to identify the two quite

* Cox, 1976.

different roles of, say, the consultant psychotherapist and the junior nurse. They have complementary tasks. Both can be therapeutic, both can improve their skills, though they may have different goals and methods of reaching them. Nevertheless, I wish to underline the fact that, however different the work of the psychotherapist and the junior nurse may be, the key dimensions of time, depth and mutuality are the dimensions used in each setting, as the therapist/nurse responds in an appropriate manner to his patient, with whom he shares therapeutic space. *Whereas their work may differ, the dimensions in terms of which their work is construed are identical.* Thus the activity of *structuring the therapeutic process in terms of time, depth and mutuality has a universal relevance.* It is pertinent to the professional work of the psychoanalyst, the school counsellor, the GP, the probation officer and many others.

The executive aspects of structuring apply not only to the out-going, incisive intervention, but also to the deliberate 'holding back' or the intensification of a sustained silence which may take place in an individual or a group setting. The therapist's participation in therapeutic space and his use of time, depth and mutuality may mean that he is reinforcing creative stillness against the pressure conveyed in the question 'Why don't you do something? Don't just bloody well sit there.' In other words, the reading of the situation leads the therapist into certain channels of activity which may be active or passive, verbal or non-verbal. The appropriate modality is determined by the dynamic underlying the therapeutic process, which is always that of enabling the patient to do for himself what he cannot do on his own. Likewise, in a group setting the group is enabled to do for itself, what the group-as-a-whole has hitherto failed to do. But the therapist does not do it for the group. He fosters the autonomous, auto-therapeutic life of the group. This is in marked contrast to the invasive, directive, administrative activity which may be necessary for a general practitioner, as he engages with a patient within a more variegated and heavily contoured therapeutic space. Nevertheless, the GP can also structure his relationship in terms of time, depth and mutuality.

Structuring the Therapeutic Process: Compromise with Chaos is published simultaneously with its companion volume entitled *Coding the Therapeutic Process: Emblems of Encounter* (Cox, 1978). Each book is complete in itself, though in many ways they are complementary. *Coding the Therapeutic Process* is a practical manual for the counsellor whatever his level of experience. It indicates appropriate notational systems and symbolic concepts for the executive task of recording the elusive and capricious, ephemeral dynamics of the therapeutic situation, which so frequently contain transient flashes of disclosure. It also suggests notation for the 'still life' of the family tree, etc. *Structuring the Therapeutic Process* introduces the concept of a nuclear disclosure, which may occur in a split second. This may convey more about the patient's inner world and his way of construing the outer world than hours of other material in which it is embedded. The nuclear disclosure reaches the archaic, yet existential, core of the patient's inability to tolerate the intolerable parts of his experience. It is a concentrated statement about the patient, by the patient and, when reflected in the presence of the therapist, it is 'received' as a statement 'to' the patient.

Ultimately it is what the patient discloses to himself that counts, though the *via therapeutica* by which this goal is reached will vary. The method of reflection of client-centred therapy and the method of interpretation and the use of the transference relationship, of psychoanalytically orientated psychotherapy, may both use monitored introspection to lead the patient to disclose facts and feelings about himself, to himself, of which he was previously unaware. This implies that, in the long run, the therapist bows out because it is not what the therapist says to the patient, but what the patient has been enabled to say to himself which is self-authenticating. Similarly, in a group setting it is what the group-as-a-whole is able to tolerate of those facts and feelings which the group-as-a-whole had previously unconsciously denied, or deliberately avoided, which points to dynamic change and is of prognostic significance. Once again, it is what the group discloses to the group which is infinitely more important than anything the therapist may bring, except the ambience of disclosure facilitation and the quality of intervention appropriate to this end.

Coding the Therapeutic Process attempts to encourage the therapist to use several heuristic devices which enable him to improve the ability to make sequential records of the therapeutic process. It also seeks to stimulate ways of 'picking up' the numerous verbal and non-verbal networks of communication which occur during the affective flow of every therapeutic process.

Structuring the Therapeutic Process looks at the way in which the dimensions of time, depth and mutuality facilitate the therapist's appreciation of what is taking place, and therefore guide his responsive initiative.

Coding the Therapeutic Process is a handbook for the therapist who wishes to make records of what is taking place. The heuristic devices described also suggest concepts which have obvious application as teaching aids and research tools. This is exemplified when students, together with their supervisor, observe a group through a one-way screen. If they each use one of the visual display systems described (the Group Therapy Interaction Chronogram), they will discover that subsequent comparison may make them wonder if they have been looking at the same group! This immediately demonstrates selective perception and differential empathy, and adds fuel to the fire of the ensuing seminar.

Though they approach the problem from slightly different angles, each book attempts to provide guide-lines whereby the therapist's capacity to 'understand' his patient can be enhanced. The 'success' of an apposite response, to the patient's disclosure-within-a-predicament, depends upon discerning the significance of verbal and non-verbal cues. This is most sharply focused in the frequent clinical dilemma: 'Is this suicidal threat a cry for help or a statement of intent?' A swimmer 'waving' to those on shore may, in the words of Stevie Smith, be 'Not waving but drowning.'*

This short poem has caught the subtle framework transposition which occurs so often in psychotherapy (see Cosmic Distortion, page 198). What is initially thought to describe a particular incident wherein a drowning man is waving, the poet translocates to a lifelong state of affairs:

> I was much too far out all my life
> And not waving but drowning.*

Both books point to various ways of reaching the man who is 'not waving but drowning'. I hope they may also help to prevent unnecessary, heroic life-saving exploits for a man who is not drowning but waving!

---

* From *The Collected Poems of Stevie Smith* (1975) by kind permission of Allen Lane, London, and James MacGibbon (see also page 119).

CHAPTER 1

Orientation:
The Centre of Gravity

It is not that we are connoisseurs of chaos, but that we are surrounded by it....
(from *The Sense of an Ending*, Frank Kermode, 1966)

... and when I love thee not,
Chaos is come again.
(*Othello*, III. iii. 91)

Our concern is with the therapist's task of facilitating the patient's disclosure of inner world phenomena, which have hitherto remained undisclosed because of his inability to tolerate the intolerable parts of his own experience. The 'centre of gravity' describes the point of a dynamic system about which all components exactly balance each other, as well as implying its 'core of seriousness'. Both meanings are relevant to psychotherapy which impinges upon a dynamic system at its emotional centre of gravity, where the patient takes himself most seriously. The approach is unashamedly anecdotal and places the highest priority upon the 'core of seriousness' of the actual words spoken by the patient. The therapist attempts to facilitate disclosure without destroying his patient's equilibrium, either by over-intrusive incursion into the patient's inner world, or by trivialisation. This may be implicit in a facial expression indicating that it has all been said before, or reaching for a prescription pad before the patient has even given his history. It takes seriously not only what the patient says, but how he says it, where he says it, when he says it and in whose company he says it. It also takes seriously what he cannot say and what he is on the brink of saying.

To take what the patient says seriously, is to take the patient, himself, seriously; therefore genuineness is a *sine qua non* (Truax and Carkhuff,

9

1967) among the therapist's attributes. Nevertheless, if the patient is to be received as a whole person, rather than an 'utterer of symptoms', then to be 'taken seriously' implies that his laughter and humour is as much part of his presentation as his formal 'complaint'. It therefore follows that the therapist's appropriate response is not always that of sombre, solemnity; indeed, shared laughter may facilitate third-level disclosures (see pages 59, 164) much more rapidly than an emotionally neutral response. Once, however, the therapist has left the safety of emotional neutrality and is involved with the cognitive–affective re-encounter and reactivation of his patient's introjected past, then his use of himself must be subject to rigorous, on-going reappraisal. Each school of counselling and psychotherapy may use different terms to describe this self-monitoring process, but I suggest that the dimensions of time, depth and mutuality would be those in which the therapeutic process is structured. At each chapter heading I have free-associated in print, giving quotations which come to mind as I think of various aspects of the therapeutic process. It is quite likely that the quotations given under the heading 'Empathy' (page 137) may be of much more value to the reader than my fumbling efforts to use technical language, which attempts to describe experiences which are often almost indescribable: 'Created as a tool to help us find our way through the world of things, our language is notoriously poor when we try to analyse and categorise the inner world' (Gombrich, 1959). There is no doubt that each reader will have his own associative experiences and quotations on, say, the subject of empathy. The sole purpose of my thematic free-association is to stimulate the reader to do likewise! I am aware of the risk of appearing to quote for quotation's sake, but it is a calculated risk. I hope it will stimulate trainees, who may have relatively little clinical experience, to recall similar incidents they have met in fiction, history, drama, film or previous personal encounters. Once the reader has 'engaged' with an incident, whether from fact or fiction, in which he felt empathy was of importance then, I hope that the ensuing technical discussion will be more meaningful. Free-association is always a personal process, and it does not matter in the least if the reader's associative responses do not match mine, because they were only given to stimulate reflection. For example, the brief phrase from *King Lear*, 'Look with thine ears', cited under the heading 'Empathy', may remind the reader of a clinical incident in which the unaccustomed use of his senses gave him a clue, which conventional appraisal had ignored. (For example, the sound of a hand-shake or the smell of a perfume-laden silence, which belies what the patient had previously said about the significance of personal 'appearance'.)

Sometimes the patient presents with finely chiselled, clearly delineated symptoms. At other times he conveys a baffling sense of swirling, inchoate, undifferentiated affective surge. He uses many words to try to describe this sense of turbulence, but chaos often seems to get nearest the mark. The disclosures listed when The Patient Speaks (Chapter 8) show how often 'chaos' is invoked to describe experience.

The psychotherapist lives at the point of his patient's disclosure and has a persistent sense of being 'on the brink of something more', as though he is a surf-rider who always wonders if the next wave will carry him further still. He is poised at the unfolding invitational edge of experience which flows out of previous experience. The here-and-now and there-and-then are inextricably interdependent, and the therapist's task is to facilitate the patient's increasing monitored self-awareness, so that the sense of inner chaos changes and what was originally perceived as inexplicable and capricious, gradually becomes coherent and purposeful.

The centre of gravity, both in the sense of his patient's balanced endopsychic patterning and the core of seriousness of what he says, means that nothing the patient discloses, fails to disclose or is manifestly on the brink of disclosing, is unimportant. The breathless, lacrymose, staccato, truncated utterance is 'saying' something quite different from identical words spoken in an even flow of bland, nonchalant tranquillity:

Jim cried a bit when he realised he wouldn't see his mum again...that's all.

Even the last two words in this disclosure say volumes, one way or another. '...that's all' may be saying 'that's everything' or, *per contra*, 'that's almost nothing'. Part of Chapter 8, 'The Patient Speaks', is entirely devoted to the words of patients, in order to underline the vital fact that what the patient actually says is more important than what he is said to have said, and infinitely more so than what the clinician wishes he had said! The patient so often has an angular way of being himself, and not obliging the clinician by offering the history he 'ought' to have given, if he was to reassure the doctor that his diagnostic formulation was correct! It was during ten years involved in the life of one local community, as a GP, that my interest in emotional disclosure was initiated and intensified, because of the daily experience of living with dying. The rich language of 1662 describes such 'daily spectacles of mortality' so that we should 'see how frail and uncertain our own condition is'. The family doctor is involved with all kinds of rejoicing and the receipt of life, and all sorts of sorrow and the relinquishment of living. A substantial part of his professional energy and skill is in helping those who 'are to the margin come' negotiate dying which is, inevitably, that most personal act of a lifetime; together with enabling mourners to mourn. I suppose few analysts have spent a large proportion of their professional energy in receiving the free-association of the dying, as distinct from that of those whose energy, and physical health, enable them to visit the consulting room. The free-association of the living is frequently concerned with dying, whether in terms of their energy to destroy others, in fact or fantasy, or in the experience of loss when those with whom they were emotionally engaged left them. There is, however, an obvious and profound added dimension when the patient is free-associating, not about the fact or fantasy of the death of another, but about his imminent 'dyingness' which pervades therapeutic space.

I find it difficult to understand why this auto-biographical, professional fact has eluded me for so long. But I am sure that the experience of being present in families, and with solitary people, at the great moments of receiving and relinquishing the capacity for living, has coloured my interest in the way they reflect upon such matters of life and death. There *is* something diagnostic about the quality of utterance upon the lips of someone who knows he is dying. In my clinical experience, there is a similar certainty that something of profound importance is being said, when third-level disclosures (*vide infra*) are made, which is quite as distinctive. Pseudo-disclosures never have this quality. As I discuss elsewhere (see page 209), great novelists have the capacity to allow the reader to discern third-level disclosures with the intensity experienced in a personal encounter:

> I've been telling you what we said—repeating the phrases we pronounced—but what's the good? They were common everyday words—the familiar, vague sounds exchanged on every waking day of life. But what of that? They had behind them, to my mind, the terrific suggestiveness of words heard in dreams, of phrases spoken

in nightmares.... *I was anxious to deal with this shadow by myself alone* – and to this day I don't know why I was so jealous of sharing with any one the peculiar blackness of that experience... I had – for my sins, I suppose – to go through the ordeal of looking into it [another's 'soul'] myself. No eloquence could have been so withering to one's belief in mankind as his final burst of sincerity. *He struggled with himself, too* [*Heart of Darkness*, Conrad: italics added.]

The theme of death, either as an inevitable subjective experience or as the goal of aggressive activity in the experience of a 'victim', may seem to permeate this book. This is no illusion. Morbidity and fear of mortality, tacitly or explicitly, demand therapy which seeks to remove, diminish or, at least, change the attitude of the sufferer to the morbidity which disturbs him. When a patient who is not depressed, and who indeed exhibits no indication of mental illness, looks the therapist straight in the face and says 'My trouble is sorrow', the therapist knows that neither medication nor physical treatments are indicated as he faces this existential dilemma. The patient has come *because* of his sorrow. Any professional approach other than that of counselling or psycho-therapy is impotent. Sorrow may be a presentation of bereavement at the loss of a loved one, but it may also be evidence of an inner dynamic loss of vitality and a diminishment of emotional resources which stretches diagnostic boundaries if 'depression' is invoked. There may be no physio-logical concomitants of endogenous depression, and although reactive depression may readily describe a bereavement situation, the patient's reaction to the loss of an internal object again stretches diagnostic credibility, if 'reactive depression' covers a loss for which even the most perspicacious interviewer can find no evidence. There are remarkable similarities in the complex cognitive–affective relationship between the general practitioner and his dying patient, and the psychotherapist whose patient may be living through intense fantasies of dying or killing during the sequential phases through which the transference relationship moves. Offender-therapy* provides a unique clinical arena in which fact and fantasy merge, and this demands a particular amalgam of executive and affective finesse in the way in which the therapeutic process is

---

* There are numerous references to the 'offender-patient'. This term refers to offenders who have been referred for psychotherapy; either as a condition of probation, or within the custodial setting of a prison or a secure hospital, such as Broadmoor. The offence may take many forms, but it always involves *action*, e.g. 'larceny of milk bottles', 'grievous bodily harm' or 'manslaughter'.

structured. Nevertheless, there is probably no better setting in which the trainee therapist can learn how to 'use' and 'be' himself.

Throughout this book there are frequent references to death, either as fact or fantasy, and this is not out of keeping with the frequency with which it enters disclosures made by the patient in the presence of the therapist.* The experience of working in general practice and offender-therapy furnishes ample evidence that even if death is taboo elsewhere, therapeutic space ceases to be therapeutic if any topic, including death, is taboo. One of the certainties that therapeutic space is, in fact, therapeutic, is that the patient is as free to talk of death as his progressively diminishing defences allow him to be. Maybe as his unconscious becomes Conscious-withheld or as this, in turn, becomes Conscious-disclosed, the patient's third-level disclosures may temporarily centre around the wish to die or the wish to kill, without even a hint that 'there was no need to trouble himself with any such thoughts yet' (*King Henry V*, II. iii. 21). A further paradox pervading therapeutic space is that at the point of confluence where psychic determinism (even if 'prompted' by organic factors) and the perennial existential 'nowness', coalesce, the patient may experience hope, precisely because therapeutic space is the only environment in which it is safe and 'hopeful' to be hopeless. It is a setting in which living is endorsed, because it is safe to express deep feelings about dying or killing.

Probably the most difficult emotional disclosures to receive are those from patients where the 'level of awareness' is low because of an organic lesion, such as an intracranial tumour or a cerebral thrombosis, and whose dynamic defences are diminished so that 'deep' emotional disclosures are on the point of coming to the surface. Such situations call for the greatest skill in reflecting and 'interpreting' disclosures which may relate to sexuality, the fear of death and, for obvious reasons, they frequently occur as a 'death-bed' scene. The general practitioner will know that it is not uncommon for such a patient to disclose aspects of his emotional life which, hitherto, have been hidden. This is a particularly specialised field of psychotherapy, because not only is there the usual dynamic of the unconscious becoming conscious, but, superimposed, is

---

* Maybe as a 'longed-for release', an intolerable 'separation', a 'dreaded unknown ending', a 'fierce' suicidal escape or 'port after stormy sea'. Dying may be free-associated with killing, which is sometimes a form of 'extended suicide'.

the neurological 'complication' whereby precisely when the 'level of awareness' becomes lower, so the patient's defences may be less effective and emotional disclosures are facilitated. Death-bed 'conversions' are well documented, but the experienced general practitioner and the geriatrician, together with specialists in the care of the dying, will know that many other aspects of emotional life other than the 'confession of guilt' may 'come to the surface'.* Thus a tough, hard-headed 'man's man' may feel safe enough in his last hours to release his taboo on tenderness, so that love and gentleness become safely expressed. On the other hand, an over-effusive, disorganised person may 'tighten up' his perception of events and show a hitherto hidden capacity for executive decision. Therapeutic space can be as intense and circumscribed as the 'space' within the eye contact of the dying patient and his family and/or his physician. There is a penetrating immediacy and a 'let's-not-waste-time-on-other-things' quality in, what may be, a last therapeutic contact between the dying patient and his physician. In many ways, therapeutic space also has this valued significance. The cynic may say that it is an 'over-valued' idea. But if he says so, it is unlikely that his prime professional involvement is in psychotherapy.

What the doctor says to the patient, how he says it, where he says it, when he says it and in whose company he says it, is also our concern; as is what he cannot say and what he is on the brink of saying. Therapeutic space encloses the temporary emotional interlocking of two or more people who meet for a specific purpose, in an agreed setting, at an agreed time. Alongside any technical clinical procedures, ranging from chest auscultation in the GP's surgery, to a hospital appointment for an electroencephalogram, is the engagement, however transient, of one person as a prime focus of perception by another. This book looks critically at the use the therapist makes of his own personality as he engages with the patient in a therapeutic alliance. This may be brief and sporadic as an outcropping of a life-long relationship, as in general practice; or sustained and regular, though with a sense of working towards a conclusion, as in formal dynamic psychotherapy. 'Bedside manner', so frequently cynically dismissed as a suave veneer, is a *sine*

---

* Williams (1972) writes: 'Yet in face of the extremity of death, curious reversals will take place.' I had not read this passage when I wrote the following sentence, but there are striking congruities.

qua non of effective medical practice. Many experienced GPs have probably developed a greater facility for rapidly entering the patient's inner world than colleagues from any other branch of the profession, including psychotherapists.

Since this book is primarily about the use the therapist makes of his own personality as he shares therapeutic space by *being with* his patients, irrespective of the nature of any technical procedure he may *do to* his patients, its relevance is not restricted to medical practice. Counselling and psychotherapeutic techniques may be used in settings as seemingly disconnected as the prison cell; the ante-natal ward; the geriatric bedside; or in the office of the chaplain, the school, student or marriage guidance counsellor, the probation officer, the ward sister, the health visitor; as well as the GP's surgery; the psychiatric department or the psychoanalyst's consulting room. In each setting the task of structuring the therapeutic process cannot be overestimated. Chaos can be intensified if structuring is inappropriate. Chaos may be floridly presented by the behaviour of a disturbed patient; it may be latent within the carefully ordered world of the obsessional; it may be a manifestation of lack of communication between the therapist and his patient; but, *a fortiori*, it may be part of the inner world of the therapist himself. In *Heart of Darkness*, Conrad described 'the triumphant darkness from which I could not have defended her—from which I could not even defend myself'. 'This thing of darkness I acknowledge mine' (*The Tempest*, V. i. 275) is echoed by all therapists as they recognise part of their own inner chaos in the inner world of their patients. When the therapist is working with the rapist or the murderer,* he is confronted by inescapably stark facts of life and death. One of these facts is the question: 'Is this patient "carrying", my murderousness?' If he is not felt to be partially personally 'at risk', the therapist will be prevented from entering their inner world and his patients will see him as a penetrating scientific probe, interested only in gaining knowledge about them. If this happens, 'knowledge about' is all he will get! Disclosure becomes sealed, insight restricted and frequently symptoms exacerbated, whenever patients sense that

---

* It becomes unwieldy if 'a man charged with homicide and found guilty of manslaughter on the grounds of diminished responsibility' is added as a description of an offender-patient who committed a fatal assault. I shall therefore use the word 'murderer', though it may be technically incorrect.

therapy is really research *manqué*. We shall consider further the different epistemological* worlds of discourse implicit in the view of knowledge as an objective, 'knowing about' category, and that of knowledge as the experience of 'knowing' a person. Both are necessary. Our present concern is with that amalgam of 'knowing about' and 'knowing', which enables the therapist to facilitate his patient's compromise with chaos, so that he discloses hidden parts of himself in the presence of his therapist, i.e. *the patient discloses himself to himself*. The realisation that in a facilitating environment it is safe to tolerate the intolerable and disclose the presumed undisclosable, has as great a therapeutic effect for the phobic housewife as it does for the homicidal psychopath. The title of Winnicott's (1965) seminal book has captured both essential elements which underly psychotherapy: *The Maturational Processes and the Facilitating Environment.*

The theme of structuring the therapeutic process will always be central, though I may illustrate various aspects of this professional activity by several oblique and tangential comments. Thus we may suddenly switch from a discussion of an individual to a group setting; from a theoretical premise to a practical illustration; from words spoken in 1976 by an East End bricklayer to a quotation from Macbeth; from describing a shared group dream to a technical point of judging the texture of therapeutic intervention or from a classification of disclosures to the psychopathology of rape. This apparently random flow is not as capricious and abandoned as appears at first sight. It is a deliberate strategy and underlines the fact that this is not a systematic basic textbook, but one which should be read alongside established texts. It presumes that the reader will have a basic orientation in terms of dynamic psychotherapy and counselling. I hope some of the perspectives offered will enable those counsellors, family doctors, social workers and others, who have not had the opportunity to join in formally arranged teaching courses, to learn how better to use themselves as they share therapeutic space with their patients. This may take place individually or in a group setting, in a 'total' institution or in the wider community.

Imagine a situation in which a tame bird, belonging to a group member, flew from its cage and landed on my head during a group session! I doubt if history will repeat itself with such precision, but my aim is not to

---

* *Epistemology:* 'theory of the method or grounds of knowledge'.

indicate what I did with a starling on my head during a group, but rather to ask the reader how he might respond in such a setting, demanding decisions in the existential immediacy of the present moment. What I actually did five years ago with a different group, in a different setting, with a different bird, is irrelevant; but the fact that the quality of response then might have led to ridicule, trivialisation and stalemate or, *per contra*, to corporate solidarity and a sense of purpose, indicates the significance of 'reading' the underlying dynamics. This raises many questions about the nature of psychotherapy, the timing and texture of the therapist's interventions, the place of humour in therapy, etc. It also illustrates the significance of a global appraisal of a total setting, and the need for a simultaneous detailed 'close-up' of group dynamics, together with awareness of the individual's inner and outer world phenomena. The therapist's response appropriate to phobic housewives and a canary might seem less so with aggressive psychopaths and a golden eagle!

The theoretical orientation underpinning this theme and variations is Janusian. It stresses that both psychic determinism and an existential approach are essential if important disclosures are not to be missed. In my experience, the therapist ignores the twin foci of psychic determinism and existential 'nowness' at his professional peril and his patient's loss. Inevitably the there-and-then of early experience, the womb, the breast, the whole body, the primary family and the secondary groups of enlarging experience, etc., influence experience of the here-and-now, in which therapeutic space is shared by patient and therapist. One of the daunting, yet invigorating, tasks of working with the offender-patient is that it is stridently and undeniably evident that at one point in his life the patient, say an arsonist, demonstrates that an early experience, 'there-and-then', has been followed by a later 'incident'; when his inner world of fantasy erupted in a catastrophic manner, such as setting fire to a school. He brings these and all the other 'there-and-thens' to the 'here-and-now' of the therapeutic session. This is of course equally applicable to the current presentation of every patient as he enters the 'nowness' of therapeutic space. In whatever technical language psychic determinism is couched (a word redolent with psychoanalytic overtones), it is an essential perspective if endopsychic patterning is to be understood. But, in my view, the existential 'nowness' of the therapeutic encounter is equally mandatory. This experience is brought home when the psychotic patient *appears* to be out of touch with reality—at least reality as we perceive it. It is easy to make a formal nosological assessment, or to describe a particular type of thought disorder. But it is more difficult to understand what such a patient is saying about himself, and most difficult of all, though undoubtedly most important, to discern what the patient means to himself.

Sifneos (1965), in his remarkable book *Ascent from Chaos*, gives the following description of his regressed psychotic patient:

> Despite his being sedated, he was extremely tense and restless. At times he ran round and round his room; then he would stop and stare at the floor, saying, 'The black rocks! It is black in there—it is chaos in there—it is nothing.' He kept repeating the words 'chaos,' 'black,' 'nothing,' as if this were the only way to describe the threat that caused his terror.

Nothing convinces the cynical, reluctant offender-patient that 'the talking treatment' is not just 'hot air' in such a startling manner as a 'group dream'. I am not here referring to a dream *about* the group, which is almost inevitable sooner or later, but to a dream described initially by, say, Pam, to which Tom replies: 'Good God, that's my dream too. I had just the same dream after the last group.' This confounds the cynic and makes him anxious, because the affective thrust of the group has obviously penetrated his inner world. An equal intensification of group awareness came when one member said:

> 'I thought you were going to have that dream', which prompted the reply 'Now I can't keep the group out, whereas I used to refuse to let it in!'

Ultimately, this restriction is beneficial, because he comes to learn that 'No man is an island' and that it is not just pop-song romance which claims 'My dream is yours, because its yours and mine'.

The bizarre history and complex psychopathology of a psychotic offender-patient who has, say, savagely assaulted and fatally wounded a complete stranger, very nearly renders the dual deterministic-existential approach impotent, in terms of helping the therapist to gain an acceptable entry of understanding into the patient's inner world. Such patients may defy the setting up of a conventional 'Therapeutic Alliance'. It was the challenging experience of trying to share therapeutic space with psychotic patients which pointed to a heuristic device called *The Expanding Frame of Reference*.

The Expanding Frame of Reference

Though this crystallised when trying to compromise with the chaos with which the psychotic may present, it has also enlarged the possibility of understanding all patients. In particular, it has furnished a growing awareness of the way in which the patient sometimes perceives and responds to a group as an aggregation of individuals and sometimes perceives and responds to a group as an irreducible whole.

The group may be experienced as supporting, nourishing and sustaining in the way that the patient either remembers mother or how he wishes mother had been, or, *per contra*, as excluding, explosive, brittle, ridiculing and distancing in a manner reminiscent of, say, father. 'The group seems to be "complete" without me...it was like this at home.' This global perception is strikingly different from the focal perception: 'Jim is like Dad...Mary is like Mum.'

The expanding frame of reference describes an attitude adopted by the therapist as he responds to whatever the individual or the group may disclose, however encapsulated or self-contained it may seem to be. It is a way of organising experience and is reminiscent of Goffman's (1974) concept of frame analysis, though its frame of reference is that of therapeutic space. But it is more than a way of organising experience, because it also implies a mode of 'entering' the experience of another, by sharing his affective response to perceived events.

The therapist asks himself *'What else might he be telling me?'* Time and again this has revealed a coherent *gestalt* and a style of conceptualising the content of a session, which had initially baffled me when viewed from a purely deterministic perspective. It seems to evoke a tangential, associative, 'lateral thinking' series of percepts, and the psychotic is manifestly relieved that someone else can see a pattern in his experience which baffles most people.

I must immediately balance these remarks by stating that *I do not for a moment suggest that such an approach, which may allow the therapist to enter the psychotic patient's inner world, does more than just that! Though dynamic change may follow such an 'accepted' entry. Appropriate medication or other physical treatment, ward 'climate control' and general nursing care are of course essential in any effective therapeutic policy for psychotics.* Nevertheless, relatively junior staff frequently ask about appropriate ways of talking to deluded or hallucinated patients, as they try to respond to the whole person. I suggest that the 'expanding frame of reference' implicit in the question 'What else might he be telling me?' can be a useful guide.

For those readers who have not yet 'conversed' with a psychotic patient, and experienced the difficulty of knowing what to say, or how to be silent, I will give a few examples of psychotic disclosures. The first two have the allegorical quality so frequently found in psychotic speech:

1. I'm blind because I see too much, so I study by a dark lamp.
2. Part of me is my mother and sister 'I ran out of reality' ... (a patient's memory of a psychotic phase.)
3. I can't bear being on my own because there are too many of me to cope with.
4. There are snakes crawling up my leg.* I *am* a snake.
   (Not confirmed by an independent observer!)

Consideration of an appropriate response to the last quotation illustrates the point, though it must never be forgotten that shared silence, interpreted and punctuated by gaze and gesture, may be far more eloquent and 'reach' the psychotic's chaos at a depth inpenetrable to words. There is a sense in which the therapist may gently and quietly need to 'follow' such a patient, till he reaches a point when he is 'invited in' to that area of experience where the psychotic has sought refuge from intolerable reality. He may be expected to share the cramped therapeutic space of an emotional hide-out for a long time, until the patient feels safe enough to risk emerging. Appropriate medication may of course be necessary, but this can never exonerate the therapist from responding to the tentative invitation from a patient whose defences are so precarious, to be with him. Yet he must respect the patient's privacy, and not force an 'invitation' if it is not offered.

It is usually safe to ask questions about the snakes to clarify 'detail'. 'What kind are they?', 'Are there always the same number?', though the

---

* Visual or tactile hallucinations ('snakes crawling') usually have an organic aetiology, and, therefore, a rigorous search for the 'cause' must be found and appropriate treatment initiated. Auditory hallucinations ('voices') are common in schizophrenia. However, our present concern is with the therapist's endeavours to understand his patient's social construction of 'reality', and also to allow the patient to understand the therapist's presence. Therefore the task of structuring the therapeutic process in terms of time, depth and mutuality is always appropriate; whether the patient suffers from an organic psychosis (e.g. due to drugs), a functional psychosis (e.g. schizophrenia), a neurotic psychogenic pseudo-psychosis (in which a patient unconsciously retreats from harsh, threatening reality into the defended preserve of a delusional system) or the pseudo-psychosis of a psychopath (i.e. a psychosis 'put on' to gain advantages for the patient). In clinical practice these divisions stand as a misleading over-simplification. Organic lesions can cause 'symptomatic' schizophrenia, which is almost indistinguishable from classical 'functional' schizophrenia.

therapist runs the risk of being perceived as a frightening interrogator. Whereas a comment such as 'of course there aren't' merely heightens the patient's sense of emotional distance and being different, and may cause a further psychotic retreat. On the other hand, to agree with him reinforces his faulty reality-testing, and is anti-therapeutic; unless there *are* snakes crawling up his leg! Having taken his patient's snakes 'seriously', because they are of 'serious' concern to the patient, the therapist will then see whether medication needs reviewing.

The expanding frame of reference implicit in the therapist's expectant attitude ('What else might he be telling me?') can frequently hold a psychotic who, through fear, has withdrawn from painful reality. For such a patient the snakes are a 'core of seriousness' and the expanding frame of reference helps the therapist to take his patient seriously and, at the same time, furthers his task of structuring the therapeutic process. The expanding frame of reference can also facilitate psychotherapy with neurotic or psychopathic patients, whose readily discernible psychopathology can still cause a locked therapeutic alliance, where transference and countertransference are almost frozen so that movement is impossible. When this happens, the question 'What else might he be telling me?', even when the therapist thinks he understands what the patient is telling him, may open the therapist's eyes to some blinding flash of the obvious which had escaped him. Nevertheless, it is the psychotic patient, whose formal thought disorder so often seems to defy dynamic psychotherapy, who posits questions about structuring the therapeutic process in the most pressing form and who most demands the expanding frame of reference. Sometimes the therapist needs to ask himself the question repeatedly, until the psychotic's idiosyncratic way of construing reality is reached. Here are two more examples:

1. Tom, a psychotic patient says in the group: 'Everyone is wearing a blue dress' (in fact only Clare has a blue dress). The expanding frame of reference indicates that Tom 'only has eyes' for Clare.

2. Mike sits in Derek's usual chair. Hilary says 'Derek isn't here today.... I didn't see that Mike *was* sitting in that chair, but that Derek *wasn't.*' Implication? Hilary can 'see through' Mike and/or Derek shares 'substance' with Hilary.

The expanding frame of reference was, for me, a discovery, but the question 'What else might he be telling me?' was known to Prospero.

What seest thou *else*
In the dark backward and abysm of time?
(*The Tempest*, I. ii. 49)

It is perhaps unusual to mention the psychotic in an introductory chapter to a book on counselling, but the examples just described introduce the next topic, which is also unusual. I refer to the group of patients known as 'borderline patients',* and I do so at this precise point for a specific reason.

The concept of structuring the therapeutic process in terms of time, depth and mutuality grew out of clinical experience in many settings, including general practice, conventional out-patient psychotherapy, psychotherapy undertaken in prison and in Broadmoor Hospital. The hypothesis stands or falls on the fact that if it really does offer a way of structuring the therapeutic process applicable in every setting, then it must do so in the most difficult 'test-case' possible. In my experience, this is provided by the borderline patient† whose history includes a serious offence against the person, such as homicide. The borderline patient has such rapidly fluctuating defences that within the course of a few minutes he may fleetingly present 'classical' clinical features of, say, obsessional neurosis, paranoid ideation, or the truculent emotional imperviousness, which is often associated with hysterical psychopathy. His endopsychic patterning oscillates as defences change; e.g. isolation of affect, projection or denial, respectively in the 'three clinical faces' just described. When a patient with such an unstable, capricious inner world has killed on at least one occasion, there may be no theoretical reason why he should not do so again. The psychotherapist may be construed as a victim-surrogate through the tinted lens of transference, and this possibility influences him as he tries to structure the process and compromise with his patient's inner chaos.

It is encouraging to note that the heuristic device of structuring the therapeutic process in terms of time, depth and mutuality has, so far, stood up to this ultimate clinical test.

* See Chapter 11 for a more detailed discussion of the 'borderline patient'. The term does *not* refer to the borderline between 'patient' and 'non-patient', but to a group of patients whose presentation fluctuates across conventional diagnostic borders.
† The borderline patient within the confines of a secure perimeter may pose many therapeutic problems; but such a patient who is free to 'come and go' in an 'open' ward, or the wider community, poses even more.

I am aware that to start with the most difficult clinical problem and then to proceed to discuss strategies of conventional counselling may be heterodox, but it is done so that the reader would not feel 'It's ok with gentle middle-class schoolgirls or passive dependent homosexual men, but I work with maladjusted kids, drug addicts, recidivists, etc.' I hope such a response will be obviated because this presentation is based not only upon ten years in general practice, but upon experience including work with the psychotic patient and the borderline homicide.

We now consider the terms of reference surrounding and permeating the meeting of therapist and patient; bearing in mind that a question which patients, research workers, administrators and finance officers constantly ask the therapist (who is also likely to be asking it!) cannot be avoided. 'Is this relief temporary or will it last?' Does the therapeutic process lead to *sustained* change? If it affords only transient symptom reduction, is it 'worth' it? This raises many ethical issues, though 'to comfort always', has Hippocratic authority, whereas 'to confront always' does not.

Shakespeare distinguished between transient relief and lasting gain.

> How light and portable my pain *seems now.*
> (*King Lear*, III, vi. 112)

> But shall we wear these glories for a day?
> *Or shall they last,* and we rejoice in them?
> (Richard III, IV, ii. 5)

Psychotherapeutic work aims to help the patient engage with the present moment (see page 221) with freer intensity, because of the resolution of inner conflict, so that he is less gripped and restricted by his past. It also seeks to liberate him from crippling anxiety about the future, particularly the prospect of his own death or that of those upon whom he depends. Though the dread of *not* dying is sometimes more fearful than the prospect of unending painful existence, living with the knowledge of 'what I've done' or 'what I've been'.

When his death and the prospect of non-being becomes a *now-event*, it is hoped that previous psychotherapy may *then* enable him to 'engage with the *ultimate present moment*' with experience based upon other, previously dreaded, 'present moments' which have been safely negotiated. If this happens, 'sustained' change will be evident.

CHAPTER 2

Terms of Reference

Loneliness ... that's the business now.

Half my life and all my troubles came flooding back.

He frightened me so much ... he was such a 'nothing' person, you could drown in him.

I kept apart, to prevent rejection.

My childhood wasn't.

There are some things I can't show, so I have to be partly here and there.

I had so many problems that I tried to solve them by *becoming a problem.*

I am rushing towards something in myself.

Since I finished the relationship, I've been less alone.

I never had a childhood.

Hiding behind your symptoms, you are nowhere near my chaos.

What I did alienated me from my own feelings.

I've no idea what is inside me ... I am not what I seem.

I ran out of reality. (Implying there was 'no reality left', or, 'I stepped out of, or ran away from reality because it was unbearable'.)

I can remember my childhood in great detail ... but I can't re-feel it.

Anyone who is not my mother, I simply don't want.

I am dustbin material. The whole of life put me in a dustbin and put the lid on.

I've got nothing to look back on.

I've been living in the future all my life ... looking ... waiting.

Fear is all around ... death is all around.

I was never sure whether I was hiding behind my mother ... or from her.

The pain (of scalding water) was big enough for all the other pain which I've felt inside for years, to flow into.

I will never get over this ... *never at the moment.*

Loving was there ... but it wasn't there. I am not me ... but it's not that I am someone else. Part of me is outside myself and can't get back in; or it's too much in me ... and can't get out.

I felt the absence of feeling and it was terrible.

The group enlarges my feelings ... it surprises me.

When I started feeling, I had to pretend to be someone else.

I felt lost in life and all that goes with it.

I wanted love and affection ... she couldn't give them and I hated her for it.

My mother's time and presence were rationed.

I want to be like what I hate.
There are the married and the single, and others who drift through life never really knowing.
Since I've been in the group I'm not so apologetic for existing.
I've got to have someone in my life, I'm that sort of person.
Chaos is a smokescreen; if I saw it head on, I'd go hysterical. (What is *it*?... 'Change'.)

Part of me is my mother and sister, so I'm not in control.
I felt as if I was in the deepest part of me.
There's nothing I wouldn't have missed for anything.
I never like doing it because it reminds me of what I've done!
I can't be a new person to my family. I can only be a new person to myself.
I'm not an individual. I'm a thing other people can enlarge on. I'm a joke.
What I did upset the flow of my life.
I'm afraid of this power that keeps me unfed.
The pain of her pain is more than I can bear.

These disclosures of inner world phenomena occurred in 'therapeutic space' (see page 40). Although they might have been made anywhere, in fact the patients chose them in a particular setting as vehicles to convey, as best they could, how they felt. The clinician may read them through 'diagnostic eyes' and even reflect upon therapeutic implications. Nevertheless, whatever drugs or other forms of treatment are indicated, the patients actually used these words. *The words of the patient call for words from the therapist.* The disclosure by the patient must evoke a response from the therapist. Our concern is with the response the therapist makes to such disclosures. When a patient says 'I never had a childhood', the therapist may respond in many ways, even by silence. An extended consideration of the factors which govern the therapist's response forms the backbone of this book.

Such disclosures* are unlikely to be part of a patient's initial clinical presentation, but they are characteristic 'outcroppings' of feeling which become evident during the course of counselling or psychotherapy, once the seam of unexpressed feeling has been reached. The analogy of drilling for oil, or mining for coal, through what appears to be a barren and unpromising surface is so appropriate. Indeed, when a particular stratum of experience has been 'tapped' then such disclosures pour out, frequently under pressure, and the patient, reflecting upon what is happening, comments: 'I never knew all this was locked up inside. I didn't realise I had such feelings.'

---

* See page 224 for 280 juxtaposed disclosures.

This brief selection of disclosures comes from patients in different settings, at different stages of the therapeutic process, from the widest extremes of intelligence, education and social class, and diagnostic category. The disclosure of such affective material *might* have occurred in any setting. Nevertheless, it is only within the professional setting of therapeutic space that the disclosure of affective material can be linked with enhanced self-understanding, so that dynamic psychotherapy can facilitate the cognitive–affective encounter with the introjected past. Dynamic psychotherapy is not a purely intellectual, cognitive process, neither is it a purely emotional, affective process; for intra-psychic and inter-personal change depends upon the mobilisation of the amalgam of cognitive–affective factors. Thus, in order for the quotations given at the chapter heading to be disclosures which would not have occurred without psychotherapy, they need to be an integral part of cognitive–affective change. For example, the patient who said 'I was never sure whether I was hiding behind my mother... or from her' could never have made this disclosure at the beginning of psychotherapy; and it was only after prolonged engagement with others in a therapeutic group that such a disclosure was possible. The pseudo-disclosure of a psychopath (see pages 140, 215) may also occur in therapeutic space. Such a disclosure acts as an 'early warning system' for the subsequent disclosure which may have the disclosure hallmark, i.e. it is a genuine cognitive–affective phenomenon. The pseudo-disclosure, by definition, does not have either component in full measure. After a prolonged period in a therapeutic group a psychopath who ultimately makes genuine disclosures will frequently reflect upon the early phases in psychotherapy when he was testing out the therapist, and the other members of the group. He recalls how, in the early days, 'my talk was just talk', whereas subsequently 'my talk has become me'. It can never be said too often that if it is presumed that a psychopath is always lying, and that every disclosure which appears genuine is, *ipso facto*, a pseudo-disclosure, then it is not surprising that if the patient is not trusted, he never becomes trustworthy. In such a situation, the therapist may be the first 'significant other', who vicariously represents other people from the patient's effective personal world, to be entrusted with genuine disclosures. The cynic may say: 'He's always lying... don't believe a word he says.' Whereas therapeutic space may be the first opportunity for the patient to begin to trust himself, the therapist and the other members of the group, so that his disclosures change from pseudo-disclosures to genuine first, second and, ultimately, third-level disclosures (see pages 59, 164).

Training in psychotherapy rests upon the three axiomatic foundations of progressive, monitored self-awareness, appropriation of an adequate theoretical conceptual framework and increasing strategic expertise. The therapist will remain ill-equipped without adequate attention to each member of this triad, and the patient with whom he shares therapeutic space will be offered an unbalanced 'therapeutic' presence.

Nothing can replace that personal encounter with self which the experience of training in psychotherapy must embrace, irrespective of allegiance to any specific psychodynamic school. Siirala (1974) has described this experience as 'a suffering-maturation process'. This steadily deepening and pervasive experience takes place slowly over months and years. It is facilitated and simultaneously monitored by an experienced therapist who enables the trainee to recognise and negotiate his own emotional obstacles, so that he becomes increasingly at ease within himself. This growing freedom experienced by the therapist allows his patient to free-associate even though this may include a wish for, or the fear of, his own or his therapist's death.

Thus, the therapist must, within human limits, be able to rest in the thought of his own death or of his patient's murderous destructiveness. The therapist faces himself as he faces his patient, and when one re-enters the orbit of his own past, he takes the other with him. Therefore the therapist is re-exposed to his own earlier experience, which might include destructive hate, engulfing love or a sense of dereliction, way-outlessness or chaos. This is rarely intentional on the patient's part, (though sadistic offender-patients may hope to cause the therapist pain) and is usually a side-effect of the disclosure of his own inner world. It means that the therapist must be able to tolerate his own murderousness, sexuality or the threat of non-being.

There are two ubiquitous and interlocking, though conceptually discrete, components which provide a skeleton for the process of psycho-sexual maturation which various theoretical schools shape and clothe in different ways and in different words. Firstly, the developmental task of adequately negotiating sequential attachment–relinquishment transitional phases, and, secondly, the flexible homeostatic mechanism of self-esteem regulation. These twin components underlie psychosexual development, and failure of one or both leads to fixation and/or deviation with ensuing disturbance of experience and/or behaviour. Self-scrutiny of both components is part of the growing self-awareness of the therapist in training, as well, *inter alia*, as furnishing a basis for understanding the psychopathology of his patients.

Training in psychotherapy therefore allows the therapist to meet himself in tolerable doses, and to discover the direction in which his developing expertise and interest lies. The therapist's life experience is integrated with increasingly sophisticated technical knowledge and awareness of the panorama of inner and outer world phenomena. Nevertheless, no therapist, however fully trained, is equally at home with all sorts and conditions of men; but to be at ease within himself is a *sine qua non* of the therapist's life, if he is to be at ease with his patient at the outset of therapy. For example, at the end of a full analysis some analysts may remain afraid of aggressive psychopaths, whereas others are threatened by lesbians or paedophils, but their training will have made them aware of their emotional assets and liabilities. No book can usurp the paramount and inescapable priority of the personal experiential component of training, in terms of personal understanding and of supervised therapy and monitored intervention.

It is equally certain that an adequate theoretical framework can only be grasped by thinking and reflecting based upon reading, seminar participation and attending formal lectures. Systematic textbooks abound and journals proliferate.

Strategic expertise is gradually gained, *pari passu*, by observing therapeutic sessions in action through a one-way screen or by using other audio-visual aids. It is also gained vicariously by reading transcripts of actual sessions or the classic early cases of the pioneers, but no learning process is quite so penetrating or indelible in the memory as that of individual personal supervision or sharing in a corporate group experience.

If experience is only gained through experience, theory is systematised and already well documented, and strategy is slowly gleaned in 'apprentice' situations, then what justification can there possibly be for adding yet another book on counselling and psychotherapy? I wish to stress, *ab initio*, that this book is not intended to provide a comprehensive survey, but rather that its heterodox executive perspective may be equally helpful to trainees of all traditions. It adopts a tangential view of the therapeutic process, so that it cannot be closely aligned with, say, psychoanalytic, transactional analytic or client-centred counselling theory. It is not an introductory book on counselling or psychotherapy. It assumes the concept of the therapeutic alliance as a core datum, in which there is an asymmetrical meeting of people when the emotional needs of A prompt him to consult B. The 'life experience-professional training' amalgam should have equipped B to *respond appropriately* to A's spoken or unspoken needs. A may have disturbed and/or disturbing experience and/or behaviour, ranging from specific symptoms to a sense of inchoate chaos, such as: the emotional poverty of a superficially 'happy' marriage; the fact or fantasy of sexual deviation; the dream, the delusion or the fact of matricide; the dread of death; the adhesive maternal bonding which is not evaded by marriage but transferred from mother to wife; the ineluctible Icarus complex of overwork and ambitious striving; the history of theft, arson, rape, buggery, poisoning or homicide. This means that B must have come to terms with these facets of emotional life if his energies are to be available to engage with A in the work of therapy, which may take the form of symptom reduction, conflict resolution and/or enhanced self-understanding.

The preceding paragraph may appear to refer to the work and training of a psychoanalyst or specialist psychotherapist, and far removed from that of, say, a GP, a school counsellor* or a probation officer. However, alongside the clearly defined clinical physical examination, the academic curricular advice and the statutory social inquiry, of the GP, the teacher* and the probation officer, respectively, there often exists an unstructured and disorganised emotional fog about the presumed inner world of the patient/client. This so permeates therapeutic space that even if the counsellor has been able to identify the problem, he is unable to formulate an *appropriate response*. Nevertheless, the emotional needs of the client do not exist alongside the 'medical', 'educational' or 'social' presentation of the client, but are an integral part of them.

The therapeutic process of counselling and psychotherapy can be structured in terms of time, depth and mutuality. *These dimensions are*

---

* A perennial debate centres upon the 'specialist' nature of counselling in schools; hence 'school counsellor'—'teacher' (see page 245).

independent of the theoretical approach adopted by the individual practitioner and of his particular professional field of expertise. These views have arisen from first-hand clinical experience, endorsed by the corporate experience of sharing with professional colleagues from other disciplines, as they pool emotional resources and concentrate upon the use they make of themselves in relationship to the emotional needs of their patients or clients. As I shared in group life with probation officers and other social workers, GPs, prison officers, marriage guidance counsellors, school counsellors, psychologists and nurses, it gradually became clear that whenever a colleague asked if he could 'present a difficult patient' he always presented certain aspects of the self–patient alliance. Structuring clarifies dynamics and helps to determine appropriate therapeutic initiative, not only with the rapist, the arsonist and the patient charged with homicide; but also with patients referred for conventional counselling, such as the teenager with an adolescent identity crisis or those seeking marriage guidance. It was discovered that the presentation of the 'difficult patient' always revealed the 'lesion' along one of the three dimensions of time, depth or mutuality. (The reader might recall the last 'difficult' patient he encountered to see whether, in his experience, the patient was 'difficult' because of such faulty structuring.) I suggest that this heterodox vantage point allows reappraisal, clarification and often reorientation on the part of the therapist independent of, say, Freudian or Rogerian theory. Whatever theoretical views he may hold, in the actual cut-and-thrust of the imminent therapeutic encounter, a paraphrase of the question the therapist usually asks himself is 'How can I optimally structure the therapeutic process at this particular point?' rather than feeling 'I wish I had greater knowledge of Freudian, Kleinian, Jungian, Adlerian...*et al.* theory.' To state this more succinctly, it could be said that logistic structuring rather than academic theory is what the therapist seeks at 'difficult' moments during the therapeutic session. It is clear that there must be a relationship between theoretical substrate and strategy, but in this book I am hoping to draw attention to the significance of structuring, *per se.* Counsellors and therapists with many different backgrounds may be asking the same question: e.g., the experienced group psychotherapist who has never before run a group of patients found guilty of manslaughter; the experienced GP who for the first time feels uneasy handling his relationship with a young female patient who seems to be idealising him, and requesting frequent consultations on the flimsiest clinical grounds,* the experienced teacher in a boarding school who finds that she is threatened by a child who appears to have become 'adhesive' so that wherever the teacher is, so, miraculously, the child 'happens' to be there too. The range of such situations and such professional disciplines could be extended almost indefinitely.

It became clear that the reappraisal of inappropriate structuring was ubiquitously relevant to the task of supervising psychotherapy and counselling. Whenever trainees presented their difficulties in handling the therapist/patient relationship, they usually indicated that they had mishandled time, depth or mutuality.

The purist may feel irritated by my paradoxical Janusian stance in which equal emphasis is laid on psychic determinism (events, conscious or unconscious, cause events, conscious or unconscious) and existential openness and invitation. This means that an event may appear to grounds that my human fallibility precludes the possibility of knowing all the causal chains of psychic determinism which may underlie the apparently 'inexplicable' events of my patient's inner world. Nevertheless, if I am to try to enter this world of experience which he endeavours to entrust to me, my response to him as a whole person must be one of openness and invitation. This means that an event may appear to be 'out of the blue' and, because I am neither omniscient nor omnipotent, it may have an existential 'nowness' about it, even though it is psychically determined. Therapists may be deluding themselves if they claim to understand the totality of the patient's inner world, however elaborate their psychodynamic formulations may be. Worse still, they may diminish, restrict and run the risk of inhibiting their patient's experience by their own personal restrictions and limits. If emotional disclosures are to occur, and the therapist is genuinely allowing his patient to free-associate, an enormous burden is placed upon the therapist's identity-retaining energy. If the patient is encouraged to *say anything*, then the therapist must be able to *hear everything*. An extreme example, which establishes and underlines this point, would be my difficulty in 'allowing' my patient to free-associate *re* strangling his child, if I had just strangled mine.

* Hitherto, she has 'been to see the doctor' many times. This time, she 'comes to SEE the doctor.'

1. AFFIDAVIT

Every man is in some respects
a. like all other men,
b. like some other men,
c. like no other man.

(Kluckhorn and Murray, 1949)

Are we not formed, as notes of music are,
For one another, though dissimilar.

(from *Epipsychidion*, Shelley)

This is not an apologia for the absence of statistics or the presence of anecdotes. '*Anecdote*. 1. pl. Secret, or hitherto unpublished narratives or details of history. 2. The narrative of an interesting or striking incident or event' (*OED*). This book is unashamedly anecdotal. It concentrates not only on the 'details of history' but also on exactly what the patient says. The experience of imminent death by three patients using different words describes three experiences, not one:

(1) I've come to the end of the road.
(2) Life is flowing out of me.
(3) I'm crossing over.

Neither do I apologise for the numerous literary quotations which permeate the text.* Not only do they furnish the long perspective of history and the longer perspective of myth, but they also provide a validating and authenticating setting for the existential disclosures of patients in the twentieth century. Acquaintance with Shakespeare (*King Lear*, *Lady Macbeth*, *Richard II*, etc.), Tolstoy or Yeats, enlarges the therapist's experience, so that he has a wider capacity to receive the disclosures of his patients. Each therapist will have his own literary 'friends' who introduce him to vicariously received experience. This, in turn, helps him to receive his patient as a person. The disclosures from history, myth and drama prepare the way for those recent disclosures listed under the heading 'The Patient Speaks' in Chapter 8. Disclosures, ancient and modern, have a quality of timeless incipience and underly the fact that the patient is 'like all other men, like some other men, like no other man'. This is also true of the therapist himself. He is confronted by the ubiquitous and timeless aspects of the human predicament, in the

---

* The Name index should be an intrinsic part of the text, and not a mere appendage after the 'substance'.

precise presence of his patient. Fortunately, he will, *ipso facto*, also discover hitherto unknown personal resources; because, if '*Any* man's *death* diminishes me ...' (Donne), then *Every* man's *life* must invigorate me. 'I'm taking this [a weeping, poignant disclosure by another patient] seriously ... because it concerns me.'

Conrad in this author's note on *Typhoon* remarks:

> If it is true that Captain MacWhirr never walked and breathed on this earth (which I find for my part extremely difficult to believe) I can also assure my readers that he is perfectly authentic. I may venture to assert the same of every aspect of the story while I confess that the particular typhoon of the tale was not a typhoon of my actual experience.

This is one of limitless examples by which the therapist's horizons of awareness extend beyond the realm of those people he has actually encountered in his personal life, or within a professional setting. The wider his experience grows, the better is he equipped to engage with the disclosures of those people he meets within the reality of therapeutic space. The more he knows of life, the less will he be shocked (or pathologically 'over-interested') by those aspects of the patient's inner world which slowly and progressively move towards disclosure.

There is an almost imperceptible transition from one conceptual frame of reference to another when an author, such as Conrad in *Typhoon*, transposes a description of outer world phenomena (usually the sea, frequently a storm) into a description of inner world phenomena, and *vice versa*. This framework transposition also occurs in the sequential phases of dynamic psychotherapy. The patient may transiently project his destructiveness upon his environment, so that it 'has' a malevolent, alien penumbra or, *per contra*, when invested with 'goodness', it assumes a benign sense of 'enlightened comprehension dwelling alone up there with the storm'. The therapist's repertoire of encounters is enlarged by meeting such characters as the crew of the *Nan-Shan* and discovering how they deal with chaos—both as an outer world event and also as an inner world phenomenon.

The following fragments from *Typhoon* illustrate the point:

> Captain MacWhirr had gone into the chart-room. There was no light there; but he could feel the disorder of that place where he used to live tidily.

> The hurricane had broken in upon the orderly arrangements of his privacy. This had never happened before, and the feeling of dismay reached the very seat of his composure. And the worst was to come yet!

The vividness of the thought checked him and for an infinitesimal fraction of a second his fingers closed again on the small object (a match box) as though it had been the symbol of all these little habits that chain us to the weary round of life. He released it at last, and letting himself fall on the settee, listened for the first sounds of returning wind.

By this awful pause the storm penetrated the defences of the man and unsealed his lips. He spoke out in the solitude and the pitch darkness of the cabin, as if addressing another being awakened within his breast.

'I shouldn't like to lose her,' he said half aloud.

He sat unseen, apart from the sea, from his ship, isolated, *as if withdrawn, from the very current of his own existence*, where such freaks as talking to himself surely had no place. His palms reposed on his knees, he bowed his short neck and puffed heavily, surrendering to a strange sensation of weariness he was not enlightened enough to recognize for the fatigue of mental stress. [Italics added.]

But it is only as his widening experience of life, aided by the writings, paintings and films of others, is harnessed to increasingly discerning technical accuracy (in deciphering defence organisation, libidinal orientation, etc., as a personal professional experience) that the therapist begins to be able to see the wood for the trees.

We shall repeatedly underline the significance of the therapist's use of himself as a participant in the therapeutic process as he meets *this* patient, in *this* way, at *this* time. A therapeutic initiative (which may imply being receptively silent for an hour) may be appropriate to the needs of *this* patient, in *this* place, at *this* time, but inappropriate to *this* patient, in *this* place, at *that* time. Writing about counselling and psychotherapy inevitably runs the risk of epistemological confusion. It must be recalled that a clear distinction exists between facts which may be *known about a patient* and the other dimension of knowing, when he is *encountered as a* person. '*Data about*' and '*meeting with*' come from different worlds of discourse, but to concentrate on one at the expense of the other diminishes the total therapeutic resources available for the patient.

The Crucial Balance: Knowledge of the Patient as 'Data about' and 'Encounter with'

In order to engage with his patient in psychotherapeutic work, the therapist needs two kinds of knowledge. He needs objective 'data about' his patient and he needs that kind of knowledge which comes from personal 'encounter with' his patient. The family doctor, the school counsellor, the psychiatric nurse (and others) all have access to sources of important specialised data about their patients, such as clinical, academic and curricular, and maybe legal information. Indeed, they would fail their patients if they did not make use of such data in an appropriate way. The knowledge which comes from encountering the patient as a person, in the unfolding course of a therapeutic alliance, includes the reception of progressive disclosures of the patient's inner world. One of the cardinal distinctions between emotional disclosure which takes place within therapeutic space and an 'identical' disclosure made in the presence of a close friend, is that in the former setting the disclosure furnishes the therapist with 'data' (such as evidence of defence organisation, libidinal orientation, etc.), which he then uses in a deliberate and strategic sense, either to facilitate further disclosure or, when necessary, to delay it. The heart-to-heart talk with a close friend may be enormously helpful. But it is not formal psychotherapy in which 'data about the patient' and 'encounter with the patient' reciprocally endorse each other, and guide the therapist as he structures the therapeutic process in terms of time, depth and mutuality.

One of the axiomatic questions which the therapist is constantly asking himself is 'How can I better understand what the patient is disclosing?' Whereas 'data about'* is relatively easy to grasp, the trainee therapist, in particular, searches for adequate conceptual tools to grapple with the problem of delineating and understanding that kind of knowledge he has of his patient when he encounters him as a person.† It is therefore impossible to proceed further without at least a passing reference to this epistemological perspective, as it applies to that specific personal encounter which takes place in counselling and psychotherapy.

There are two epistemological themes which must be considered. The first is the approach to knowledge through analogy and the second through dialectic. Each principle is one-sided if not supported by the other, and the cognitive–affective communication within therapeutic space makes much use of both analogy and paradox. The former is concerned with metaphor, so that knowing is due to expanded concentric circles of recognition. This means that anamnesis (literally 'unforgetting',

---

* 'Hard', objective 'data about' the patient may be of prime importance in determining an appropriate therapeutic policy; but such information is not our concern here.

† This is closely linked to the facilitation of the kind of knowledge the patient 'acquires' about himself. It may occur as a flash of insight or as an almost imperceptible change in the level of tolerable awareness.

using this word in a wider sense than is usually implicit in psychoanalytic literature) is facilitated by areas of recognition overlapping,
affirming and complementing each other. There are innumerable
examples supplied in the text. Thus the group-therapist's role is described as that of the conductor of an orchestra, the prompter for a play,
an interpreter for people who do not speak the same language and
who even need interpreters for their 'mother' tongue. There are also
musical analogies whereby the therapeutic task of interpreting material
as the unconscious becomes conscious, and the Conscious withheld becomes the Conscious-disclosed, is likened to the musician's
task of modulating into a relative key, which is not too jarring and
intolerable to be accepted by the listener. Painful disclosure, if clumsily
interpreted at an inappropriate time, and without sensitively relevant
affect, may cause the patient to 'hear' painful discords from which he
needs to withdraw (page 204). Indeed, it is often the transposition of the
perspective from which events in the outer world are perceived, or events
in the inner world are experienced, which mobilises the patient into a
cognitive–affective encounter with himself. (See, for example, the different
ways of 'looking' at the Thames (page 197). When a patient volunteers:

'I suppose the Thames ... in a way ... is like the flow of my life',

the changing frame of reference and the enhanced possibilities of interest
and absorption in life are obvious.) Thus the language of analogy not
only describes activity, it also has instrumental initiative. Each of these
metaphors is partially true, so that their summation gets nearer to conveying a total *gestalt*. Obviously the therapist is not actually the conductor of an orchestra or the prompter of a play, etc., but each conveys a
partial facet of his work. Likewise, with the patient. Under the cloak of
disclosure we may discern his way of 'living out' his own metaphor. In
other words, his totality of life-style 'says' things about him, not only
in terms of body-language but also in the wider setting of cosmic location (page 198). The act of disclosure has a dynamic impact upon the
discloser and those who 'receive' the disclosure.

The dialectic of opposites is the second main epistemological avenue
by which both patient and therapist 'know' with ever-growing clarity
what is 'going on'. It is illustrated by paradox which permeates the
book, and was stated explicitly at the outset (page 1). Examples are
legion: the therapist is involved-yet-detached; he is 'in' the world of his

patient, but not 'of' it; love is seen most clearly in the presence of hate and the more hating becomes intensified, the more does quality of love declare itself. Psychotherapy is permeated by ambivalence:

> I love and hate at the same time.... I'm a battlefield and fighting on both sides at once, that is why I'm tired all the time.

The more a man is involved in affective commitment to another, as in a progressively deepening marriage, he will make such paradoxical statements as:

> The more I live shared life with my wife and we become one, the more I become myself.

The paradox is most intense in the statement of vicarious presence, so that each becomes the 'unlived life' (page 139, 222) of the other.

These opposing, but complementary epistemological perspectives, need to be stated explicitly. During the subsequent detailed discussion of the relationship between therapist and patient, the process of psychotherapy and the different phases of the sequential emotional alignments during the early, middle and late phases of transference, many clinical examples will be given, using analogies and statements of dialectical opposites, in the form of paradoxes. Both perspectives are necessary for our purpose, yet both leave so much unsaid. The therapist will always need to 'know' his patient as a person but also to 'know about him'. If, for example, he is to understand-with-a-view-to-treating a young man with an overactive thyroid who has become phobic in any social situation, since a girl, he was particularly attracted towards, found his 'bulging eyes frightening'. 'Knowing' and 'knowing about' are inextricably enmeshed, and a genuine, professional therapeutic presence demands both. The twin approaches of analogy and paradox facilitate the task of enabling the patient to be 'put in touch with his feelings' so that he meets himself, and in so doing, finds that the self he meets changes! The disclosures listed in Chapter 8, 'The Patient Speaks', afford ample evidence of the analogy–paradox quality of his way of construing both inner and outer world phenomena.

> Knowing doesn't even get us half way there.... *Just* knowing.... It only gets you there when you *feel* it, too (a 'fragment' from a therapeutic group).

There could be no clearer statement in basic English about the inescapable fact that insight and the enhanced self-awareness of being 'in touch with feelings', at both an early infantile level and at the 'growing point' of maturation, depend upon a cognitive–affective process. The dynamic pervading therapeutic space depends upon this cognitive–affective quality of the relationship between the therapist and the patient.

Sometimes a patient on the brink of disclosure has the 'knowing-feeling' awareness that he is talking of one dimension in terms of another (see Chapter 8, section on Cosmic and Semantic Distortion, as disclosure characteristics). For example, 'When I was talking of a ball-game (or, say, "making an opening"; not "rising" to anger; being a "sucker", etc.), *I knew I was talking of something else.*' This invitational edge of disclosure can be facilitated by the therapist or other members of a group; but, a 'switching off' may occur.... 'No one understood what I was trying to say, so I stopped trying.' This is a 'tidal' phenomenon and the therapist must wait for next 'high' tide.

The patient hopes to disclose (or conceal) his anxiety. The therapist hopes that his own personality can be appropriately used on his patient's behalf and tries to prevent, on the one hand, unnecessarily harsh intrusion into the therapeutic space he shares with his patient, and, on the other hand, over-anxious distancing.

A patient can be interviewed and examined, a diagnosis made, a therapeutic policy initiated and the clinical information thus gained, processed and quantified, without the patient ever having been 'met' as a person.

> They didn't ask me who I was; I was a card with 'bronchitis' on it.*

I am not disputing the fact that my unknown informant might have been part of an essential statistically based survey on the use of a new drug used for the treatment of bronchitis, which may be life-saving for thousands. However, this book is not about such things, vitally necessary though they may be, but it stresses the impact such handling of even the briefest personal encounter can have on the patient. She felt that she was 'just a card' and had obviously gained the impression that she was construed as being nothing other than bronchitis. Every clinician will know from a professional standpoint, and every reader will know from the

---

* At the precise moment of writing the original draft of the preceding sentence on the back of an envelope in a London café, a lady in her seventies, with a grey coat and with a matching expression, described the impact of a recent medical consultation to two neighbours on an adjoining table! (See footnote page 84).

experience of being a patient, that recuperative energy and even the natural history of an illness can be influenced by the penumbra and ethos which surround and 'invade' the patient. To be 'just a card with bronchitis on it' may be an indication of the low self-esteem found in depressive illness, but, in any event, it was indicative of the way the lady thought she was construed. This highlights the fact that the highest priority must be given to the significance of the meeting of patient and doctor (and client and counsellor) and the need for the therapist to try to do what sounds impossible! By this I mean that not only must the patient be viewed through the therapist's eyes, so that an accurate history can be taken, a diagnosis established and appropriate treatment initiated; but, simultaneously, the therapist also needs to see the patient through the patient's eyes, as well as trying to see the therapist through the patient's eyes! This essential clinical and counselling skill is discussed in Chapter 6, Empathy. The outcome of the clinical/counselling/psycho-therapeutic meeting may well depend upon empathy, which is an infra-structure and foundation upon which the fluctuations and vicissitudes of transference and countertransference move (see Chapter 5). It can never be established perfectly, but it can be improved with increasing professional skill and experience. I hope the ideas presented in this book may help the reader to further his understanding of himself, so that he becomes increasingly able, not only to listen to his patients, but to understand them. And then (most difficult of all) of being able to convey that he understands them.

2. SETTING THE SCENE

(a) Therapeutic Space*

This term is used in several ways by different authorities. Thus Moreno uses it to describe the 'stage' upon which psychodrama is enacted, whereas others use it to describe intra-psychic space, i.e. that realm within the personality in which there is room for manœuvre and growth.

There has recently been a growing interest in the concept of thera-

* The first part of this section is incorporated in a chapter entitled 'Dynamic psycho-therapy with sex-offenders' (Cox, 1977) in *Sexual Deviation*, Rosen I. (ed.), 1977.

peutic space. Khan (1974b), in a paper entitled 'The role of illusion in the analytic space and process', writes:

> Clinically the unique achievement of Freud is that he invented and established a therapeutic space and distance for the patient and the analyst. In this space and distance the relating becomes feasible only through the capacity in each to sustain illusion and to work with it.... It is my contention here that Freud created a space, time and process which potentialize that area of *illusion* where symbolic discourse can actualize.

The clinical experience of working with many patients whose lives have included incidents involving the 'basic' crimes, such as murder and incest, has convinced me that therapeutic space, though symbolic, is much 'firmer' and part of a joint reality that can be conveyed by the word 'illusion'. Khan writes: 'the relational process through which the illusion operates is the transference.' The transference may be an illusion, but without genuineness, which endorses reality, transference might not have a chance to grow. 'The basic movement of the life of dialogue is the turning towards the other' (Buber, 1947). It is not the whole content of dynamic psychotherapy, though its inherent dynamic pervades it.

Psychotherapeutic work with the offender-patient can provide a corrective emotional experience for the therapist! By this I mean that it reminds him that the ubiquitous and timeless fantasies of murderousness, and other destructive activity, may erupt into reality in a catastrophic manner. Much literature on psychotherapy often states explicitly, or conveys by an implicit *timbre*, that destructiveness is confined to intrapsychic fantasy or attenuated in the clinical presentation of verbal abuse or hostile silence. Though this is often the case, the exceptions are obviously of great significance. When the patient has actually killed someone the conceptual boundary between 'that area of *illusion* where symbolic discourse can actualize' and that area of *reality* where the 'hard' non-symbolic facts are disclosed is of paramount importance. It is the merging of the *fact* that Donald killed his father with the *transference* '*illusion*' (when the therapist may transiently vicariously represent the un-killed father, or whoever Donald's father stood for in his social construction of reality) which sharpens the significance of reality-testing. Such dynamic events are part of an established therapeutic alliance (whether on an individual or group basis) within therapeutic space. In my view, there is a danger of simplistic reductionism if the concept of therapeutic space is restricted to an illusion, on the one hand, or 'these four walls', on the other. In the same way that a patient who has actually killed his father reminds me that fantasy may become fact, so therapeutic space which may be an illusion can become enclosed within concrete boundaries.

The setting in which much offender-therapy takes place may be 'secure' so that therapeutic space takes on a literal 'concrete' quality, readily discernible in the form of bars at the windows and locks on the doors. These are constant reminders to both patient and therapist that therapeutic space has undeniable boundaries. Such therapy may be conducted in the 'group room' set aside for this purpose in a hospital, or prison, or a probation officer's office. In this sense, therapeutic space is the exact opposite of an illusion. My experience is that such custodial emblems as bars and keys intensify, rather than diminish, the affective flow of the therapeutic encounter. 'We are in this together' has a double meaning. There is the symbolic illusion of therapeutic space but this 'takes place' in a physical space (confined by a secure perimeter) which is also therapeutic. This existential blending, of the symbolic and the literal, intensifies transference phenomena and therefore facilitates individual and group dynamic psychotherapy when conducted within a secure setting. When a group is conducted within such a secure setting, it gives the angry patient something to 'storm into' or 'storm out of'. Such acting-out is impossible through an impenetrable high security wall. A group, therefore, provides an opportunity for the language of movement, for which there is ample opportunity in conventional therapy and patients in a secure setting need it no less. Indeed, because of more restricted avenues of expression, such 'safe' gestures of defiance very likely reduce the incidence of less acceptable 'explosive' language of movement.

In view of the many connotations of the term therapeutic space, it is essential that I clarify my own perspective. I regard it as a term which can be used metaphorically to describe an invisible boundary to the 'space' within which the therapist and patient meet, and where the phenomena of transference and countertransference are 'housed'. It may therefore embrace both an individual therapeutic encounter or a total group matrix, involving eight patients and two co-therapists. In a more global sense it could include all the space within a hospital. Who would not regard the hospital football pitch, in which a patient might learn to improve physical co-ordination and at the same time learn the values of team-work and personal sacrifice, as therapeutic? However, the term usually refers to that space within, and between, those who share in a formal psychotherapeutic alliance. In other words, it includes the intra-psychic space of both patient and therapist and the inter-personal space between them. It is the shared air they breathe.

Even without bars and keys, I could not work if I felt that the therapeutic space which I shared with a patient was ever *solely* an illusion. I regard it as a 'concrete' existential fact that the patient and I are 'in this together'. Winnicott (1945), describing the feeding of the infant, writes: 'I think of the process as if two lives came from opposite directions, liable to come near each other. If they overlap there is a moment of *illusion*—a bit of experience which the infant can take as *either* his hallucination *or* a thing belonging to external reality.' Dynamic psycho-therapy with sex-offenders frequently needs to get back to this early nurturing situation and this implies that the therapist may become a transitional object. This links closely with Balint's (1968) concept of the 'basic fault'. He so accurately describes both the dynamic within, and the ambience of, therapeutic space with many offender-patients.

> The patient says that he feels there is a fault within him, a fault that must be put right. And it is felt to be a fault, not a complex, not a conflict, not a situation. Second, there is a feeling that the cause of this fault is that someone has either failed the patient or defaulted on him; and third, a great anxiety invariably surrounds this area, usually *expressed as a desperate demand that this time the analyst should not—in fact must not—fail him*.... Although highly dynamic, the force originating from the basic fault has the form neither of an instinct nor of a conflict. It is a fault, something wrong in the mind, a kind of deficiency which must be put right. It is not something dammed up for which a better outlet must be found, but something missing either now, or perhaps for almost the whole of the patient's life. An instinctual need can be satisfied, a conflict can be solved, a basic fault can perhaps be *merely healed* provided the deficient *ingredients* can be found; and even then it may amount only to a healing with defect, like a simple, painless scar. [Italics added.]*

This domestic, 'homely' choice of words reminds us that certain psychotherapeutic tasks require the therapist to be an 'ingredient' (or an ingredient-surrogate for earlier faulty ingredients), so that 'a basic fault can perhaps be *merely healed*'. This is a demanding role and is certainly not 'inferior' to that needed in dynamic, interpretive analytic therapy.

When the therapist is working at such a primitive level with his

---

* For example: The more that things are hurled at you, the less painful it becomes....
It's like *scar-tissue*.   (Anon., 1972)

patients, he may be perceived as a transitional object but this is only while his patients need to perceive him in this way. It is of the essence of psychotherapy training that the patient's prevailing needs determine the therapist's response. In this instance it would be disastrous if the therapist's personal 'need', to be seen as a transitional object, 'over-ruled' the fact that his patient had now reached a stage where he could safely relinquish such transitional maturation facilitation. It is pathologi-cal to depend upon a permanent transitional object, and therapy has ceased to be dynamic if the patient's emotional needs and perceptions of the therapist do not change. Winnicott's comment about infant feed-ing is also exactly on target at the deepest level of dynamic psycho-therapy with the sex-offender: the nourishing experience may be taken 'as *either* his hallucination *or* a thing belonging to external reality'.

Sommer (1969) discusses why the individual needs a concept of personal space, also known as portable territory, and how 'some people find no place to hide in society and turn within themselves for solace. Strange mannerisms, bizarre dress, and crazy talk are all means for keeping other people at a distance.' Other patients need an intensely shared space, and are, *per contra*, unable to turn within themselves for solace. The links between personal space and the concept of therapeutic space are self-evident. He describes the sociofugal space of a library where interaction is discouraged, and the sociopetal space 'that orients everyone toward the centre [which] makes it difficult for people to retreat'. This is reminiscent of the customary room used for group therapy, where retreating out of the circle, either into the corners or by actually leaving the room, is always seen as a symbolic retreat from the emotional situation currently carried by the group. For example, the patient may be retreating from arguing parents as he did in childhood. The patient's perception of therapeutic space is influenced by innumerable contingent factors, as exemplified by the final meeting between a probation officer and his client [in the 'condemned cell' of a prison] who would be aware of the physical boundaries of therapeutic space. He might also have an added intensity of awareness that this was the last occasion he would share it with his probation officer. He might find it difficult to let his probation officer leave the therapeutic space, which would then cease to be therapeutic. At the other extreme, during the phase of an intense nega-tive transference, a patient may be totally unaware of the physical surroundings in which he meets his therapist who, at that stage in therapy, may be vilified and seen to be everything to the patient which his harsh father in reality represented.

> My cage is within me
> Not without
> The bars as well as the key
> Not without
>
> The cage is without me
> Let me out
> The bars as well as the key
> Let me out.

These verses, written by a hospital patient, are an eloquent presentation of some of the issues discussed by Sommer under the heading of 'The Axiology of Space' in which he considers the different ways in which people value space. 'The cage within' or 'the cage without' highlights the patient's sense of being restricted by both his inner world or the outer world of the environment, and both colour his perception of therapeutic space.

(b) Therapeutic Process

The term therapeutic process refers to the sequence of integrating energies released in a patient as a result of his interaction with the therapist, and I am using it in its least specialised and restricted sense. It is a process in which the patient is enabled to do for himself what he cannot do on his own.* The therapist does not do it for him, but he cannot do it without the therapist. It is inseparable from the interpersonal relationship between therapist and patient, though it is conceptually distinct.

Dynamic psychotherapy involves a deliberate cognitive–affective re-engagement with those aspects of the introjected past which were previously inadequately negotiated. This means that there may be areas of emotional development which were 'bypassed'. In more technical language, this 'shut off' part of the personality may be described as an endopsychic enclave. The impact of this failure to negotiate certain

---

* When a group is the therapeutic focus, the group-as-a-whole is enabled to do for itself what the group-as-a-whole cannot do on its own.

maturational phases implies that the patient experiences a restriction in the quality of his current living. This may present as a specific symptom, as a disorganised sense of chaos, or an awareness of purposeless drifting rather than having any fixed point of reference or goal. Nevertheless, whatever the clinical 'presentation' there is usually failure of unfulfilling loving, so that the patient is either unable to 'let go' of his possessive hold on another, or, *per contra*, he is unable to 'open up' and share life with another. This sharing of life is infinitely more complex than the capacity to enjoy simultaneous sexual orgasm with a partner; though a sexual relationship in which this is not part of shared living usually gives other evidence of corporate defensiveness. Denial or sublimation then 'justify' the poverty of sexual intimacy, however enriching other aspects of life may be. Lack of satisfaction in a sexual relationship is a common reason for seeking professional help. It may take the form of an obsession with 'peak performance', as though the patient expects a five-star orgasm on each occasion. Such anxieties are so widespread (Crown, 1976) and patients may consult their family doctors or seek help through counselling agencies. On the other hand, the lack of satisfaction may lead to overt, and possibly dangerous, sexual deviations (Rosen, 1977).

Once the corrective emotional experience has enabled the introjected past to be re-negotiated, then the patient is better equipped to face the inevitable emotional hazards that await him.

The task of the psychotherapist is to facilitate this cognitive–affective re-engagement with the past, so that the patient is enabled to discover his hitherto unrealised capacity for coping with assaults he experiences, both from his outer and inner world. This facilitating process implies that receptivity is a hallmark of the therapist. So that when the patient feels he wishes to disclose *anything*, however ludicrous, lurid, trivial or traumatic it may sound, the therapist will not merely tolerate his disclosures, but will endeavour to invite and help the patient to accept his own feelings. Such receptivity depends upon a Janusian amalgam of a carefully studied unfolding sequence of events necessitated by the concept of psychic determinism, together with the constant possibility of being 'surprised' by the existential openness of the present moment which calls for an alert sense of expectancy. If anything 'new' is to happen within the immediacy of the 'nowness' of the clinical encounter, then the therapist must not restrict the patient's capacity to have new experiences. The paradoxical amalgam demanded of the therapist, no matter whether the setting is that of a clinical consultation, formal group psychotherapy in a total institution or in an individual psycho-analytic session, is that of providing an 'invitational ethos' of in-evitability–surprise, predictability–unpredictability, surpriseless certainty or 'anything goes'. These twin facets of the therapeutic presence are discussed in greater detail later. But, at this point, it must be stated that, in my view, when the patient is offered a therapeutic presence which is solely based upon psychic determinism (or, *per contra*, when it is solely based on the existential current 'predicament-ness' of both patient and therapist) then something less than the fullest facilitat-ing environment endorses the patient's maturational processes. In my experience, the corporate life of a therapeutic group illustrates these twin approaches so clearly. Psychic determinism underlies the comment from one member of the group to another: 'I knew you were going to have that dream.' The existential exigency of the present moment is evident in so many ways when extraneous events suddenly impinge upon the life of the group; so that novelty, surprise, the unexpected, cause infectious giggling which escalates into 'helpless laughter' or cor-porate disquiet gives way to overt anxiety. It is felt at the 'unexpected' arrival of a noisy new group member, who is not only waspish, but actually is a wasp!; or a window-cleaner's eyes study the group through a transparent 'two-way screen'; or a torrential haemorrhage or an epileptic fit, though they are experienced by an individual member of the group, underline the fact that the group-as-a-whole has to cope with the existential predicament. Such unpredictable events frequently yield a harvest of disclosures. A wasp may frighten any of us all the precise moment in which we are proclaiming our audacity in other fearful circum-stances! A therapeutic group is not slow to seize upon such a 'gift'.

All meetings between patient and doctor either enhance or diminish the therapeutic process. Thus the physical examination or the blood test contribute to an emotional climate which may be therapeutic or the reverse; and there are parallel factors in the professional relationship between, say, the social worker and her client. In this case it may be the mobilisation of social resources, the provision of home help, aid with housing, etc. A probation officer will likewise have contingent factors which impinge upon the relationship which cannot be construed as 'pure counselling'. For example, undue compliance in a prison interview might be attributed to the need to impress the probation officer if a decision was soon to be made about granting parole.

In essence, we are concerned with the therapist's structuring of the therapeutic process, although this never occurs in 'pure culture'. There are always material factors which not only impinge upon the relationship, but actually pervade and may virtually sustain or destroy it. Such factors may be medical, social or legal. Important though they are, they are not our prime concern.

3. DRAMATIS PERSONAE

(a) Patient/Client

My refusal to be drawn into a detailed distinction between a patient and a client is not because I am naïvely simplistic or escapist, but because it is an almost purposeless debate for our present purposes. Both words cover the person who seeks help from a professional who has been specifically trained to offer such help. I adopt the word 'patient' with reference to clinical matters, and 'client' for the rest. The same person may, within ten minutes, assume both roles. When John Smith reports to his probation officer and shares his anxieties about rising hire-purchase premiums, which restrict him, he is a client; when, ten minutes later, he visits his GP, with whom he shares anxiety about rising blood-pressure which restricts him, he is a patient. I shall therefore use the word which seems appropriate, and do not apologise for using either word as our discussion moves from setting to setting.

The concept of structuring the therapeutic process, which applies right across the board in any counselling or psychotherapeutic situation, may therefore occur as part of a more complex relationship in the instances already cited, such as general practice or social work. In the more specialised field of psychoanalysis and, say, group psychotherapy, the therapist works with 'nothing other than the relationship'. This must be the most absurdly generous restriction of all time! The fact that there are no other contingent factors in psychotherapy, such as the physical examination in general practice or the mobilisation of social resources with the social worker's client, does not imply that there are fewer emotional components to the 'pure' psychotherapeutic relationship. It is precisely because of the apparent barrenness of contingent, material, executive facets, which allows the psychotherapeutic relationship to assume its many-faceted, multi-level pleroma of recapitulatory, conscious and unconscious factors which add momentum to the dynamics of psychotherapy. The dimensions of structuring the therapeutic process already outlined, namely time, depth and mutuality, are equally applicable to the 'pure' psychotherapeutic process and the 'consultation' in general practice.

(b) Therapist/Counsellor

Psychotherapy and counselling are both gigantic umbrella terms with many subdivisions, frequently jealously guarded with almost religious fanaticism. I wish to disassociate myself from this distinction. Our focus is upon structuring the therapeutic process, irrespective of the theoretical school espoused by the 'psychotherapist'. I adopt whichever word seems appropriate to the setting described. The important distinction between counselling and psychotherapy is not a question of territorial preserve, duration of training or the prerequisite of a personal analysis. The distinction lies in the therapeutic process itself as a function of depth structuring. In other words, 'superficial psychotherapy' may be much less profound and incursive into the patient's personality than activities normally termed 'counselling'; such as the work of a probation officer involving reality restrictions and the specialised aspects of transference, when, say, a rapist on parole* reports regularly to a female probation officer for 'counselling'. Counselling is often belittled as though it is a poor relation of psychotherapy, which, in turn, is Cinderella compared to the rigours of formal psychoanalysis. In many instances this is far

* Throughout the book our attention is upon changing aspects of the professional relationship between, say, the probation officer and his client. The legal technicalities, important though they are in their own right, are not our concern here. Therefore, in future passages, I shall refer to 'the rapist who meets his probation officer for counselling', and I am not in each instance adding 'on statutory after-care' or 'on parole' after the word 'rapist'. It is taken for granted that the reader is aware that a rapist is very rarely 'put on probation' as a definitive sentence. The important personal relationship with a probation officer may start during the client's life in prison or a secure hospital, and will continue after his release/discharge.

from the truth, when the counsellor, in the kind of professional therapeutic work just described, has an infinitely harder task, and runs many
more professional risks, than the psychotherapist. There are, indeed, great
differences between psychotherapy and counselling, and, in practice, these
depend largely on depth control. For example, there are many ways of
responding to the statement 'I had a dream about you last night'. The
setting influences the quality of an appropriate response in terms of time,
depth and mutuality. This will depend upon whether it is part of prolonged psychotherapy; a casual remark in the GP's surgery; whether it
occurred out of the blue with an almost flirtatious giggle; whether it
occurred at the end of months of many weekly sessions, in which dreams
were described, or whether it was the first occasion when a patient felt
he could describe a dream about the therapist. It might also be that he
had recently had his first dream about the therapist, which is an example
of the Conscious-withheld becoming the Conscious-disclosed.

A dream may be regarded as an existential message (whatever the
physiological 'explanation': see *British Medical Journal*, 1976b) and when
a patient says: 'This is the dream I've been waiting for ... *because it
will tell me something*' there is no doubt that he tells me his dream, because
he wants to tell me something! The nature of my response will either
make it easier for him to make disclosures, or more difficult.

'I had a dream last night about the group ... when Dr. Cox left he had become
a cripple.'

(Anon., 1977)

4. ACTION

(a) Structuring

This may be primary or secondary.

(i) *Primary*

Primary structuring refers to the therapist's personal presence in therapeutic space. It is *what he is* in therapeutic space. This is an exceedingly
complex phenomenon because it involves what the therapist's presence
means to the patient, and during the sequential phases of therapy this
is inevitably coloured by transference and countertransference.

It may appear that duplicity is implicit in the suggestion that the therapist may structure 'what he is' in therapeutic space; though it denotes 'presence modification'. The therapist must, at all times, be himself. He will fail his patient and become either rigidly hyper-defensive, or chaotically unbounded, if he does not remain 'himself' as he engages with the patient in the hard work of therapy. It makes demands upon the therapist and the patient, though the nature of the demand is different. Primary structuring is therefore concerned with the intensification of those aspects of 'who he is', which further the therapist's task of making available aspects of 'what he is' to which the patient can respond. It is difficult to grapple with this concept, but all therapists and patients will, I think, know what I am trying to say! Nevertheless, in the ultimate analysis, if the patient ever senses that the therapist is 'not being himself' with any hint of lack of being genuine and a real person, then the development of transference, without which formal psychoanalytically based psychotherapy would never flourish, is cut off at the roots. It is easy to see that 'who he is' within the context of therapeutic space differs from the 'who he is' of family leap-frog on the beach. Though the distinction is something deeper than simply adopting a different role. It has something to do with a genuine ontological emotional engagement, rather than the adoption of a professional role.

(ii) Secondary
Secondary structuring refers to the therapist's executive initiative in maintaining an optimal disclosure level on behalf of the individual or the group. He achieves this by discriminating differential modification of time, depth and mutuality. It is *what he does* in therapeutic space. These concepts are interlocking but clearly demarcated facets of the therapist's presence.

In non-structured social settings even a fleeting glance may imply an evocative invitation, an incursive penetration, a furtive desire for increased emotional distance or an engaging 'ask me another' ambience. But in the professional setting such factors of non-verbal communication and body-language assume even greater significance. Both primary and secondary structuring depend upon posture, gesture, facial expression and numerous other para-linguistic overtones which 'colour' the spoken word. Structuring therefore depends upon the total 'climate' and not only upon what the therapist says.

Structuring is an activity and carries connotations of work, initiative and energy expended in an executive act, but for what purpose and by whom?

Primary structuring refers to the therapist's use of himself, i.e. how much he gives of himself within therapeutic space, whereas secondary structuring refers to his degree of control of the range and depth of interactions which occur within therapeutic space. The distinction between primary and secondary structuring is shown most graphically by considering the group setting, where the number of possible interactions is so much greater than within the therapeutic space of individual psychotherapy. The distinction between primary and secondary structuring is not purely semantic or academic, because of the wide spectrum of possible interventions ranging from clarificatory or confrontational incursive activity, to personal disclosure by the therapist. The concept of structuring the therapeutic process in terms of time, depth and mutuality applies whatever theoretical school the therapist follows. And like all therapeutic agents, it does not escape the stricture that if, properly used, it can be beneficial to the patient, then, *ipso facto*, improperly used, it may be harmful to the patient. If structuring can be advantageous, then it must, *per contra*, carry risks. In the affective flow of the therapeutic session it may be difficult to distinguish donor and recipient. The patient responds to the therapist and the therapist responds to the patient. The therapist may be active or passive, but when he appears passive he is still attentively monitoring the therapeutic process, and his passive activity is deliberate.

Depending upon exigencies and theory, he may focus on the individuals or the group-as-a-whole. Sometimes the therapist's activity in a group conveys the impression of the circus juggler, who keeps many asymmetrically balanced plates spinning on the ends of canes by means of intense, transient, discriminating activity if poise and balance is to continue. On other occasions his activity is more reminiscent of a timekeeper in a chess tournament, whose silent presence reminds players that there is a limited time in which to move.

Primary structuring, whether on an individual or group basis, is reminiscent of the 'controlled emotional involvement' suggested by Biestek (1957), whereas secondary structuring has implications of controlling events within therapeutic space, which includes the 'response' component of Biestek's triad.

the controlled emotional involvement is the case-worker's sensitivity to the client's feelings, an understanding of their meaning, and a purposeful, appropriate response to the client's feelings.... There are three components in the case-worker's controlled emotional involvement: sensitivity, understanding, and response.

Biestek has certainly touched upon the core of the matter, though I suggest his 'components' are ultimately dependent upon the structuring of time, depth and mutuality. The therapist needs to be able to enter therapeutic space in a natural spontaneous way, although to be 'spontaneous' in such an emotionally charged and often frightening situation can take years of training. It is to be hoped that the therapist gradually develops an increasing sense of being at ease within himself, so that he may enter the orbit of his patient's experience along an appropriate trajectory.

Structuring by the therapist and disclosure by the patient are closely related, though obviously distinct activities. Thus structuring may include the ability to discern, impose or evoke the patient's awareness of form, pattern or meaning in an otherwise inchoate and fluid field. This is an intrinsic part of the activity–passivity spectrum of the therapist's *modus vivendi* concerned with discerning–imposing–evoking awareness of the cosmos behind chaos.

Central to my thesis is the fact that structuring is an activity equally valid in all professional 'helping' relationships. Thus alongside the specialised clinical work of the doctor, or inextricably involved with it, is the use he makes of his own personality. An identical situation pertains to the work of nurses, social workers and counsellors of every discipline. There is an almost endless list of possible professions that might be mentioned, but these must stand vicariously for the rest. Each discipline has its own technical procedures, which may involve physical examination of the patient, environmental manipulation of the client, and many other variations on this theme. In addition to these practical, executive and highly specialised activities there will always be the personal relationship between the patient/client and the therapist/counsellor. This relationship may be brief and intermittent or extended and sustained. The occasional visit to the family doctor is an example of the former, and the patient in regular psychotherapy or psychoanalysis is an example of the latter.

The reasons why a patient is referred for psychotherapy are legion, ranging from the need for symptom relief, or the resolution of internal conflict, to the reduction of social isolation and anomic experience, or the

modification of anti-social behaviour. It may be stated in general terms
that the therapist's attention and initiative is aimed at facilitating the
patient's increasing self-awareness, at a depth and pace which is tolerable,
as he is confronted by those aspects of his life which were hitherto intolerable and thus banished from consciousness. This effect is accelerated
and intensified in a group situation, where the patient is confronted by
many images of himself reflected in other group members. The therapist
may be able to discern patterns in their shared therapeutic space, which,
to the patient, becomes temporarily increasingly frightening and bewilder-
ing, as established defence patterns change. Such bewilderment and confusion may border on malignant chaos, with the attendant risk of the
development of a psychogenic psychosis. The patient is often described
as being 'put in touch with his feelings', and it is the sense of having
a gradual introduction to himself, mediated by the therapist, which
demands the most stringent perception of his levels of tolerance. Yet,
patients frequently say, in one way or another,

> I know that one capsule taken three times per day is not an answer to a personal
> problem, although it made me feel less anxious. I've got to face things about myself
> which I've been running away from for so long.

He embarks upon psychotherapy expecting that it may be painful, but
also aware that growth cannot avoid such pain. The therapist therefore
facilitates or delays emotional disclosure *by* the patient, *to* the patient,
for the patient ... depending upon prevailing psychopathology. It cannot
be over-emphasised that the prolonged silence of the psychoanalyst is
just as much a deliberate structuring activity as the sustained reflection
of the client-centred Rogerian therapist. (*Patient:* 'I'm annoyed with myself
and the whole damn world.' *Therapist:* 'You're annoyed with yourself
and the whole damn world?') It must not be assumed that there is only
one correct way of structuring. The classical Freudian psychoanalytic
situation and that of the Rogerian client-centred therapist provide two
clear-cut examples. The trained professional in either discipline acts in a
different way, and structures the therapeutic process according to certain
theoretical frames of reference. I submit that the difficulty will arise for
each therapist when structuring, according to his own premises, becomes
inappropriate and ineffective. We are therefore not comparing different
styles of structuring between, say, the Freudian and the Rogerian, but
rather indicating that *difficulties in psychotherapy occur when the therapist*

is not at ease with his patient because of faulty structuring, when viewed from the vantage point of his own discipline and training. For example, the trainee analyst may be so concerned with presenting an emotionally neutral, blank screen to his analysand, that he cannot decide whether he should say 'All the best for the exam tomorrow' to his analysand sitting his finals on the subsequent day. In general human terms it seems reasonable to do so, but seen against the background of psychoanalytic theory and the particular stage of therapy, it may be inappropriate, and the trainee may be unsure of structuring because of his feared risks of a marginal modification of mutuality. Mutuality is one of the dimensions of structuring which will be discussed subsequently. The reader may dismiss this as a trivial example, but it is, in fact, a real one.

The concept of 'structuring initiative' poses many fundamental questions about the activity of the therapist. Is it merely a question of seeing what is already there but is scarcely visible, or is it a question of changing what is present, so that it takes on form, pattern or meaning? An even more fundamental question is to ask who it is that structures the therapeutic process, the therapist or the patient. It might be presumed that it is usually the therapist, however casual, colloquial and spontaneous it may appear. It may come as something of a surprise to compare three references about counselling and the activity of the counsellor. Who does the structuring? 'Once feelings begin to be expressed, an emotional involvement starts, and *it is up to the counsellor to decide* the extent to which this shall be allowed to continue and the amount of control he should exercise' (Heaseman, 1969; italics added). 'The point to be clear about is that the client is the arbiter; he controls what can be disclosed, *not the counsellor*' (Venables, 1971; italics added). 'But *the counsellor needs, if possible, to be a little bolder than his client* and sense when is the time *to bring the discussion back* to more personal concerns' (Wallis, 1973; italics added). I suggest that the resolution of these conflicting statements itself depends on other aspects of structuring initiative. By this, I mean that we shall discover that the overall gauging of the depth of the inter-personal encounter between therapist and patient should be, within human limits, at the level of the patient's encounter with himself. It is to be hoped that the therapist will facilitate rather than prevent the patient's increasing self-awareness. The answer to the question of who takes the initiative, the therapist or the patient, lies primarily with the therapist, who will allow the patient such initiative as is 'appropriate'. This was put in inverted commas, because it implies a whole range of clinical judgements about the patient's mental state and his current pattern of defences, which will indicate how much of the unacceptable parts of himself the patient will be able to accept. It is difficult to write about such a complex matter, and though it will be amplified in subsequent chapters, there is no substitute for clinical supervision from an experienced therapist. This paradox may be stated simply, though appreciating such matters in the therapeutic situation requires great finesse. The therapist takes the initiative by structuring the therapeutic process in such a way that *the patient is given adequate scope for disclosure initiative*, compatible with his current mental state, so that he feels that he has the initiative to say whatever he wishes. At times the therapist senses that certain disclosures would be too overwhelming for the patient to express, so that the possible field of the patient's initiative is in fact restricted. In other words, the therapist's initiative controls the overall 'disclosure potential', but as far as the patient is concerned, he feels that he is free to say whatever he wishes. Obviously, he will not be aware of unconscious repressed material. The minutiae of such structuring initiative on the part of the therapist is associated with his scanning attention to everything accessible about the patient; such as the quality of speech, the nature of silence, gestures, postures, rate of respiration, the sweating on his hand or forehead, and so on. Such clinical aids, as well as intuitive discernment, give the therapist's initiative a scanning quality which changes from discerning form, pattern or meaning to evoking the patient's awareness of these qualities. The therapist's structuring activity is not only to discern form in an emotional fog, but to delicately impose a pattern and invite awareness of a meaningful process in the place of inchoate turbulence, primitive violence or disorganised and inexplicably insatiable hunger for love or protection. Analogies can sometimes convey meaning in such a vivid, concentrated form that many pages of technical, arid description are obviated. The structuring process may be exemplified by considering the therapist and patient walking in mountain mist. Neither can see the summit. Whereas one may panic and be aware of chaos, the other searches for the compass and the next cairn. However turbulent the transference, the therapist tries to retain contact with landmarks. Jung (1954) implied this when he spoke of the therapist being more conscious than the patient, in his discussion of the transference relationship.

The psychotherapist needs not only the highest possible clinical acumen and diagnostic expertise, with a ruthless concern for precision, such as an adequate conceptual model of defence, but simultaneously (and this is the rub) a sense of sharing experience with his patient. He must be regarded as 'safe' to be invited into the patient's inner world, with its universal fantasies of loving and killing. Books on psychotherapy tend to describe patients as either experimental objects, to be worked 'on' and studied, or to describe them in experiential, almost religious terms, so that clinical grasp is elusive. To try to have a foot in both camps may invite disaster, but the experience of working with offender-patients continually confronts the therapist with this Janusian dilemma. Thus a rapist of 26 can be described as 'an aggressive psychopath, with poor socialisation and high impulsivity', his sexual drives can be assessed and his penile erections can be measured for speed, strength and duration. At the same time he can be known as a man with low self-esteem, which dates from early parental rejection, and the awareness that his adoption was instrumental in enhancing parental prestige, rather than parental affection. Such an experience may be extrapolated to indicate that no one, male or female, would ever want him for himself, and therefore, because he would never be loved spontaneously, he had to force himself into a sexual situation and 'get' what he would never be given. During the course of psychotherapy such a patient may come to trust the therapist in a way that he has never trusted anyone else, and there will be rare and fragile moments of deep personal disclosure which have never been reached before. Nevertheless, the gentle building up of such a patient's ability to love and be loved must be seen over and against a history in which another person was severely wounded and possibly killed. Psychotherapy with such patients strongly reinforces the necessity for adequate structuring of the therapeutic process.

The mental defence mechanism of repression may keep the emotionally painful fact that a man has recently fatally stabbed his brother beyond the reach of introspection. The clinical presentation may therefore be as a circumscribed, focal amnesia for the event. When such a patient embarks upon psychotherapy, the therapist may so structure the initial sessions that feelings about the brother were not deliberately evoked because they would be intolerable. And any therapeutic thrust in this direction would be counter-productive and lead to more fiercely entrenched amnesia. Alternatively, if the therapist senses that the patient is keen to discuss the details of the events and get the feelings 'off his chest', it would scarcely be therapeutic to prevent this. He therefore structures the therapeutic process in such a manner that the patient may be slightly anxious, to the extent that such anxiety provokes disclosure; but not to such an extent that the patient experiences catastrophically overwhelming anxiety. This might lead to explosive acting-out or accelerated emotional distancing.

A similar need for the discretionary decision of discerning an optimal therapeutic strategy is presented in a particularly vivid way by the adolescent patient. The commonest clinical presentation of the adolescent referred for counselling is that of an identity crisis. The patient is manifestly no longer a child, though he has not yet reached the stage of adult autonomy. Adolescent ambivalence towards authority is shown so clearly in the following disclosure:

> I blamed them for *letting me* get out of their grasp.

The therapist tries to avoid the two pitfalls of making the individual either more, or less, of a 'patient' than he needs to be. Unnecessarily frequent therapeutic sessions may reinforce the adolescent's sense of being a 'patient', and therefore different from his peers who 'do not need to see a psychiatrist regularly'. Whereas the opposite risk is that of not taking the patient sufficiently 'seriously', by not providing a much-needed therapeutic presence, which the young patient, already uncertain of his own identity, may desperately need but finds it difficult to ask for. Put bluntly, the dilemma facing the therapist is to avoid making the individual either more or less of a patient than he, himself, feels that he is. Coleman (1974) discusses relationships in adolescence and studies the way in which the adolescent perceives his 'effective personal world', to use Laing's phrase. The structuring of time, depth and mutuality with such patients can be extremely difficult. Yet, when judged correctly, can ease a difficult transitional phase for the patient and reinforce the therapist's sense of gaining effective clinical discretion.

The ability to appropriately structure the therapeutic situation, which depends upon overt clinical evidence and intuitive reading between the lines, is an invaluable asset for the therapist. If this ability is intuitive, can it be taught? The appropriate use of his own personality in the therapeutic situation is a central topic in all psychotherapy training and supervision. I hope that some of the ideas suggested about structuring the therapeutic process may be helpful in equipping the therapist to appraise his relationship with his patient, in terms of the crucial dimensions of time, depth and mutuality. The therapist has to think hard about the ultimate value of his structuring skills when a widow tells him that she received most help from a visitor who said

> I don't know what to say.

Structuring finesse without 'the meeting of people' would be abortive.

(b) Disclosure and levels of disclosure

> I have seen
> Hours dreadful and things strange, but this sore night
> Hath trifled former knowings.
>
> *(Macbeth,* II. iv. 2)

This is the subject of Chapter 8 and pervades much of the text, but it is introduced at this point as it is a key concept in our terms of reference.

In dynamic psychotherapy movement always occurs in the direction of disclosure, by which I mean that the unconscious becomes conscious. It has already been said that further therapeutic movement in the same direction implies that the total process can be regarded as follows: Unconscious→Conscious-withheld→Conscious-disclosed. For obvious reasons the therapeutic group provides the ideal *milieu* in which the change from Conscious-withheld to Conscious-disclosed is facilitated. Macnab (1965) describing group therapy with schizophrenics endorses the value of disclosure in a corporate setting: 'The patient may disclose to one, but may be in semblance with the rest of the world. Thus the group assumed vital significance, for it represented more faithfully the shock of self-disclosure to the patient's world.'

The concept of disclosure refers to three 'levels'* of emotional 'revelation' ranging from the trivial, 'bus-stop', inconsequential chat of the first level, e.g. 'I thought I saw frost this morning' to the extremely personal (either treasured or 'banished' because of shame or resentment) third level, e.g. 'I never had a childhood'. It will be seen that these levels are moving in the direction of greater disclosure. This means that a third-level disclosure occurs in individual or group therapy as 'Conscious-withheld'

---

* See page 164 ff for further consideration of levels of disclosure.

becomes 'Conscious-disclosed'; indeed, this important transition is, *ipso facto*, always in the form of a third-level disclosure.

Disclosures have the characteristic quality that the patient appears to be startled by what he has said. They are often truncated, internally contradictory, 'poetic', telegrammatic, primary process utterances and are usually accompanied by the physiological concomitants of anxiety (or the reduction of anxiety).

The *therapist must discern what the disclosure means to the patient and not what it would mean to him (the therapist) if he had said it.* What would be a third-level disclosure for me is not necessarily so for my patient, and *vice versa.*

The different levels of disclosure form excellent teaching foci and link closely with heuristic devices known as the 'disclosure profile' for an individual and the 'differential disclosure profile' for a group (Cox, 1978, *Coding the Therapeutic Process*). It may be baldly stated at this stage, though it will be elaborated further on, that one of the features distinguishing counselling and psychotherapy is varying disclosure-level control. For example, free-association, an essential part of psychoanalytic technique, has no bar to disclosure levels, whereas group counselling, which might be 'problem-orientated', would limit emotional disclosures about, say, dreams which were not strictly relevant to the problem under consideration.

Celebration

In psychotherapy the patient is encouraged to say whatever comes into his mind and it is not surprising that the areas of life which many people find difficult to disclose, though obviously influenced by culture and social setting, relate to their personal experience and inner world of fantasy and dream. This frequently includes destructiveness, eroticism, rivalry, sexual deviation and the like. Nevertheless, he should not be discouraged from saying whatever comes into his mind if it happens to be in the nature of joy, thanksgiving, affirmation or celebration. It is a perverted idea of therapy to presume that it is only masturbatory fantasy or oedipal problems which are indicative of what is buried in the patient's unconscious, and so 'acceptable' as free-association! There may have been experiences which were more in the nature of a celebration which had been banished from consciousness by, say, a frightening mother. If the patient is encouraged to say whatever comes into his mind, then he must be allowed to share the joy and excitement, maybe, of a fifth birthday party, and not only the repressed anger towards his mother, who subsequently cast a shadow over the celebration by confiscating his most important present. It is unusual to find such words as joy, thanks and celebration in the index of a book on psychotherapy, but the training for psychotherapy must include the development of a sufficient degree of freedom 'from himself' for the therapist to be able to 'take' whatever the patient discloses. It would be a caricature of therapy if the therapist could only hear about impotence, failure or the fear of failure, and dismiss any joy and celebration as his patient being 'defensive'. The therapist is confronted by himself in the patient with whom he shares therapeutic space. The therapist's personal *weltanschauung* may be called into play at any time, and it is essential that he has a wide enough frame of reference to include the capacity to accept whatever his patient needs to disclose. The disclosure may obviously relate to psychopathology, without which the patient and therapist would never have met. As therapy progresses, and the patient feels safe enough to make fuller disclosures many enjoyable, 'good' events and experiences may be shared. Thus the therapist must be able to take not only his patient's disclosures about psychopathology, which so often involves sexual and aggressive drives and may have led to killing or rape, in fantasy or fact, but he must also be able to rejoice with those that rejoice. *The therapist may be threatened if his patient's joy is greater than his own.* It may be safer for the therapist to hear of his patient's failures than of his successes, if the therapist's homosexuality, impotence or need to be successful, outweigh his joy, celebration and experience of love. The patient may be less afraid of death than the therapist's *weltanschauung* allows him to be.

Laughter: defence or achievement?
Every experienced therapist knows that the manic defence is a reality. Trivial giggling, incongruous gaiety, may be, and often are, ego defence mechanisms. Nevertheless, to belittle all humour and genuine shared laughter is to trivialise what can be one of the deepest human experiences.

When laughter is not a defence it may be an enriching reinforcement of corporate solidarity. The ability to laugh at himself is, paradoxically, an indication that a man is able to take himself seriously. Similarly, a group that dares to accept laughter, will also be able to tolerate tears. At the end of his book *Tensions: Necessary Conflicts in Life and Love*, Williams (1976) writes: 'And although we are still on our journey, when we laugh we know that really we have already arrived. The party has begun and we are there.'

> The lamentable change is from the best;
> The worst returns to laughter.
>
> (*King Lear*, IV. i. 5)

In ordinary social intercourse, or the world of literature or drama, there is a clear distinction between hearty, insensitive, robust jocularity; the trivialising, tedious quality of hectic gaiety or perpetually infectious ebullience and the capacity to laugh, and thoroughly enjoy it, as the occasion demands. This is a function of an integrated personality, just as much as is the ability to cry, in appropriate circumstances. There is no conceivable reason why the patient in psychotherapy should not aim towards what is, after all, the norm, i.e. the ability to laugh or cry, as the occasion demands. I always find that the answer to the question 'When did you last laugh?', during an initial interview, is extraordinarily revealing. A similar question, 'When did you last laugh at home?' is even more revealing.

'Home! Laugh!... Never... the two just did not go together', or, 'We never stopped... it was a riot from start to finish'. There are many other variants between these extremes. The fear of laughter so often borders upon paranoid ideation, as though laughter is always at the expense of the hearer. 'I heard people laughing... and I knew they must be laughing at me.' There are echoes here of the distinction between the depressed patient who enjoys nothing, and therefore all laughter is a waste of time, i.e. he is truly anhedonic; and the hysterical patient who insists that he enjoys nothing, though he obviously enjoys telling you that he enjoys nothing. This is 'pseudo-anhedonia' and is an important point in distinguishing the depressed patient, whose energy to be depressed is anger against the self, from the hysterical patient whose defence mechanism is that of denial. This is not only an unconscious defence mechanism but it is frequently overt and intentional, i.e. the patient denies what he is telling you during the very act of doing so. It is for this reason that the pseudo-anhedonic patient flares up, if there is even a flicker of an indication that the therapist is aware that the patient who 'enjoys nothing', appears to be enjoying relating the fact. It would therefore not be prudential to raise an eyebrow in an initial interview when this phenomenon occurs; although it is an important point in differential diagnosis, influences prognosis and is likely to carry considerable weight in the decision about the suitability of embarking upon a particular form of psychotherapy.

Laughter, and the lack of laughter, is inevitably closely bound up with the patient's emotional life. The changing qualities of laughter (its spontaneity, its congruity, its insularity, its degree of corporate participation, its 'controllability', its affective concomitants, etc.) furnish invaluable clinical material.

Thus the capacity to laugh, the capacity to tolerate being laughed at and the capacity to laugh at oneself are closely linked with ego-strength and indicate an ability to 'tolerate' the 'intolerable'. The catalytic effect of group laughter, at an object of mirth *outside* the group, can lead to the acceptance of a group's ability to laugh at *itself*, i.e. the group-as-a-whole. Once this has occurred it becomes a group which can 'tolerate itself', and individual disclosures follow, almost too fast to assimilate.

For example, group laughter may 'spontaneously' lead almost 'casually' to a patient's description of how he felt excited as he broke into a house, and this experience of entering forbidden territory was similar, though less intense, to the sexual experience of breaking into a forbidden woman. The therapist is able to be with his patient as he gradually understands things about himself, either individually or within the context of a group, relating to, say, rape. But he must also be able to take the joy of his patient. It says a great deal about the therapist if laughter is always regarded as a manic defence, or he writes 'heavily defended' in his notes if a patient describes himself as being happily married. This attitude may say more about the therapist's marriage than that of his patient!

If the therapeutic process only consisted of laughter and thankfulness, it would indeed be pathological! However, it may embrace forgotten joy, banished affirmation and crushed celebration. The patient would not have embarked upon the therapeutic process without adequate motivation and psychopathology which the therapist felt could be modified by psychotherapy. Nevertheless, if the whole person is to be acceptable to himself, by way of the shared experience with the therapist, then his repressed joy must be made conscious just as much as his guilt. My experience with many groups of patients from all social classes, including mixed groups of patients whose histories include killing, is that it is often during sessions of deep sharing in the group (where group cohesion was possibly at its highest and maybe fostered by an amusing 'happening', a poem written by a patient, or waves of laughter) that the deepest disclosures, perhaps concerning the wish to kill or the actual killing of a relative, occurred. If the patient is to be accepted as a person in his own right, then his joy just as much as his psychopathology must be acceptable to the therapist. The forgotten birthday party, when 'I was too happy to remember... since Mum died', might be a gateway to the realisation that the patient had a capacity for joy and previous good experiences which, along with his mother's death, had been repressed. Shared joy can lead to the most painful disclosures: 'Am I a man or a woman?'... 'I wouldn't mind if only someone wanted me because I was me,' but, *per contra*, it often surprises the patient to discover that an even deeper disclosure was that he can be 'surprised by joy' (a phrase deliberately borrowed from Lewis, 1955). Becker (1962) makes the fascinating comment, 'the psychoanalytic view was not complete ... the child reacts not only to the threat of despair but also to the overwhelmingness of the miraculous. Both of these dimensions of experience dwarf him and threaten his power and sanity.' Thus the therapist must be able to let his patient's joy and love come into therapeutic space if he is to let depression, anger and destructiveness do likewise. *To preclude any disclosure is to prevent free-association.* Such free-association may in time include fantasies of incest, penis envy, the dentate vagina, the frustrating breast and other psychoanalytic concepts which permeate the literature. Further, free association may permit crushed celebration to surface into conscious awareness. The celebration which had been crushed is as important for the patient to accept, as is the wish to kill an omnipotent parental figure who may have caused the crushing. However, there are people whose lives have been so impoverished and unnourished since their moment of birth, that they have no good experiences whatever to fall back on. Their environment has always failed them. This also the therapist must be able to accept. Such patients will inevitably make greater demands upon the therapist in terms of dependency and the need for nurturing and sustenance, because he is supplying them for the first time. Because of their inadequate ego-strength, and their inability to 'use psychotherapy', they may be sent back to the referring GP who will have endless demands from such patients for the emotional feeding they have never had as a child. They therefore present as a perennial 'child' in the doctor's consulting room or the social worker's office, needing endless support. The mere juxtaposition of such words as 'joy' and 'celebration' with such patients underlines the point.

Disclosures can threaten the therapist

    The therapist may be threatened by the patient's need for support, and therefore refer him back to his GP because he is not 'suitable' for psychotherapy. The therapist may be threatened by the joy in his patient if it is greater than his own; this is of special relevance in the world of personal relationships and, in particular, to marriage, family life and the deepest meta-psychological frame of reference within which he and his patient meet. Both he and his patient will die. The fear of death and separation is therefore an almost universal topic at some stage in psychotherapy (see *The Denial of Death*, Becker, 1973). Indeed, the avoidance of death would be just as much a defensive manœuvre as would be the avoidance of joy. All laughter is not a manic defence, and it can be the strongest bonding between therapist and patient which facilitates subsequent disclosure of a profound dread of separation. There are hints here of Jung's concept of the shadow self, which extend to the shadow group. Behind the shared group dream there may be group solidarity and an awareness of cohesion which permits the group to tolerate internal confrontation. I return to a fundamental tenet of psychotherapy that if association is to be free for the patient, then the therapist must be able to 'take' whatever the patient discloses as buried, unconscious material enters consciousness. The therapist is, in a sense, at his patient's mercy, because he may be confronted at any moment by rape or rapture. The grotesque as well as the generous may show up the therapist to himself, as the patient comes to terms with himself. One of the reasons why psychotherapy may be prolonged, in what was originally described as a negative therapeutic reaction, can be because the patient wishes to retain contact with the therapist. He senses that one way in which to 'keep' the therapist is by concentrating on psychopathology. 'If I was well, he will not see me again, therefore I will remain ill.' 'Whenever they said "You're getting better", I did something else!' Many different factors come into play if repressed happiness is as acceptable, via free-association, as repressed hell. In this instance the patient cannot 'keep' the therapist by being ill!

If free-association is to live up to its name, it must permit not only the disclosure of torment and dread, but also love and joy. Kierkegaard (1844) ends his study of anxiety with a prophetic sentence: 'So soon as psychology has finished with dread, it has nothing to do but to deliver it over to dogmatics.' Dogmatics of any kind, including those of the psychiatrist and the psychoanalyst, may stifle disclosure, prevent free-association and thus intensify a patient's sense of chaos.

CHAPTER 3

The Sense of Self

Where had they come from?
Out of my joy, out of my sorrow,
Living entities sprung into life from the dust
Of my existence, taking wing, making song?
Or were they there already before I came
Along into my room, waiting
Until my joy should open eyes to see them,
Until my sorrow should reach down
Into the depths of being, and there find them,
Find such a company of living multitude?
(from *The Company*, Kathleen Raine, 1956)

Here coincide
The long histories
Of forms recurrent
That meet at a point
And part in a moment,
The rapid waves
Of wind and water
And slower rhythm
Of rock weathering
And land sinking.
(from *The Moment*, Kathleen Raine, 1956)

Dynamic psychotherapy involves the meeting of at least two people, and whatever theoretical position the therapist holds, he will inevitably reflect upon the meaning of shared space, in terms of the relationship with his patient.

The Sense of Self is important to both the therapist and patient as they share therapeutic space.* The therapist tries to maintain his sense of self, though it may be temporarily modified by countertransference, which makes demands upon his identity-retaining energy. The therapist

---

* 'The real feeling is battling with my own worth' (a patient's disclosure which the therapist recognises as his own).

also tries to enhance his patient's sense of self. This is true not only for the depressed, anhedonic patient whose self-esteem is obviously low, but, paradoxically, it is also true for the narcissistic* patient who appears to radiate self-confidence. Such patients may be enabled to discover sufficient certainty of their *own* identity that they can *share* life with others, rather than constantly needing to impress the 'audience' of the environment in a flamboyant, peacockesque manner. This finds its most obvious expression in the difference between the satisfaction of sexual intercourse as part of shared life, in which each partner becomes the 'unlived life' of the other, and the self-defeating, despair-reinforcing autogenous act of masturbating in front of a mirror.

Khan (1974a) in *The finding and becoming of self* discusses two styles of relating to patients: the first is 'covered by interpretative work' and is related to the deciphering of meaning, whereas the second is 'more in the nature of providing coverage for the patient's self-experience in the clinical situation. The knack of any psychotherapeutic work is to strike the right balance within these two types of functions in the therapist.' I entirely endorse this experience described by Khan. The 'knack' is a clinical skill based on theoretical premises and modified in the light of personal experience. When 'the knack' fails it is because the structuring of the therapeutic process in terms of time, depth and mutuality falters. The therapeutic presence offered by the therapist is then inappropriately loaded towards 'deciphering meaning' on the one hand, or 'holding', on the other.

If the therapist is to enable the curative inter-personal process of change to take place, such dynamic psychotherapy will not only facilitate change in the patient but, possibly along other dimensions, the therapist himself will change too. If I was exactly the same person, seeing life in exactly the same way after a thousand hours of sharing therapeutic space, with a group of murderers or rapists, I would be dangerously immune to the affective flow of my patients' experience.

The life of a group inevitably impinges upon the therapist. Whereas a group may always have a fixed constitution of, say, four male and four female patients, each group so constituted will have its own orchestration and its idiosyncratic sonorities. If the patients are to experience 'the find-

* See *The Restoration of the Self.* Kohut, H. (1977) International Universities Press, New York.

ing and becoming of self', the therapist must do so too, because the becoming of self is an open-ended process which extends, at least, until death. (Whether it extends beyond death takes us into another realm of discourse which is not appropriate here.)

Each therapeutic encounter contains moments of existential choice for the therapist. This is true whether he is working in an individual or group setting, or whether the therapy takes place within a total institution or in the wider community. He must act in the immediacy of the present moment and cannot defer decision about technical problems, such as judging the texture or timing of an appropriate intervention. Therapy may call for physical activity such as dealing with a patient who has an epileptic fit during the session, or is about to explode in a catastrophic manner which may endanger other members of the group or the patient, himself. There is therefore always a preserve of clinical discretion and autonomy which cannot be evaded. Events in therapeutic space 'now', call for appropriate response 'now'. The gradual discovery of the therapist's personal threshold of awareness is an essential part of the suffering–maturational process of psychotherapy training. If he is unduly anxious at the slightest provocation, he prevents effective dynamic flow within the group; whereas to sit back and give a commentary on the dynamics of the situation while several patients assault each other can scarcely be termed therapeutic!

The therapeutic task of enabling the patient to redefine faulty self-definition, is one which bridges the nosological gap between neurotic and psychotic 'categories'. A disturbed sense of self may be the experience of all patients, though each category presents this psychopathology in a different way.

It is not only psychotic illness which distorts patients' construction of reality. There is a certain similarity between the activity of the psychotic patient who eats his clinical notes, as a way of destroying his past, and that of a non-psychotic patient whose intention to change her name is not merely to escape recognition and stigmatisation, but also in the deep conviction that she will, *ipso facto*, actually become another person. Her intention was not merely to achieve a disguise by wearing the mask of another name, but to so transform her identity that she actually became someone else. There are interesting parallels between this clinical instance and the predicament of Lord George Hell in Beerbohm's (1897) *The*

Happy Hypocrite, in which the ugly lord falls in love with a beautiful girl and he can only win her hand by wearing a mask. There is an anticipated moment of fearful vulnerability when he is denounced, but when it is stripped off it is seen that he has become like the mask. In fact the relationship had made him become what, previously, he had only seemed to be. I submit that this is a parable of an axiomatic component of dynamic psychotherapy with many patients who are stigmatised by society, either on account of deviant activity or physical deformity, and who therefore seek other avenues of self-esteem regulation. By this I mean that, for example, a psychopath who 'wears the mask' of honesty may actually become honest, as the maturing process is accelerated by psychotherapy. Gloucester, who later became King Richard III, was aware that he was so 'unfashionable / That dogs bark at me, as I halt by them...'. He gives such a vivid account of a man's precarious self-esteem when severe and obvious physical deformity threaten him, that it must be quoted in full:

> But I, that am not shap'd for sportive tricks,
> Nor made to court an amorous looking-glass;
> I, that am rudely stamp'd, and want love's majesty
> To strut before a wanton ambling nymph;
> I, that am curtail'd of this fair proportion,
> Cheated of feature by dissembling nature,
> Deform'd, unfinish'd, sent before my time
> Into this breathing world, scarce half made up,
> And that so lamely and unfashionable
> That dogs bark at me, as I halt by them.
>
> (Richard III. I. i. 14)

The subsequent development of the play is a classic example of how self-esteem regulators of destructiveness and ambition follow in the wake of stigmatising experiences. A 'corrective emotional experience' at the optimal time might have changed him (and history!).

A poignant search for enhanced self-esteem, and a clearer sense of identity, is that described by a young offender-patient,* who, hitherto, had impoverished and almost non-existent self-esteem. The first time he could recall being wanted was when he featured as someone '*WANTED*' in connection with a crime. An identity parade, pointing fingers and a

---

* A further example is given by a girl who asked for an extra copy of an 'official photograph' because no one had ever wanted her photograph before.

unanimous 'He's the man' (*Ecce homo*) made him feel 'I became a real person for the first time in my life'. Dynamic psychotherapy with such a patient must inevitably suggest other pathways to achieve a sense of self, as well as redefining his personal sense of value and being valued. Thus he might ultimately learn that he was wanted for being himself, and not because of what he had done.

A young psychotic patient referred to an 'incident' caused by him when he was disturbed. 'That was me *then*'; he demonstrated the break in continuity of a sense of identity which thought disorder can 'cause'. The 'me *then*' was not the same as the 'me *now*... we're different people.' This is in marked contrast to the logical, rational approach of the philosopher. Lewis (1969) writes:

> I recognise myself in the past experience to be the person I am now, not, as I have stressed, because of any particular content of the experience it is, but more expressly in the proper reconstruction of the experience as a whole. I recall, in other words, not just what happened but its *happening to me as the person I know myself to be now*. [Italics added.]

This passage comes from *The Elusive Self*; the 'self' is particularly elusive for the psychotic patient.

Sensitivity, flexibility and the ability to use the existential immediacy of the 'off-the-cuff' situation within a theoretical framework of psychic determinism, are likely to be personality characteristics of the would-be psychotherapist. He will spend the remainder of his days wishing these attributes could be improved. It is the paradox of purposeful spontaneity which governs both the structuring initiative of the therapist and the free-association of the patient. It is because the therapist's personal experience is always 'at risk' when sharing space with his patient, that selection procedures for training in psychotherapy and counselling must be rigorous, with the result that they are often assumed to be unnecessarily harsh and exclusive. However, much depends upon the therapist's personal *weltanschauung* which must be broad enough to embrace whatever the patient may disclose. When the therapist invites the patient to 'say anything', there is an implicit assumption that he is able to 'hear everything'. This is a less than modest claim, because it means that the therapist is equally at ease in the presence of his patient's disclosures about loss, loneliness and death; power, position and prestige; politics, pacifism and prostitution; religion, rape and racism; Marx and the Marquis de Sade; violence and virginity, and the almost limitless variation of sexuality; heterosexuality, homosexuality, and deviant sexuality of every kind. Clearly, no such idealised human being exists! Nevertheless, the therapist is in the presence of another person who has been encouraged to 'say anything' and his painful personal experience may, at any moment, be recalled. Unless he is sufficiently secure within himself, he may be preoccupied by his own sexual or aggressive fantasies while listening to his patient's disclosures. He is then unable to focus unconditional concern, either upon what his patient says, or upon those para-linguistic overtones which may 'disclose' the silent facts of resistance, rebellion or retreat.

There are certain therapeutic initiatives subsumed under the heading of structuring which enable the patient to relinquish the use of primitive defences such as projection and denial. Basic English makes the point far more effectively when it is stated that the therapist's aim is to put the patient 'in touch with his feeling', though at an acceptable depth and pace. Like many clinical activities, or such complicated manœuvres as driving a car, there seem to be so many variables which alarm the beginner. But it soon becomes clear that with experienced supervision, it is possible to control, in an optimal fashion, several variables at the same time. If this does not occur, accidents follow, in psychotherapy no less than in driving!

The interrelationship of self, space and sharing, which are universally important variables in every counselling setting, can be exemplified by two brief vignettes.

The first took place in a long hospital corridor, where Jeremy, an introverted, intermittently psychotic, frail, frightened young man, noiselessly glided towards me and whispered:

> Dr. Cox, everyone hears voices ... (*long pause*) ... don't they?

What does an 'appropriate response' mean in this situation? What would be optimal primary and secondary structuring? If the answer given is 'No', however warmly or reassuringly, it would accentuate the young man's sense of being different, and run the risk of increasing his social and emotional distancing; with the attendant possibilities that his hallucinations would return, as he withdrew into himself from such an unfriendly environment. On the other hand, if the answer is 'Yes', it would not only be untrue but, in the long run, would not be ultimately therapeutic and beneficial. It would certainly be a tempting expedient, which might temporarily reassure him, but it might impair Jeremy's reality-testing, already manifestly precarious.

Could there be a response which took into account the feelings and expectations of the patient and yet, at the same time, be honest ('Everyone does *not* hear voices') and still be therapeutic?

Would the answer 'I am sure everyone has his own private world', which is both existentially and ultimately true (and yet would not block a deepening relationship with the patient because it is no deception or betrayal), be a reasonable structuring of the therapeutic process, in terms of this casual meeting in a hospital corridor? Would the appropriate response be different if the same patient had asked the same question in a group setting, and would the therapist's primary and secondary structuring be different for both immediate and long-term logistic purposes? This deceptively simple question epitomises the therapist's dilemma, and demands the conceptual framework of a structured therapeutic process.

The second example is taken from a group in which a patient comments upon my new shoes!

> I like your shoes ... what size are they?... I could do with a pair like that!

There are many possible 'appropriate' responses in this situation. The therapist might give a direct answer to the individual; he might deflect the question to the questioner or generalise it to the entire group; he might remain quietly attentive and await events; he might comment on the prevailing mood of the group (e.g. the group might appear to be disastrously relaxed if, in another setting, this apparently trivial question was asked while a known arsonist had just set fire to the curtains!); he might note the fact that long-standing latent homosexual identification was at last at the brink of disclosure; he might hint that it seems to be safer deliberately to draw attention to male clothing, because it is further removed from the risky fantasy world of the transvestite, who prefers female clothing, etc. Each of these responses *might* be appropriate, depending upon the patterning within the group matrix and the endopsychic patterning of the individual patient, in this place, at this time. If this fusion of psychic determinism and existential immediacy applies to the therapist's discernment of an appropriate response to such an apparently inconsequential and trivial 'starter' as 'I like your shoes', then how much more important does structuring become when parataxic distortion, transference and countertransference, identical dreams about the group by members of the group and other such sophisticated dynamic patterns, are added. Secondary structuring describes what the therapist 'does' within therapeutic space, in terms of an almost limitless variety of interventions, which may be verbal or non-verbal. Gesture, posture and expression convey meaning to the group-as-a-whole and each individual patient differently, depending upon previous experience. The parataxic distortion of current perception, together with transference-induced 'colouring', of both the other members of the group and the therapist, add to the pleroma of composite experience.

There is no such entity as the 'correct response' to the remark about my shoes, though the patient is entitled to expect consistency from the therapist; so there might be a way in which my patients would expect me to answer, whereas a colleague might respond in a different way. This exemplifies a paradoxical facet of psychotherapy training, namely, that the therapist learns to be spontaneous. For what it is worth, I would always try to gain maximal therapeutic advantage of a situation, such as this 'shoe incident'. If I had naïvely replied 'They are 9½', which might be a literal answer to a specific manifest question, it would put a fullstop to the end of an expression, where I would hope that my response might serve as a comma. The aim is to foster disclosure rather than closure. A tangential reply which, in this instance, might have opened up a whole area of the patient's inner world (or of corporate though hidden group life) which, hitherto, had been almost sealed off, might have been some such reply as 'This is the first time *"standing in my shoes"* has been mentioned, although the group has often made it clear what it would do in my shoes.' Brian had difficulties about authority, rebellion, identification with older men, and other factors, which made me feel that for him, at that time, in that place, this seemed an appropriate response; though a corporate attitude vicariously voiced by Brian may indicate a generic response to the group as a whole.

There is no 'correct' way of dealing with such a situation. The group analyst, the client-centred group counsellor, and colleagues from many other disciplines, might each deal with the situation in a different way. My contention is that every therapist and counsellor, whatever his theoretical perspective, will be structuring the therapeutic process in terms of time, depth and mutuality. His structuring initiative would be both primary, i.e. what he *is* in therapeutic space, and secondary, i.e. what he *does* in therapeutic space.

Whatever may be written about the professional skills of structuring the therapeutic process during the formal therapeutic session (whether individual or group), there is always the casual, 'off-the-cuff' encounter which may take place at the bus-stop, in the canteen or as a chance meeting in the hospital corridor. Such encounters are always important, and possibly even more so when the majority of the time, when therapist and patient meet, is in a formal setting. One such incident may illustrate the point. I was coming down the stairs of a busy hospital ward where patients were waiting to go into the dining room. Open arms and a loud cry greeted me as I turned the corner:

> 'How much do you love me, Murray?'
> 'How much do you want to be loved?'
> 'A pound of sugar and a quarter of tea!'
> 'That's too commercial for me, Sarah!'
> 'Cheers.'
> 'Cheers.'

(This brief encounter seemed to be satisfactory, for the patient, me and the numerous onlookers! Any attempt to provide a 'serious' reply would have met with ridicule from Sarah, an extremely intelligent girl, who knew that the setting did not call for a 'professional' response. On the other hand, to walk briskly by as though I had not heard would, by any standards, be inhuman. The fact that our brief encounter ended with a reciprocal smile and 'cheers', did, I think, prove the point that this casual meeting was a friendly indication of mutual recognition. I am not claiming that this was a therapeutic process to be structured in any formal sense but, in retrospect, it seemed a useful way of using time, depth and mutuality; although, when it happened, it just happened!)

Another brief encounter which, though superficially trivial, raises fundamental existential issues of identity and self-esteem, is as follows:

[Setting: *A crowded hospital corridor where I meet a patient, normally encountered only during a formal weekly therapeutic group.*]

'Whatever may be said ... underneath ... *really* you're just a professional therapist and I'm just a patient.... Anything else is on the surface!'

'Or could we be ... underneath ... *really* just two people saying 'Good
to see you' ... and anything *else* is on the surface?'
'Could be....'

Professional boundaries

The doctor, the teacher, the probation officer, the generic social worker,
the nurse and the members of other professions are well aware that there
is a boundary defining their preserve of professional expertise, which is
also an interface with that of a colleague in the next 'territory'. It may
be presumed that the adequately trained professional operates with
appropriate knowledge and matching technical skill if confronted by a
challenge, the nature of which is well within his sphere of competence.
Nevertheless, there are many marginal situations in which he does not
feel fully at ease in himself, and yet he can think of no other discipline
readily accessible and available for his 'patient', so that relatively untrained in this particular field as he is, he still has to act to the best of
his ability. If he does not do so, he is diminishing the reservoir of professional help to which his patient is entitled. These strictures apply to us
all. No single professional can possibly be equally fully versed in clinical
matters, education, social policy and the law, to name but a few. The
number of full-time professional counsellors and psychotherapists is
infinitesimal compared with the demands for counselling and psychotherapy made upon the teacher or the doctor. The latter have not had
full professional training in counselling, yet they are confronted day by
day by pupils and patients whose presenting problems are often an
amalgam of educational or purely 'medical' matters, and the individual's
emotional response to the predicament in which he finds himself. It is
not only in the comparatively safe confines of the specialist psychotherapist's consulting room that the structuring of therapeutic process is
important. It is at least as significant, if not more so, for the work of the
GP, the probation officer or other social workers, the school counsellor,
etc. Each of these disciplines will have had its own professional field
adequately covered during their training. For example, the probation
officer will know in detail about the legal aspects and constraints of his
work. He will know about writing social inquiry reports, attending court,
visiting clients in prison, etc. But, as far as the actual dynamics of
counselling are concerned, he may not have received a systematic course

on dynamics, underlying the actual face-to-face encounter as he sits interviewing his client in a prison cell. The advantage of the concept of structuring is therefore relevant to workers from many professional fields who, though feeling competent in their own professional territory, understandably feel on quicksands when involved with those aspects of their work subsumed under the heading of counselling, for which they have not been fully trained. It is at this trans-marginal area of expertise that I hope these ideas will bear fruit. The probation officer is unlikely to have had extensive psychoanalytic training, but he may well be involved in situations which even the most experienced therapist would find difficult to handle. For example, a female probation officer may be seeing a client with two convictions of rape. During the course of the session, the client mentions his dissatisfaction with his hostel where there is too much noise to allow him to sleep properly, and then adds: '...I think I saw the place where you live, Miss...funny, but I had a dream about you afterwards and then thought I'd try to follow you to see if you really lived there, and whether it was like my dream.' At one level this was a formal office appointment in which a client on parole was reporting to his probation officer, and therefore all was well. At another level, the probation officer's perception of what he is saying may have been profoundly disturbing. She could not be unaware that her response to the client's statement about his dream might influence their subsequent relationship, depending upon whether she facilitated greater disclosure, e.g. 'Do you want to tell me about it?' or precluded further disclosure, 'I'll look into the possibility of changing your hostel and we can talk about it next time'. I am certainly not claiming that either response is, *per se*, correct or incorrect, but rather that her response at such a pivotal point could steer subsequent sessions in very different directions.

'Practitioners' from many disciplines often say 'I wish I had some kind of conceptual framework so that I could understand in greater detail and with finer precision what is "going on" between my pupil (client or patient) and me. I have always dealt with these matters intuitively, but I would feel on firmer ground if I could understand the rationale behind my decision to be warm and supportive to Mary Smith and be firm and confrontational with Mary Brown.' In essence, they are saying that they can assess and initiate appropriate management in terms of, say, educational or therapeutic policy, but they feel on uncertain ground when it comes to conceptualising the emotional problems presented to them, with sufficient clarity and precision.

The concept of structuring the therapeutic process can provide a frame of reference which allows a professional relationship to be monitored, so that fresh bearings can be taken if necessary. Endless sympathetic listening may, in the long run, be as unhelpful as staccato probing in vulnerable areas. Structuring can help the counsellor to feel more at ease within himself and to have greater available energy for his client, because he has a clearer idea about what is 'going on' and what he and his client are 'aiming for'.

The dynamics implied in structuring the therapeutic process are also useful logistic concepts for supervision in the 'Use of Self', particularly with seminars which are heterogeneous as far as the academic, clinical and personal life-experience of the participants is concerned. Visual Display Systems (described in *Coding the Therapeutic Process* Cox, 1978) can convey ideas about levels of disclosure, the welding of here-and-now and there-and-then, and the texture and timing of interventions, in a manner which the student and trainee find stimulating and easily remembered.

One of the frustrations of being relatively junior and inexperienced is that there is very little professional experience upon which to draw. The trainee therefore has to learn vicariously through the experience of his teachers or from the sterile and 'remote' descriptions in textbooks. The experienced senior surgeon knows how to reassure Abraham Brown by humorous anecdotes, and with the confident assertion that the next patient on whom he performs the same operation will be taking him into four figures! A completely different bedside approach is needed for Abraham Jones, who regards any humour as trivialising and feels so unique that the idea of 999 similar patients is intolerable. To the student, the surgeon explains that he 'senses' the way to deal differently, 'and I do it *off the cuff*'. The difficulty is that the inexperienced junior has very little 'cuff' to fall back on, yet he feels insecure if he is told that as far as the counselling aspect of his caseload is concerned, he will 'pick it up as he goes along'. The concept of structuring the therapeutic process in terms of time, depth and mutuality offers workers of all levels of experience a coherent frame of reference, which can accelerate the gaining of 'experience' and discernment, so that understanding can reinforce the intuitive 'gut feeling'. Primary and secondary structuring can equip the trainee GP or the junior nurse to describe in technical, repeatable, 'seminar-worthy' terms aspects of their relationship with patients which, previously, they had found different to conceptualise: 'I just knew it intuitively'; 'I felt it was right'; 'I did it off the cuff'. The nurse in a psychiatric hospital would 'know' that when Jean was in trouble she needed to talk 'then and there', whereas when David was in trouble 'he could wait until the group on the following morning'. This intuitive awareness can now be framed in terms of structuring the therapeutic process, by thinking of time, depth and mutuality, so that the nurse's understanding of her use of herself within therapeutic space is maximised. A self-fulfilling prophecy thus emerges. As the nurse's confidence in structuring the therapeutic process increases, so does her efficacy and so does the patient's confidence in her and so does her efficacy, etc., etc. This leads us to a subsequent chapter on empathy, which is fostered by appropriate structuring of the therapeutic process and in turn fosters disclosure by the patient which, to complete the circle, reinforces empathic bonding.

The following are indications for differential initiative expected from the therapist, by patients who are struggling to jump the disclosure gap from Conscious-withheld to Conscious-disclosed. Each expects enabling activity on the part of the therapist, and each necessitates different structuring initiatives:

> a. 'For God's sake stop cueing me in ... I've got to get it out myself.'
> b. 'Can you pull it out? ... I can't do it on my own.'

> (If the reader only sees these comments through psycho-sexual 'eyes', he may need to ask himself whether any other perspective about these disclosures could yield richer affective material.)

Each calls for the therapist's 'sense of self' to be used in a different way to facilitate the further crystallisation of the patient's 'sense of self'. Structuring the therapeutic process therefore intensifies a specialised use of self, because it provides an orientating frame of reference within which the therapist engages with his patient in 'purposeful abandon'. When a patient can say 'It's becoming increasingly easy to be me,' the authenticity of being fully human is endorsed, and selfhood is restored.

CHAPTER 4

The Therapist's Personal World

I was very glad afterwards to have had the interview; for, in her face and in her voice, and in her touch, she gave me the assurance, that *suffering had been stronger than* Miss Havisham's *teaching, and had given her a heart to understand what my heart used to be.*

(from *Great Expectations*, Charles Dickens)
(Original version: italics added)

For earth's days and nights are breaking over me
The tides and sands are running through me,
And I have only two hands and a heart to hold the desert
and the sea.   (from *The Moment*, Kathleen Raine, 1956)

1. THE CHANGING SYMMETRY OF 'COMING TO GRIEF'

When therapist and patient meet, they do so with a degree of implied reciprocity rarely discovered in other clinical settings. There is no impressive machinery or other equipment, not even a stethoscope. From a physical point of view the space is often literally symmetrical, either being part of a circle or in symmetrically placed chairs.* In this sense therapeutic space sustains genuine sharing. The asymmetry of the sharing of symbolic space is, certainly in the early stages of psychotherapy, that of seeker and sought, or, non-commitment, but as the therapeutic process deepens, and counter transference begins to impinge upon the identity-retaining energies of the therapist, a more pervasive and multifaceted sharing of therapeutic space develops.

The poverty of ancillary aids and the lack of impressive professional

* NB. The classical psychoanalytic setting is deliberately *not* symmetrical. The analysand lies on a couch. The analyst sits.

79

equipment intensify the wealth of significance of the meeting of patient and therapist. In one sense they are nothing but people meeting. The words, the smiles and the tears of the patient are not a prelude to a more important activity, but are of the essence of disclosure. How does the therapist's initiative facilitate the surfacing of third-level disclosures? How does he handle the disclosures when they occur? How does this influence his further handling of the situation in the light of the long-term therapeutic aims? More penetrating questions follow: Why does he do this? When does he do this?

Systematic training and the development of a coherent theoretical framework, which underlies his psychotherapeutic technique, will equip the therapist to come to terms with emotional assaults from his patients. He will have to face, say, the generous patient who highlights his own jealousy; the agnostic who highlights the primitive dependency of his own 'faith'; the religious patient who faces him with his fear of adult dependency or the delusion of autonomy; the rapist who did what he would like to have done, but lacked the courage; the almost chaos of the patient who highlights his own obsessional rigidity or the well-ordered, structured life of the patient who highlights his own barely disguised chaos. His blind spots and idiosyncrasies must have been painfully worked through during training, to prevent his personal world distorting his 'reception' of that of his patient. This means that his own early experience of grief, pain and loss must be re-negotiated during the suffering–maturation process of training; so that when his patient comes to grief (in either present experience or recapitulatory transference experience) the therapist can endure the phases of an asymmetrical 'coming to grief'.

The literature sometimes gives the impression that no mystery remains, and that the psychodynamics of every patient and every group situation are crystal-clear. Could this be because mystery has 'untidy' edges? Sometimes the dynamics are as clearly discerned, and as intricately and predictably interwoven, as a Bach fugue, with theme, counter-theme, recapitulation and resolution. At other times there is an air of uncertainty with the sense of uneasiness of walking on thin ice, when a step in any direction might be wrong. This conveys the impression 'I am safe where I am and will be all right as long as I do not move'. But there is a yet more pervasive and disturbing situation when a group is more like eight people stranded on a rapidly melting block of ice, and tension increases when it is realised that there may finally be no platform whatever on which to stand. It is in situations such as these that the individual and the group learn that one either sinks or learns to swim very quickly.

Such analogies may be unpalatable and unfashionable, but there is a risk that technical terms like 'externalisation of a toxic introject' may convey an aura of science and certainty into what may be, at times, a capricious and pervasive sense of chaos. I stress this point because when such subjects as counter transference or the classification of disclosures and the differential disclosure profile are discussed, it may appear that the therapist always has an explanation for everything, which is far from the truth! A patient may say 'My chaos is bearable here', and this is, in part, because the therapist is not immune from chaos himself and, in part, because he perceives a matrix where the patient only experiences chaos.

A penetrating question is asked in the Heidelberg Catechism, compiled in 1562: 'What doth it help thee now, that thou believest all this?' Similarly disturbing questions may arise at any moment, apparently 'out of the blue' in the course of counselling or psychotherapy. However sophisticated his professional training may have been, a Heidelberg type of confrontation may face, say, a probation officer whose client says

> Would you like to see photographs of my victim?

The probation officer finds he is asking himself

> How does it help you now that you 'believe' or know all this?

about appropriate handling of such a situation or just what controlled emotional involvement means in these circumstances. Morbid curiosity might provoke a desire to see the photographs; nausea at the prospect of a mutilated body might cause revulsion. This could lead the client to feel that if his probation officer was revolted by what he did, he would therefore be revolted by the client himself. A circle of diminishing disclosure and increasing distance between counsellor and client might ensue.

This factually based incident serves as a starting point for the consideration of the therapist's personal world and how it influences his way of construing that of his client. It also raises the unavoidable question of what training in counselling and psychotherapy seek to achieve. Such training cannot possibly be mass-produced, and there can be no monopoly of patent processes which guarantee to produce uniformly trained and emotionally equipped psychotherapists at the end of the 'process'. Each therapist reaches the point of starting his professional training after, say, twenty or thirty years of life lived in different circumstances, with a variety of relationships dating from his birth. Thus, sibling rivalry will be a new experience for an only child as he enters the competitive socialising world of his first school, whereas a child with many siblings will have begun to adapt, for better or worse, in his earliest days. This does not mean that the only child or the child from a large family make better or worse psychotherapists, but they may each have different emotional hurdles to negotiate in the course of their subsequent professional training.

Is it possible for one person, by professional training involving self-scrutiny at depth, to become sufficiently free from his own emotional 'bias' so that, relatively uncluttered by himself, he can focus concern on the current needs presented by his patient? This is the fundamental desideratum of training in psychotherapy and counselling, and it will be amplified in subsequent chapters on counter transference and empathy. The challenge is unavoidable. Somehow or other, by the process of training and supervision, the potential therapist has to learn how to respond to the needs of his patient. These may be plain from the spoken word, camouflaged behind verbal veneer, or even demonstrated most audibly by the quality of the patient's silence. He must not confuse the needs of the patient with what the therapist projects from his own experience. Untrained volunteers, with almost limitless compassion and genuine desire to help, often come to grief by not understanding that their carefully thought-out 'advice' fails to be effective because, either overtly or implicitly, they have said '... if I were you'. The realisation comes home to the recipient of their beneficence that 'he is not me', with the emotional concomitant which makes him feel 'How could anyone know what it was like when my mother died; my father was paralysed; I failed an exam and my engagement was broken; I came out of prison with nowhere to live ...' and so on. Training in counselling should equip the counsellor so that, literally and metaphorically, he does not 'come to grief' as he comes to grief.

I am not equipped to write with any depth of personal experience of the problems confronting the training of the teacher or the probation officer, etc. Nevertheless, there must be similarities between implicit tensions and potential emotional pitfalls in my experience with a patient who perhaps has anxiety which I myself experience, and, say, the probation officer who interviews a client who is about to appear in court, having been charged with an offence which the probation officer himself committed (unlikely!), might have committed (more likely), or, at least, had fantasies or nightmares about committing (very likely!). The professional worker must be sufficiently at ease with himself to avoid voyeuristic, unnecessarily detailed inquiry about, say, sexual perversion on the one hand, at the same time allowing his client freedom to share his anxieties about, say, rape or homicide if he wishes to do so. *It is the gauging of what the client needs and not what the counsellor wishes him to need that is the guideline to optimal structuring of the therapeutic process.* An added complication is that as the relationship between client and counsellor develops, so the needs of the client will change, hopefully in the direction of making greater disclosure and thus entering into a richer sharing of therapeutic space. Therefore the counsellor is constantly on emotional tiptoe as he tries to discern what the client needs *now*, which may well be quite different from what his client needed ten days or ten weeks ago.

There are two basic requirements, without which the psychotherapist is unable to function effectively. Firstly, he needs an adequate conceptual framework which allows him to formulate a dynamic hypothesis so that he can construe the patient's dilemma in terms which make sense to him (the therapist). The security which such an exercise gives the therapist allows him to accept the inchoate, chaotic, disorganised, unstructured part of the patient which has probably brought him to the point of needing therapy. At this point I do not wish to digress into the field of psychodynamic theory, except to cite as an example the numerous theoretical views which are offered on *the* psychopathology of murder (Cox, 1977). There is no single psychopathology behind all homicidal events, and anyone who writes on *the* psychopathology of the murderer must have limited first-hand experience of treating such patients. A Freudian, a Jungian or an eclectic therapist may be equally 'effective' in treating murderers, and their efficacy as therapists probably depends, not so much upon their theoretical standpoint as upon their emotional accessibility and ability to tolerate their patients' disclosures. This means that providing the therapist is able to hear, the patient is 'free' to speak, and therefore his patient's silence may indicate internal resistance. The process of reducing the patient's resistance to making disclosures is well grounded in psychodynamic theory, and is probably the ultimate skill the therapist can acquire. He thus permits further disclosures to occur at the time, the rate and the depth which is acceptable to the patient; though he must avoid the Scylla of seductive encouragement on the one hand and the Charybdis of premature deflection to a safer topic, or termination due to his own anxiety, on the other. The therapist's orientation and training allow him a measure of independence and autonomy and, paradoxically, a modicum of diplomatic immunity, so that within limits he is 'safe when all safety's lost'. The turbulence, sometimes amounting to typhoon proportions, encountered in negotiating certain critical transitional phases of transference and counter transference can be endured and used, because training has equipped the therapist with a dynamic framework and adequate motivation.

The second basic requirement is adequate motivation to persist in what may be a frustrating and apparently thankless task. The exact nature of such motivation is a highly personal matter. Intense clinical interest in his patient as a person often borders on a sense of wonder,* and is the motivation least influenced by *kudos* or status. Buber (*vide infra*) has influenced many psychotherapists. *Between Man and Man* and *I and Thou* convey the sense of wonder which a therapist may feel towards a patient who is not interesting because she shows the psychodynamics of schizophrenia or psychopathy, but because of the sheer fact that she *is*! Such 'amazement' intensifies critical discernment and diagnostic acumen. He needs to 'see' his patient against the background of all the similar patients he has seen, and yet to note her idiosyncratic, peculiarly unrepeatable personal qualities. He will have gained experience from the earliest days of his clinical training, and will have seen many 'cases' demonstrated. He will know the percentage of patients suffering from A, who have complication B. However, as far as emotional illness is con-

---

* 'There is an *interesting* patient in bed 3.' A remark frequently heard in any staff-room. Does it imply that the patients in beds 2 and 4 are *not interesting*? Are they aware that their neighbour is '*of interest*'? N.B. *Structuring always intensifies interest.* (See footnote page 39).

cerned, he can have a much broader backcloth. There is timelessness about mental illness, and the phobias of the housewives trapped in high-rise blocks of flats may be the modern counterpart of their ancestors trapped in caves by prowling predators. Behind each patient he can see not only other patients from his own clinical experience, but those he has met in history or in the realler than real characters of drama and myth. Behind a suddenly bereaved parent can be heard the voice 'in Ramah, lamentation, and bitter weeping, Rachel weeping for her children; she refuseth to be comforted for her children, because they are not' (Jeremiah 31. 15). Or King David hearing of Absalom's death: 'And the king was much moved, and went up to the chamber over the gate, and wept: and as he went, thus he said, O my son Absalom, my son, my son Absalom! would God I had died for thee, O Absalom, my son, my son' (II Samuel 18. 33). Or a distraught Macduff, unable to accept the news, carried by Ross, that his wife and children have been savagely slaughtered.

> All my pretty ones?
> Did you say all? Oh hell-kite! All?
> What! all my pretty chickens and their dam
> At one fell swoop?
>
> *(Macbeth*. IV. iii. 216)

King Lear's is the archetypal cry of devastating loss,

> Thou'lt come no more.
> Never, never, never, never, never!
>
> *(King Lear*. V. iii. 308)

Bereavement may be negotiated successfully, but it can be a life experience which may cause a patient to seek psychotherapy. To be present at the dying of another reinforces the neglected possibilities and 'unlived life' which may yet be lived. This search for 'unlived life' is one way a patient may 'present', and a sense of unfulfilment is a common reason for referral, alongside a sense of impending chaos or a neatly circumscribed, focal symptom.

There are risks of depersonalising people by referring to them as using projective identification or denial, which can sometimes lead dangerously near the point of reductive reification. The sense of wonder ensures that the mechanism never becomes more important than the person. It has already been said that it is morbid to think that only the pathological, the symptom or the 'bad news' is acceptable currency in individual or group psychotherapy. The 'good news' of passing an exam or successfully surviving a testing and dreaded ordeal may be as significant as a patient's fear of authority or his masturbatory fantasies! A poignant aspect of the sharing of therapeutic space is shown so vividly when a patient says 'You are the only person whom I thought would be interested to know that I was chosen for the choir .../... went in for a sponsored walk'. The fact that a patient felt able to share such experiences with the therapist or the group, without feeling trivialised, belittled or sensing implicit disinterest, makes it more likely that he will be better able to offer third-level disclosures about homosexuality, the fear of death, or whatever else comes from his 'insidest inside' (to use an expressive phrase a composer wrote on the original score of the music he felt said most about him).

Our concern here is with the motivation for embarking upon the 'suffering–maturation process' of training in psychotherapy, prior to engaging in the highly specialised meeting 'between man and man' known as the therapeutic alliance. The patient can readily discern whether the therapist is interested in him because he is who he is, or whether he is perhaps making up a controlled sample for a research project.

> He looked at me as though he was wondering whether he had dropped my card into the correct slot, rather than looking at me as another human being.
> He changed, and suddenly became 'clinical', so I shut up and wouldn't say any more.
> I was lying in bed in the ward and heard him talking about 'the sample', and to my horror I found he was referring to me.

These quotations reflect the patient's anxiety, which is so readily understandable. None of us would like to be regarded as a specimen, part of a sample, or of interest to our medical adviser simply because he was doing research! This highlights a dilemma which is almost gossamer-thin in the therapeutic alliance between therapist and patient. The intelligent patient is aware that the therapist has had training about defence mechanisms, transference, interpretation, and so on. Yet the minutest indication on the part of the therapist that he is using any particular technique or structuring process, in response to a profound disclosure, possibly withheld for years, can evoke an almost vicious backlash from the patient. 'Here I am giving you things I've never dared to tell anyone else, and all you can do is to be "technical".' This poses for the therapist a knife-edge existential decision. In the long run, being genuine to the extent of not deceiving the patient, and certainly not pretending to know all the answers or have infallible technique, will enhance the sense of sharing therapeutic space. It will also have a homeostatic regulating function within the therapeutic alliance.

No therapist or counsellor can be taught to be genuine, but he can learn how to bridge the gap so that the patient can accept the therapist's entry into his inner world as a reinforcing activity, rather than an attack.

In order to diminish the risk of treating his patient as less than a whole person, the therapist must give balanced weight to the inner world and the outer world of his patient. These are inter-dependent, and if either is belittled or ignored, the therapist is acting to the detriment of his patient. Thus an elderly refugee widow, described as having 'no significant event in her history to account for her depression', stretched clinical credulity to the limits when a subsequent paragraph stated 'the last time Mrs. X saw her parents was when they were walking into the gas chamber in a concentration camp'. The death of her parents was an event in her external world whose anniversary had brought the memory of their death back to life, so that her inner world and its emotional resources were again at risk. A psychodynamic orientation shows how inextricably involved are the inner and outer world of every patient. Just how close the demarcation between the fantasy of, say, killing a parent; the fact of killing a parent; and the extension of this destructive intent by killing parental surrogates can be, demands the highest possible clinical judgement, using every conceivable source of collateral information. Transference phenomena may lead to the murderer ephemerally perceiving the therapist as a victim surrogate. It is the experience of undertaking psychotherapy with the offender-patient which makes me stress that any theoretical approach which claims to have a monopoly of determinism, by concentrating on either the outer world or the inner world of the patient, to the exclusion of the other, is taking a dangerously unilateral view. This may have serious consequences, not only for the individual patient, but also for the society in which he lives.

Our attention is therefore upon those inner and outer factors which have made the patient who he is, and which we hope to modify through psychotherapy so that his inner and outer world will enable him to love more deeply and experience less restricted living. In Chapter 8 the patient will speak for himself. William Osler, the famous clinical teacher, used to say to his students 'Listen to the patient, he is telling you the diagnosis', and if they could not make sense of the clinical material during the first interview, he would make them return to listen to the patient again and yet again. There could be no better advice for the psychotherapist; listening 'with every possible sense' or, as one patient put it, 'listening with the whole body and not just the ears'. It requires limitless listening for detail, greater detail and still greater detail. It is as though the therapist's listening enabled the patient to change the fullstop at the end of his sentence into a comma, so that what had seemed to be a cessation in the flow of disclosure, became in fact a prelude to yet greater disclosure. This is considered in more detail in Chapter 6 on Empathy. For the purposes of this description the therapist's response to the patient is paramount, though in actual practice, the doctor examining his patient, prescribing appropriate medication and 'structuring the therapeutic process' of the emotional involvement does so simultaneously. Furthermore, the patient may be presenting corporate pathology, i.e. he acts as the carrier of disease for the family or local community. The concept of the individual patient and the individual therapist is deficient, as though each lived and worked in isolation, in some way immune from the forces of the environment which inevitably impinge upon them. Rapoport (1968), in *Community as Doctor*, and Richter (1975) in *The Family as Patient*, draw attention not only to the pathology of the family and the community at large, but also to the therapeutic policy of treating not one sick patient but a 'disturbed and disturbing' community *by* the community. The 'community as patient' may be the counterbalance of *Community as Doctor*. Both books were heralded by the writings of Clark-Kennedy (1954), which invigorated and refreshed junior clinical students because they came across real-life situations of humour, pathos and pathology, so that they felt as though they really knew the people described in *Patients as People*. The significance of what illness may be saying about and through the patient has been persuasively described in *The Voice of Illness* (Siirala, A. 1964).

It is an enigmatic fact that in many large textbooks of clinical medicine it is still impossible to find the word 'patient' in the index! In hundreds of pages on pathological processes and management strategies, comparatively few are spent considering what becoming a patient or adopting 'patienthood' means. The reasons behind this omission are obvious. The pathological processes taking place within the person who is the patient are, of course, a focal point of clinical concern, but so is the patient himself, with his own reactions to these processes, which will undoubtedly influence the mode of presentation as he consults the doctor. Clark-Kennedy and Bartley (1960) speak of the 'incontrovertible, and yet neglected fact that diseases are not things which exist independently of the patients who suffer from them'.

It is this suffering quality which colours the changing symmetry of 'coming to grief' in areas of concern as seemingly diverse as general practice, formal psychotherapy and say, school counselling. However, in each setting structuring the therapeutic process facilitates the changing symmetry of 'coming to grief'.

2. THE EXPERIENCE OF BECOMING A THERAPIST

He resembled a pilot, which to a seaman is trustworthiness personified. It was difficult to realize his work was not out there in the luminous estuary, but behind him, within the brooding gloom.

(from *Heart of Darkness*, Conrad)

In this brief passage, Conrad has caught several aspects of the experience of becoming a therapist. The analogy of the pilot speaks for itself. He is not the captain of the ship, but may facilitate the captain's negotiations of unknown and treacherous waters. One of the skills which the therapist can never fully master is that of discerning *the* moment (*kairos*) or turning point during sequential psychotherapy sessions, from the moment (*chronos*) which may not be a turning point. The patient may need to turn from free-association about the pathogenic past (the brooding gloom) to exploratory free-association about what he might become, as he is caught up in the expanding flow of his personal life in relationship to others (the luminous estuary). In actual clinical practice there is rarely one such moment. A whole series of moments occurs when the patient's preoccupation with who he was, and where he has come from, swings towards reflection on who he might be, and where he is going.

He is also concerned with who and where he is. Ontology must be influenced by teleology and this is reflected in the psychotherapist's clinical experience.

Every professional training involves the acquisition of essential factual knowledge and learning of certain skills. Medical training is no exception. This means that the clinical student not only has to incorporate factual information imparted as he proceeds from one speciality to another, but also has to tolerate his own emotional responses to the different clinical situations which confront him. Thus the birth of a baby who dies four days later posits a harsh emotional confrontation for the student, particularly if the mother was an elderly woman who would have no chance of a further pregnancy. This may be readily accepted in terms of obstetric complications. It is less easily tolerated as a sudden emotional reversal, where what might have been excited preparations for a christening have turned into funeral arrangements. The poignancy of the situation is brought home to the student as the forlorn father describes how he registered death within a few days of registering a birth. The medical student may meet such a disturbing incident on his first day in the wards.

Fox (1957) has written on 'Training for uncertainty' and reviews those experiences in which the medical student learns to cope with different types of uncertainty, which he will later encounter in clinical practice. One of the indubitable facts about clinical responsibility, which legislation can never remove, is that the doctor may need to make decisions in the presence of uncertainty and incomplete knowledge. The development of clinical judgement grows with experience, but in the last resort the clinical decision is made by the physician on the basis of his previous clinical experience. Fox's paper has particular implications for psychiatric training in general and psychotherapeutic training in particular. There is often great uncertainty, but clinical action is always inescapable if the therapist is not to avoid his responsibility.

The experience of becoming a therapist depends firstly on the personal characteristics of the individual concerned, and secondly upon his particular professional or academic training hitherto. There are certain generic aspects which involve new patterns of response, as well as specific areas of re-learning which differ for, say, the doctor, the psychologist or the probation officer. Foren and Bailey (1968), Hamblin (1974) and Meeks (1971) respectively, touch on these important issues as far as social casework, teaching and counselling, and psychotherapy with the adolescent are concerned.

Clinical training quite correctly stresses the importance of detachment,* so that the doctor can act effectively, with compassion but without over-involvement, in the presence of chronic need or catastrophic tragedy. The mutilated casualty lying by his motorbike needs a surgeon who will get on with his job, rather than spend time on saying how sorry he is. This point it so obvious that it scarcely needs to be made, except to stress the risks of taking the 'ultra-clinical' road-accident medical model as being equally applicable to less dramatic medical situations. Alongside his increasing professional distance from suffering, the student needs to be kept in touch with the world of feeling and anxiety by such eloquent and poignant descriptions of love, terminal illness and the inevitability of bereavement as found in *All the Days of His Dying* by Marlena Frick (1972) or *The Death of Ivan Ilyich* by Tolstoy. 'Chekhov, himself a doctor, said that if he were teaching medical students, he would spend half his time teaching them what it feels like to be ill' (Royal College of General Practitioners, 1972).

He has spent much of his time trying to distance himself from sorrow and grief so that he can come to an 'objective appraisal' of the situation, and he needs to unlearn, or rather, learn new ways of entering the orbit of his patient's experience. Any session in any general practice contains moments when 'success' or 'failure' depends upon the ability of the doctor to convey that he 'understands' the life of his patient. Indeed, the difficult art of providing long-term support is one which the family doctor develops to a high degree. This particular skill applies not only to organic illness but to many chronic emotional cripples, who need long-term support, and for whom the family doctor may be an 'alter-ego'. The support involved in managing chronic physical illness, and enabling a patient to negotiate and accept the increasing restrictions of advancing years, used to be a grossly undervalued and neglected dimension in clinical training. This is partly because it does not have the dramatic display quality of, say, cardiac surgery, and also because it takes place at the geriatric bedside rather than as a presentation at an international conference. Consider this example:

---

* Parsons describes 'affective neutrality' as one of the values which characterises the physician's role. (Parsons, T. (1961) *The Social System*. Free Press, New York).

[Setting: A 74-year-old widow, with chronic arthritis, waits in a cold upstairs bed-sitter for girl guides to bring up her coal. She is seen *in bed at twelve noon.*]
'Twelve o'clock and still in bed, Mrs. Pathos?'
'Yes, doctor, I stay here *till it's time to go to bed.*'

Supportive therapy of every kind; psychotherapeutic, mechanical, medicinal and social are needed for such a poignant psycho-geriatric problem. Appropriate supportive psychotherapy is sometimes seen as less 'significant' than penetrating, interpretative, dynamic analytically based psychotherapy in which there is dynamic change in the patient's inner world, and in which the endopsychic patterning is not fixed. In actual practice, very different skills are required in giving such long-term psychotherapeutic support, but I would strongly contest the suggestion that supportive psychotherapy is 'easier' to do than say, dynamic group psychotherapy which has an intrinsic buoyancy and vitality of its own.

History is in the making and it may be argued whether a psychotherapist needs full personal psychoanalysis, but there is no doubt whatever that he needs prolonged personal supervision and monitored introspection of his own responses to the significant life experiences involving love, sex, violence, family relationships, authority, death, etc. In other words, this suffering–maturation process should lead to a point where the therapist is at ease in the presence of any experience which the patient wishes to disclose. This will depend partly upon his basic personality characteristics, the duration and depth of his training in dynamic psychotherapy, and his personal *weltanschauung*.

Superimposed upon the medical student's clinical training, in which he is taught to distance himself from his own feelings so that he can act efficiently, is the 'reversal' of psychotherapy training. This can impose a considerable strain, because it puts the trainee 'back in touch with his own feelings'. This has been styled the 'beginning psychiatric training syndrome' (Merklin and Little, 1967), in which the specific 'obstacles' in psychiatric training are discussed as additional factors superimposed upon the universal 'adaptational pressures shared with other medical residents'... 'a review of the literature on psychiatric training reveals an emphasis on the teaching of basic principles and therapeutic techniques. While there is plentiful discussion of the difficulties of supervision, there is little investigation of the residents' subjective response to this training.' The psychotherapist in training is therefore required to effect a fundamental change in his affective approach to patients. To begin with, he has distanced himself so that he can act with the compassion and emotional distance necessary for effective clinical work. He is then to be sensitised again to the feelings which the patient evokes in him. Having been in remote clinical orbit, he now has to re-enter his patient's atmosphere and yet, *pari passu*, remain sufficiently separate to function effectively as a sounding-board.

Balint (1957) pioneered the study of the possibilities and limitations of psychotherapy in general practice, and his book *The Doctor, His Patient and the Illness* is a landmark in transforming what had hitherto been a no-man's land, between the GP and the 'specialist' psychiatrist, into a specific arena of focused therapeutic activity. He explores the relationship between GP and patient at a depth hitherto unknown, and instead of making the doctor/patient relationship a brief introduction to the main body of the book, as so frequently occurs in textbooks on clinical medicine, he made the relationship and its dynamics the core concern. Balint and Balint (1959) write:

> Knowledge can be learned from books and lectures; skill must be acquired by doing the thing, and its price in psychotherapy must always be *a limited though considerable change of one's own personality*. Without this, psychotherapy, so-called, is a well-intentioned, amateurish exercise; it is this change of personality that raises it to a professional level.

The therapist is fallibly human, however fully analysed. He hopes that his construction of the reality his patient presents to him, in no way restricts what the patient might disclose. Two philosophers use phrases which are forcefully relevant. Harrison (1974) in *On What There Must Be* discusses 'what there must be in any world which might possibly be intelligible to us, and so what there must be in our own present world'. In other words, in view of the history of his patient and the current clinical presentation, the therapist is often aware of 'what there must be' in the patient's inner world which he has not yet been able to disclose. Heelan (1971) describes a heuristic structure as conveying the 'anticipation of a known unknown'. These phrases, 'on what there must be' and the 'anticipation of a known unknown', so accurately convey the sense of being open to whatever disclosure the patient is about to make. Yet, at the same time, the therapist has a rationally based intuition of what is about to be disclosed because of his knowledge of the previous history, the current presentation and the discernment of a predisclosure state. No therapist can ever fully master this clinical skill, but part of his training is to make sure that his own personality does not intrude and so prevent what was about to become conscious for the patient, from doing so. The therapist's experience must never limit or confine what the patient may be about to discover about himself. It is for this reason that I maintain the therapist needs a dual approach to his patient, the first is deterministic and the second existential. The latter gives a sense of shared reality with the patient, sometimes almost amounting to a sense of standing on tiptoe with the patient waiting for some disclosure to come to them both. Siirala (1963) describes the 'delusion of primary autonomy', in other words, the 'mature' adult is one who realises how dependent he is for nourishment upon everything that sustains him, and how far removed from the 'self-made man'. Bally (1956), referring to the psychoanalytic encounter with schizophrenics, talks of the radical change which implies 'the crushing of not only one but *two* delusions: that of the patient and that of the therapist. The therapist's heart is wounded, but not mortally.' Siirala continues:

> What are the therapist's delusions? A central feature of the delusions of the healthy seems to be the unconscious assumption that they possess reality, the criteria of what is worthy of notice acceptance, sharing, and how it is to be shared. This means that the healthy believe they have an absolute and autonomous ability to see the facts.... Thus they are subject to the delusion of not being caught by any delusion.

Elsewhere Siirala (1969) writes:

> Neglected possibilities, unlived individual and collective life, unintegrated potentialities—a man feels guilty because of these. He feels them as an 'unpaid debt'— a failure to respond to life with life, to pay his potentialities into the fund of life that he has drawn on. This existential guilt, this sense of an unpaid debt, is signalized through 'causes' of disease and disturbance, which are the manifestations of unlived life, unpaid debts, guilt. But, as such, they have a positive aspect. Amidst all the factual devastation, unused resources are at stake and are suggested by the situation. There is an implication of talents, possibilities, reserves, potentialities, and, as it were, treasures that have partly remained unrealized and even been partly destroyed. Now they are indicated, there is the possibility of their being realized.

Other existentialist therapists stress that the confronting of death gives positive reality to life itself, and it is patently clear that however much life experience the therapist himself may have had, he will not have experienced physical death at the time of the therapeutic session. He must be free enough to allow his patient to be free enough to say how frightened he is of dying, how much he wishes to kill someone, or, as is common in psychotherapeutic work at Broadmoor Hospital, what it felt like when he *was* killing someone. The verbalisation of depth experiences of this quality, whether on an individual or group basis, bring us to the very edge of linguistic existence and the fundamental problems of being *versus* non-being, and the dialectic of yes *versus* no, which Tillich (1953) discusses in *The Courage To Be*. Psychoanalytic training may or may not have altered how a therapist himself behaves, but it should have made him aware of areas in his life which are at risk. No therapist will have negotiated his own personal physical death, and therefore he and the patient together are facing 'a known unknown'. May (1958) writes: 'Death is ... the one fact of my life which is not relative but absolute, and my awareness of this gives my existence and what I do each hour an absolute quality.' This theme is extended by Boros (1965), in a penetrating study of man's attitude to the certainty of his own approaching death, *The Moment of Truth.*

What it is that allows the therapist to 'take' whatever disclosure the patient wishes to make, when he wishes to make it, is a philosophical, meta-psychological and may be a theological problem. It impinges upon the therapist's personal view of life, although it has nothing whatever to do with any particular creed or affiliation. The questions which, in a paradoxical way the therapist enables 'the patient to ask the patient', inevitably impinge upon the therapist's personal answer to such questions as that asked by Jeremiah (5. 31): 'But when the end comes, what will you do?' The cardinal fact here is not that the therapist answers the patient's questions, but he must be sufficiently free to allow the patient to ask the questions and, as so often happens with third-level disclosures (see page 164) in any sphere of life, it is discovered that as the questions are asked, so the answers begin to crystallise. The therapist therefore cultivates an emotional climate in which the patient is safe enough to ask his own questions. The psychoanalyst finds that psychoanalytic theory provides coherence and a framework for understanding his patient. He is safe enough in himself to let his patients genuinely free-associate. It is absorbingly interesting to speculate on what other frame of reference, if any, could provide counsellors with this capacity. 'A sword will pierce your own soul too' (Luke, 2. 35) conveys the potential vulnerability which is a prerequisite of effective therapy. If the patient senses that the sword which penetrates him does not penetrate the therapist at all, he will be construed as being cold, remote and 'clinical'; if, on the other hand, the sword is felt to penetrate as deeply or even deeper than it does the patient, then therapy is again blocked, because the patient cannot express his feelings for fear of wounding the therapist too deeply and perhaps annihilating him.

The therapeutic process should lead to the enabling experience in which the patient feels that she is sufficiently understood, so as not to feel inaccessibly incomprehensible, but, *per contra*, not to have the devastating experience of being completely understood. Each patient likes to feel that there is a preserve of idiosyncratic 'me-ness' which does not fit into any easy category, so that the doctor will not see her as 'just another one of those'.

Erikson (1959) reminds us that 'we cannot lift a case history out of history', by which he meant that the clinical events always take place somewhere, some time, when the context of suffering and the penumbra surrounding the predicament will influence the predicament itself and the patient's adaptive response. Bettelheim (1967) took the 'single liberty of changing a desperate question to a statement' when he spoke of his staff who could 'minister to a mind diseased', in contrast to Lady Macbeth's physician, who could 'not minister to a mind diseased'. He added that the poets have understood human needs since the beginning of time, but the progress has been in the 'art of tendering help'.

Winnicott (1963) has spoken of the corrective experience which may occur in the course of psychotherapy, though he states 'the corrective provision is never enough' ... 'in the end we succeed by failing—failing the patient's way'. The therapist is often said to be involved with emotional 'climate control', which implies that he tries to enhance the 'support-confrontation' ratio so that therapeutic space *is* therapeutic. Ultimately, the patient finds he can 'go it alone' and can safely relinquish therapeutic space. The idea of a 'safely-failing' environment as the patient's capacity for autonomy grows, recalls *The Maturational Processes and the Facilitating Environment* (Winnicott, 1965).

Many analogies have been offered to convey the role of the group psychotherapist. The leader, the facilitator, the enabler, the conductor are all words that have been used, and Foulkes (1964) describes the 'discrimination activity' of the therapist: what he is, what he represents and what he does. It is however thanks to a hospital patient that I owe the perceptive and perhaps best description of all: 'You are the prompter for the group ...' but, paradoxically, 'a prompter who does not know the lines!' This, surely, is exactly on target. The psychotherapist prompts and facilitates disclosures which neither he nor the patients know, but his function is to make the unconscious conscious and the Conscious-(hitherto) withheld, become the Conscious-disclosed. This links closely to the declaration of a 'known unknown'. When a disclosure occurs, the patient is surprised by himself:

> 'I never thought I had it in me!'
> 'If the final of the football cup is between two houses in which you have groups, then please come down as a "*neutral supporter!*"'

This splendid remark was a patient's answer to the dilemma facing me, when two of my groups were identified with opposing football teams. The phrase could not be bettered as a description of the involved-yet-detached work of the therapist. He is a *neutral supporter*!

3. TOWARDS A PERSONAL 'VIA INTEGRATA'

Having frequently referred to the therapist's personal *weltanschauung*, it seemed escapist not to amplify the way in which this makes its impact upon the character of therapeutic space. The psychotherapist, who may spend an hour in total silence with his patients, is inevitably bound to reflect upon the significance of their corporate silence. Both in terms of the immediacy of current psychodynamics, and also in terms of the 'worthwhileness' of this professional undertaking. It almost amounts to negligence if he has not thoroughly thought through what the significance of their meeting is, and what therapeutic space might hold for the patient. It therefore follows that the psychotherapist is always called upon to integrate the totality of his clinical experience (and he will always wish he had more!), his focal preoccupation with the therapeutic task confronting his patients (and therefore confronting him), and the global 'setting' in which this work is done. It must be stated dogmatically that in this section there is no hint of an implication that my patient should, in any way, grow in the direction of sharing my personal *weltanschauung*, even if he knows what it is. He may do so. He may not do so. In either event, it is his own emotional growth, in his own way and at his own time that is the determining factor. However, at this point we are concerned with how the therapist's *weltanschauung* colours the way in which he construes the totality of his relationship to his patient, irrespective of the minutiae of transference interpretation, or the meaning and quality of a confrontational intervention, etc. These details, however technically 'correct' they may be, always take place in a therapeutic setting which has a particular ethos and is likely to be coloured by the significance of a therapeutic encounter in ultimate terms.

The next few pages are autobiographical, personal 'small-print' and can be skipped without losing the theme. However, after much thought, they are included because each therapist has to grapple with technical material, clinical material and 'himself'! The reader will find no difficulty in recalling those areas of his own life which are called into question during his training as a therapist. Nevertheless, in addition to his psycho-sexual maturation (and the blocks thereto), it is likely that the fundamental and axiomatic issues of life relating to ontology (being), teleology (destiny), the presence or absence of a transcendental frame of reference, the place of psychotherapy in a particular social and political arena will form the main areas of confrontation with self, for each therapist. It is highly unlikely that the reader will share my personal task of trying to integrate psychic determinism and a theological frame of reference. Nevertheless, he will undoubtedly share the generic nature of the task, which is to integrate what he has learnt about himself with the cognitive–affective dynamic of the therapeutic process and its impact upon the emotional growth of his patient. As I tried to integrate these areas of knowledge and experience, I grew increasingly frustrated by fundamentalists from both camps. It seemed to me that the psychoanalytic fundamentalist was quite as inflexible as his Christian counterpart, and there were risks that each group had surrounded itself with impenetrable defences and claimed a monopoly of truth. The difficulty lay, not so much in understanding those who need direct access to an unquestioned authority (whether that of 'Vienna' or a religious 'Mecca'), but that it did not seem technically sound or intellectually honest to adopt a superficial syncretism. Nevertheless, I slowly found that wide areas of congruence between Christian belief and psychodynamic psychotherapy seemed to emerge. Zilboorg (1967) discussed the possibilities for a synthesis between Freudian psychology and Christian belief, and my clinical experience supports these convergent lines of thought.

The emotional need for a poised balance of confrontation and support seems 'common ground' between psychotherapy and religious belief and is truly 'independent' of a transcendental frame of reference.

Offender-therapy, as always, brings such matters home to the therapist in a particularly vivid way. For example, when I spend one and a half hours in the presence of eight murderers, I am bound to reflect, not only upon the dynamics underlying their murderousness, but the dynamics underlying the fact that I have not murdered. How do I cope with my aggressive impulses? Am I over-controlled, like some of my patients who are over-polite then, suddenly, explode in a catastrophic way, with fatal consequences? What does their sexual drive (its direction, its intensity and its stability) say to my sexual drive? What does the rapist 'say' to my 'non-rapingness'? This brings me face to face with my own *via therapeutica*; not only about how I learned various technical aspects of clinical medicine, or how I tolerated the 'suffering–maturation' process of psychotherapy training, but also how it became integrated into my personal *weltanschauung*. What sustains me in the face of constant battering of my own defences? My professional life is almost totally occupied with responding to deflected loving and/or hating, or idealisation and/or vilification by others. In the following section I discuss the extra dimension which I found the existential approach to psychotherapy afforded me. This is because it provided an integrating principle. It linked closely with the work of Moltmann (1967, 1974):

> Freud never entered into serious discussion with the theology of the theologians of his time. His critique of religion is directed at 'the external forms of religion' and at 'what the common man understands by religion' (1974).

Moltmann states the supreme paradox when he develops the theme that God may be met by 'all the godless in their godforsakenness ... !' There is an alluring fascination about this paradox. It might be regarded as a defensive mechanism which ensures that God is always there even to the godforsaken! And it is strikingly similar to the charge levelled at the psychoanalyst, who also appears to 'have it both ways'. By this I mean, that once psychic determinism has been accepted, then what the patient says may be a statement about the 'state of affairs'; whereas if he forcefully denies such a state of affairs, then this may be regarded as an unconscious dismissal of what (in the mind of the analyst) must be the state of affairs! Psychic determinism is either a 'con' or true. It cannot be half true. Though, as I hope to suggest, it is only one among other perspectives which sustain the cognitive–affective power of therapeutic space. However, behind these teasing paradoxes, both from the world of theology and psychoanalysis, there is an implicit demand made upon the therapist which takes the following form: 'What is the frame of reference within which all this takes place?' (where 'this' refers to, say, the relationship between the therapist and eight sex-offenders in a mixed group). This brings me to the point that if the patient is to be allowed to free-associate (and if he is not allowed to do so, it can scarcely be called dynamic psychotherapy), then *my* frame of reference must be large enough to allow *my patient* to do so. Like all therapists, I have my blind spots. Though, like other therapists, I hope I can 'see' them better as my experience of life grows, so that therapeutic space is less restricted by my limited horizons. The therapist's attitudes 'colour' the atmosphere of therapeutic space. He is never as 'neutral' as he thinks! Clothing, accent and the quality of his smile 'speak'. I wonder how much Freud's patients were really allowed to free-associate about, say, a transcendental frame of reference (whether or not this had a particular religious texture)? Did Freud's *weltanschauung* influence the ease with which disclosure of religious phenomena took place? Might his analysand sense that he was furnishing support for *The Future of an Illusion* (1927), if he expressed ambivalence towards his human father and gave evidence of displacing such feelings in religious rituals? If the therapist has a transcendental frame of reference, does it admit the patient greater freedom to free-associate re finitude, the dread of non-being or an 'Everlasting Now'; than if, to the therapist, such disclosures are likely to be manifestations of an illusion predominantly obsessional, ritualistic or otherwise of 'heavily defended' significance?

Conversely, what restrictions to free-association may occur if the therapist has categories of experience his patient does not share? Does my frame of reference enlarge or restrict the response of my patient in his task of free-associating? Each therapist must ask himself these questions, because, however thorough his training, he cannot be 'all things to all men'. All patients cannot feel equally 'at home' with me;

but neither can they with my colleagues. *It is a matter of profound importance that the personal views of the therapist must not set a limit on the person his patient is becoming.* These were (are still?) the cutting edges of my personal grappling with my world view and the accumulated weight of my patients' disclosures. The reader will have his own 'cutting edge' to sharpen his concepts against the disclosures of his patients.

Ramsey (1964) writes: 'The only distinctive function theology can or need claim is that of being the guardian and spokesman of insight and mystery.' Psychotherapy is frequently held to be the guardian of insight, but it is impoverished if it cannot co-exist with mystery. The ability to tolerate mystery, ambiguity and uncertainty alongside psychic determinism is linked to the therapist's *weltanschauung* and how he construes the nature of his task.

It is for reasons such as these that I have written these 'personal' pages, which are tangentially connected to the theme of structuring the therapeutic process. In my view, time, depth and mutuality, which are the dimensions of structuring, and the patient's capacity for disclosure, are the *sine qua non* of the therapeutic alliance. I find it difficult to see how the therapist's *weltanschauung* does not impinge upon the frame of reference of the therapeutic encounter. It therefore falls within the scope of this chapter on 'The therapist's personal world'. By the law of averages, it is unlikely that the reader will share my point of view, but he will have other areas of experience where his *weltanschauung* will influence his patient's freedom to free-associate. It is not uncommon to hear the therapist say that he cannot '*work well* with … Marxists, priests, Conservatives, homosexuals, Jews, etc.' I suggest that the frame of reference within which the therapist lives must influence what he can offer his patient in the way of a therapeutic presence, for better or worse. This will facilitate (or inhibit) disclosure; and increase (or decrease) his patient's affective options.

Hope:

Love is seeping into my hopelessness, in spite of me.

(Anon., 1977)

If the defect lies in us and not in the character of life, life is not hopeless.

(From *Beyond Tragedy*. Reinhold Niebuhr)

It will be noticed that hope features in several disclosures listed in Chapter 8. The concept of hope is rare in literature on psychotherapy, although wishing and wish-fulfilment are a recurrent theme in psycho-analytic literature. The relative poverty of a discussion, in depth, of hope in clinical writing is strange, when it is recalled how often the patient's hope (or lack of it) can substantially influence the course of an emotional, or even a physical illness. Siirala (1965) discusses the relationship between thought and hope from the standpoint of the psychotherapist. A patient referring to his reflections upon his own disclosures said 'Having admitted it... is halfway there. Having it accepted is three-quarters of the way there. Having it illuminated so that I can live with it would be the whole way there.' Hope is implicit in this sequence of responses in the experience of a patient in the depressive position, using Kleinian terminology. The essential distinction between wishing and hoping is that whereas the former carries connotations of desire, the latter includes desire *and expectation.* Hope is, paradoxically, often against hope. The dictionary inserts 'to have trust', 'confidence' under the entry on 'hope'. It is hope which undergirds emotional growth, whereas, wishing may be purely a 'fantasy' to be 'treated'.

Consider this vignette from a weekly group:

'I am grateful for your hope because I haven't got any myself.'
'I feel that, but isn't this the one place where we can dare to say we are hopeless?'
'What can I bloody well hope for?'
'Hoping is a risky business ... it's safer not to hope, then you've got nothing to lose.'
'I suppose being hopeless and sharing hopelessness is, in a funny way, the one thread of my hope. After all, I do come to the group, which I wouldn't if I was hopeless.'

Kierkegaard described hope as 'a passion for what is possible'; and the 'hopeless' patient seeking treatment 'hopefully', does so because of implicit hope.

The organic clinical description of one patient would be n.a.d. (nothing abnormal demonstrated). The nosological psychiatric description might be 'a depressed introvert'. A psychodynamic formulation might indicate ambivalence towards exciting and frustrating objects, with aggression towards the self leading to a poverty of relationships.

Each of these assessments might be correct as far as it goes, yet they somehow remain tangential and have not really engaged with the totality of a patients 'presentation'. It was not so much disagreement with concepts I had been taught, but a sense that in some way they seemed to fail to 'reach' the patient. This challenge the human predicament of the patient forced upon me. I had received no formal training in existential psychiatry, although, since an undergraduate, I had a personal interest in existential theology and vaguely knew of Tillich, Bultmann,* Macquarrie, etc.

It therefore came as something of a surprise to discover that it was only *after* I had begun to formulate concepts which were currently of working value in my work as a psychotherapist, in prison and later at Broadmoor Hospital, that I came to realise that it was the dimensions of time, depth and mutuality which somehow permeated the therapeutic space which I and my patients shared. It was exciting to discover that these dimensions had been described by other therapists, infinitely more experienced than I, but of whose writings I was totally unaware. I had found such dimensions essential in coming to terms with the immediacy and simultaneous timelessness of the psychotherapeutic encounter. Binswanger (1963), using the words 'temporalization', 'spacialization' and the 'communio' of love and 'communicadio' of friendship, writes of the same dimensions; time, depth and mutuality. '... only there can height and depth, nearness and distance, present and future, have so much importance that human existence can go *too far*, can attain to an *end* and *now* from which there is neither retreat nor progress.' There is remarkable matching of dimensions forged in the intensity of clinical experience, with the murderer, the writing of Binswanger just quoted, and a letter to a group in Rome: 'for I am persuaded, that neither death, nor life... nor things present, nor things to come, nor height, nor depth ... shall be able to separate us ...' (Romans 8. 38–39).

[The city of Rome, and what it stood for, exerted a repeatedly powerful effect on both Freud and Jung, though our theme permits no more than a passing reference:

> Jung... himself could never bring himself to visit Rome because—as he admitted—Rome raised questions 'which were beyond my powers to handle. In my old age—in 1949—I wished to repair this omission, but was stricken with a faint while I was

---

* Pond reversed Bultmann's stress on demythologising the gospel: 'To put it in current religious terms, after the demythologisation that culminated in the Death-of-God school, we need to re-mythologise our deepest human fantasies.' Pond. D. A. 1973. *Counselling in Religion and Psychiatry*. Riddell Memorial Lectures No. 43. Oxford University Press. London (see first paragraph, page 280).

buying tickets. After that, the plans for a trip to Rome were once and for all laid aside' (1965). What are we to make of all these giants fainting at the prospect of what to us seems simple tourism? Freud, too, had not been able to visit Rome until later in life and turned back each time he approached the city. (Becker, 1973).

Freud also experienced derealisation when he visited the Acropolis. Fainting and nausea are 'unignorable' symptoms, and both Freud and Jung must have known the emotional chaos of psychosomatic symptoms in the presence of 'questions beyond my power to handle'.

Freud (1941) wrote:

> It must be that a sense of guilt was attached to the satisfaction in having got so far: there was something about it that was wrong, that was from earliest times forbidden. It was something to do with the child's criticism of his father, with the underestimation which took the place of the overestimation of earlier childhood. It seems as though the essence of success were to have got further than one's father, and as though to excel one's father were still something forbidden.
>
> As an addition to this generally valid motive there was a special factor present in our particular case. The very theme of Athens and the Acropolis in itself contained evidence of the sons' superiority. Our father had been in business, he had had no secondary education, and Athens could not have meant much to him. Thus what interfered with our enjoyment of the journey to Athens was a feeling of *piety*. And now you will no longer wonder that the recollection of this incident on the Acropolis should have troubled me so often since I myself have grown old and stand in need of forbearance and can travel no more.
>
> I am ever sincerely yours
>
> Sigm Freud]

Needleman (1963) writes:

> Daseinsanalyse cannot but seem impotent and superfluous if it is treated as an erzatz for scientific psychiatry. One must realise that its strength is of a different sort than that of natural science, a strength sorely needed if scientists are to succeed in taking man as its object.

4. TOWARDS A THERAPIST'S 'EFFECTIVE' PERSONAL WORLD:

(a) The Synergism between Psychic Determination and an Existential Approach*

I am not suggesting that the existential approach is, *per se*, comprehensive; but that its absence may preclude an avenue which could lead the therapist in the direction of understanding his patient. This, in turn,

* See also L. L. Havens (1944), The Existential Use of the Self, *Amer. J. Psychiat.* **131** (1) 1–10.

might influence the formulation of an appropriate point of therapeutic entry into the patient's inner world. In my clinical experience, the existential approach complements other perspectives. During my training I had gradually become aware of the existential factor as the answer to a deficit I had previously sensed, but been unable to demarcate. Basic psychiatric training had led to classical phenomenological descriptive psychiatry, and I found that subsequent psychodynamic theory and experience provided a partial answer to the question 'Can these bones live?' However, I still felt there was a dimension missing. As though formal medical training and the indubitable significance of organic pathological processes, descriptive psychiatry and psychodynamic understanding had almost, *but not quite*, provided an adequate frame of reference to equip me to work at the invitational edge of patients' disclosures, when killing and 'wayoutlessness' were both metaphorically and literally true. Organic, descriptive, classical psychoanalytic and other behaviour-modification-through-learning perspectives may fail to enable me to come to grips with the significance of the patient and his being-in-the-world; though they frequently act with great precision in elucidating focal psychopathology. The first disclosure below conveys more about the patient and his sense of 'placement' in the world than the clinical note: 'depersonalisation, due to separation anxiety'. This comment might apply to the first example which follows, though existential significance would in no way diminish the vital importance of accurate diagnostic formulation, both in terms of possible organic aetiology and also in terms of a psychodynamic formulation.

(1) When he comes back to me, I become real again.
(2) Mum is not *a* stranger, but she *is* stranger.
(3) When people feel attractive they become attractive.... He thinks I'm beautiful, so I'm beautiful.
(4) I was rejected by the rejects.

There may be an organic basis for depression; chromosomal abnormalities may be present in a small group of aggressive psychopaths; 'castration anxiety' may underlie some cases of impotence, but, in addition to these factors, there is always 'the voice of illness'. The illness is saying something through the patient and also to the patient. This may be missed if the therapist is so preoccupied by symptoms, that he misses what the fact of having symptoms is 'saying'. A symptom is, by definition, what the patient complains of. But the very fact of having a symptom is, in itself, also declaring events in addition to the complaint! In other words, the state of being-in-the-world is, *ipso facto*, a disclosure long before a focal disclosure is made. Therefore 'focal' psychopathology must be seen in a global setting. Indeed, 'focal' is only a meaningful category if a 'non-focal' or global category also exists. To use Erikson's important words yet again 'We can never lift the case history out of history', and the patient's being-in-the-world implies an historic context. The therapist is particularly concerned with his patient's 'effective personal world' as a fragment of his being in the world; and in his effective personal world the patient's depression, aggression, homosexuality, frigidity or impotence will influence his engagement with, or his retreat from, the present moment (see page 221).

This tautologous and circuitous paragraph is endeavouring to say that the presence of the patient not only 'sets the scene' for disclosure, but is an intrinsic part of disclosure itself. The symptom is not only a complaint about something, but the very fact of 'symptomness' and the seeking of therapeutic space is, in itself, an implicit complaint about the unfulfilling quality of the patient's effective personal world. In my view, the existential perspective buttresses and reinforces the essential clinical tasks which are concerned with, for example, blood sugar levels, the exclusion of brain tumours, current endopsychic patterning and the like. It is easy to fail a patient by not taking his symptoms seriously. But it is also possible to diminish his potential for emotional growth by failing to grasp the implications of his 'symptomness'. This may be before he even complains of a specific symptom and, probably, long before he makes any third-level disclosures during the course of psychotherapy. This aspect is closely aligned to the patient's disclosure potential (see page 194). *It must be stressed that determining all the disclosures listed in Chapter 8 will be the strength and direction of libidinal drives, defence patterns and other aspects of the psychic apparatus; but the disclosures, as listed, also imply existential qualities of 'how it is'—in the world.*

> I felt like a rabbit caught in car headlights. Terrified. Not knowing which way to go, but too frightened to stay where I was.

Sometimes this 'frightened rabbit' attitude is expressed about the experience of being exposed in the glare of self-awareness. As though the light which guides is also the light which exposes. The patient may turn to psychotherapy for the former, with the later realisation that it is only attainable with the latter. This experience is conveyed more intensely using another analogy. The patient often fears that psychic determinism acts as a 'guided missile' which will always penetrate any emotional smokescreen and find its target. Therapeutic space is indeed constantly and rigorously surveyed in a searching sequence. The therapist scans, with every sense available to him, the quality of silence, the content of the spoken word and the patient's ability to free-associate, particularly when this touches upon painful areas of psycho-sexual experience. The theoretical basis for psychoanalytically orientated psychotherapy implies that repressed infantile sexuality, and its plethora of adult psycho-social manifestations, may underlie a vast range of socially acceptable relationships and activities, as well as deviations and destructive activities of every kind.

I suggest that much of the fear of psychic determinism is removed when the therapeutic process is simultaneously viewed from two perspectives. The existential quality of therapeutic space redresses the potentially frightening thought of psychic determinism acting as a 'guided missile' from which the patient cannot escape. The existential nature of the encounter guarantees that both the therapist and the patient share ontological insecurity. Therapeutic space is therefore a continuous suffering–maturation process for both the patient and the therapist. This is because the therapist (unless he has already died!) will continue in emotional growth in every professional encounter. It is naïve to assume that any course of official professional training can possibly be co-terminous with the end of the therapist's own emotional growth. Therefore, when the therapist also experiences ontological insecurity, it can ease the burden for his patient who does not have to 'go it alone'. The therapist can never be a merely neutral, impassive facilitator of cognitive–affective self-awareness for his patient, because he also shares the predicament of humanness. Paradoxically, it is precisely because of the ontological insecurity in the therapist, that the patient dares to trust him enough to risk the 'abandonment to therapeutic space'. In my view, there is a risk whenever the therapist, himself, comes close to losing his ontological insecurity. He can become dangerously near the anti-therapeutic experience of being 'over-safe'. This, like so many other facets of psychotherapy, is shown *par excellence* when working with the patient who may have killed a victim. It would be ultra-dogmatic to state that interpretation is always the appropriate response, with no exceptions. I have never heard a therapist experienced in offender-therapy who has shared this view. The offender-patient keeps the therapist 'on his toes' by constantly challenging the therapist's grasp on reality. I am aware that my own ontological insecurity serves as a corrective balance to the almost fiercely incursive 'tracking down' quality of those confrontational aspects of my 'engagement' with a patient in therapeutic space. It is my partial insecurity which gives the patient the freedom to engage in the suffering–maturation process of psychotherapy. This, *en passant*, must continue to influence my own growth.

The therapist's 'double-barrelled weapon' of free-association based upon psychic determinism, together with an existential shared onto-logical insecurity with the patient, underlies much of the technical skill of structuring the therapeutic process in terms of time, depth and mutuality. I experience maximum facilitating potential when my patient is encountered simultaneously in both ways. Whereas psychic deter-minism alone, or the abandonment to an existential predicament alone, without the counterpoise they can afford each other, provide less than a full therapeutic presence for the patient.

The relationship between psychic determinism and the existential concern with ontology and the predicament of the present moment, is illuminated in a particularly vivid way by a consideration of therapeutic space. Here previous encounters colour the current encounter (psychic determinism) yet, simultaneously, there is imminent 'nowness' in the meeting of therapist and patient (existential preoccupation with the present moment). Writers from other disciplines (philosophy, psychology, etc.) may discuss the relationship between these approaches from various standpoints, but it is only on the basis of clinical experience that I am equipped to enlarge upon the interdependence of these conceptual per-spectives. Empirical clinical experience validates the working-value of linking these concepts in guiding the therapist's executive task.

I regard the existential significance of the patient's predicament, which may be verbalised in the form of a disclosure, or indicated by other specific attributes of his 'predicamentness', as an indication that the patient is 'ready' for a therapeutic intervention which may expose underlying psychopathology. Thus, psychic determinism and endopsychic patterns may be influencing current experience, though the patient, himself, is still unconscious of its existence. The analogy of bomb-aiming or gun-sighting may illustrate what I mean. It is as though the existential significance comes 'into line' with what psychic determinism, based on classical psychoanalytic theory, suggests must be there. When the two 'sightings' come into line, the therapist is not only aware that he is 'on target' but he also has the assurance that the patient is ready to receive emotional facts about himself which, previously, he might have hotly denied or found hard to tolerate. The superimposition of underlying psychopathology and its existential significance, either in terms of what the patient says or in terms of his predicament, furnish the therapist with ample evidence that the timing is appropriate for an intervention. Furthermore, the actual words of the patient provide a means of gaining emotional 'access' to his inner world. Existential phenomena thus permit an entrée, because the therapist is, in effect, quoting the patient to himself. The phrases which follow—

> 'It's all pointless', 'I knew I'd had it, right from the start', 'I'm getting on but I'm not getting on'

—*might have been said at a cocktail party but they were not.* They were made within the context of therapeutic space where the patient is taken seriously and psycho-sexual difficulties are 'in the air'. Such disclosures frequently represent the patient's inner struggle to express the inexpressible and he often feels relief that the therapist had 'drawn the deeper meaning out'. 'I'm glad you picked that up.' Disclosures are usually in 'Basic English'. It is their cognitive–affective quality, the setting and the therapist's facilitating response which sharply demarcates this profound increase in self-awareness, from the same words casually tripping off the tongue in the 'club' when there may, or may not, be someone 'listening'.

Let us take the example of the phrase 'it's all pointless'. This may be the complaint of a patient suffering from a depressive illness who is describing the colourless, anhedonia (a state of mind in which 'nothing pleases') which is characteristic of endogenous depression. It may also indicate existential, ontological and teleological insecurity if the patient describes his anxiety which is focused on an uncertain sense of being, and little sense of purpose and destiny. Thirdly, the phrase 'it's all pointless' may be an overtly genital statement describing his impotence; not only is his life pointless, but it has become increasingly so during a recent situation when his potency was on trial. So that at the precise moment when his life needed point, his penis failed to measure up to the demands of the situation and he was, literally, pointless. His self-esteem may have been further threatened if his sexual partner commented that the encounter had been a pointless exercise and that he was 'useless'. The therapist is always on his guard lest he miss organic illness or fails to perceive that drugs or physical treatments may be indicated by a sudden turn of events. Nevertheless, he must also ensure that he does not miss psycho-sexual phenomena which are crying aloud. Paradoxically, there is a risk that precisely because the patient is describing his predicament in psycho-sexual terms the therapist may not take it at 'face value'. The impotent man may complain that if girls don't stop laughing at his wilting performance, he will 'use a knife' to ensure that he is 'taken seriously'. It is therefore essential that the therapist takes him 'seriously'.

The synergistic way in which psychic determinism and the existential approach buttress the certainty of the timing of the therapist's interventions is therefore evidenced in the example just cited. This means that when classical psychoanalytic theory makes the therapist aware that the patient is discussing castration anxiety and, simultaneously, the existential statement about 'pointlessness' coincide, then, he is reassured that it is safe to pull the trigger of interpretation. Indeed, on such occasions, I may be depriving the patient of what he desperately needs if he is to come to terms with himself. To fail to pull the trigger at the 'right' time may mean that it is months, or even years, before the patient reaches another stage where unconscious, psycho-sexual phenomena, come so close to out-cropping; in terms of such an overtly conscious predicament of being 'pointless' which, simultaneously, is exactly 'on target' as far as hidden psychopathology is concerned.* (See Semantic Distortion, page 196)

I am aware that I have described this in what is, perhaps, unnecessary detail, but the timing and texture of interventions is a *sine qua non*

---

* Other examples are:

That's not my strong point.
I've got nothing against her.
I don't have a sexual inclination.
It smells when it gets to the tip (cigarette stub; ejaculation).

of all therapeutic work. The therapist must wait until these two sightings are superimposed if the patient is to be aware that the *kairos* (*the moment*) which may, to him, seem to occur almost at random in an endless sequence of chronological moments, becomes *the* moment of insight *and* emotional relief.

This description was couched in Freudian, psycho-sexual terminology. But the superimposition of sightings is equally applicable in terms of psycho-social maturational phases, using Erikson's terms, particularly in the stage of generativity *v.* stagnation. Examples of the pragmatic, working-value of linking psychic determinism and the existential approach in day-to-day clinical encounters, within therapeutic space, are legion. Thus, the homosexual who describes his panic at falling down a 'manhole'; the teenager who is 'struck' by the tone of his father's voice; the frail wife whose asthmatic 'attacks' induced by the prospect of her husband leaving the house, which have the effect of making him the 'victim' of her asthmatic 'attacks', are all examples of the relationship between underlying psychic determinism and the spoken or unspoken existential predicament. These examples are not confined to the psychoanalyst's consulting room, but permeate all therapeutic space. It is as important to understand these phenomena in the GP's surgery and the counsellor's office. It is the merging of present predicamentness with the 'inevitable' course of psychic determinism which underlies many of the penetrating qualities of emotional disclosures, such as those given at the heading of Chapter 2 and in the second part of Chapter 8 entitled 'The Patient Speaks'. It is the superimposition of different frames of reference which give disclosures their particular quality, and the variants of semantic and cosmic distortion make it clear that the patient is talking of 'several things at once'. '... When I was describing the attack ... I felt as though I was talking of something else.' (In this instance the patient is calling out for an interpretation and is on the brink of an autogenous interpretation.)*

One of the most difficult decisions that the therapist has to make is gauging the exact timing and texture of his interventions. And it is at this critical juncture that I find the psychic determinism of a psychoanalytic

---

* Framework transposition is often a central feature of an 'appropriate' interpretation; though, ideally, it implies fostering the evocation of the patient's awareness of 'another frame of reference', rather than 'forcing' it upon him.

approach and the existential immediacy of the present moment an invaluable guide. Psychic determinism may have led the patient to the brink of disclosure, so that material which has hitherto been unconscious is about to enter consciousness. This strictly determined component of his experience could happen irrespective of any existential concomitant events. However, the existential factors guide the therapist in fusing optimal qualities such as 'colour', texture, weight with such qualities as incursiveness or evocativeness in his intervention. Thus, when a patient refers to the nourishing/frustrating experience of his early life and his recent experience in the phrase 'I knew I'd had it... right from the start', he was referring to events in two conflicting senses. He knew he had had it, there was something he had been given 'right from the start'. This something was satisfying. *Per contra*, he knew he had had it, in the sense of not having a chance, being overcome and almost liquidated, before he had a chance to live...'right from the start'. This disclosure was made in therapeutic space. Psychic determinism underlying his unfolding anamnesis ('unforgetting') enabled a dynamic formulation to be made about the patient's defences, libidinal orientation, etc., but the actual quality of my intervention was governed by the existential specificity of his disclosure 'I knew I'd had it... right from the start'. I regarded this phrase as an indication that he was willing to receive certain aspects of emotional information about himself. It is as though the existential component is a kind of emotional range-finder, which indicates that the dynamic formulation based on psychic determinism is 'on target', so that the patient responds to an intervention by feeling 'how true', rather than 'how dare you'. In this particular instance feeding, nourishment, hunger, frustration, incorporation, part-objects and whole objects had all featured as shared, corporate disclosures in a group setting prior to my specific invitation. I use the word 'invitation' quite deliberately. In my experience, the patient is almost on the brink of inviting the therapist to make interventions. Thus it comes so close to the state of affairs whereby the patient actually makes his own interpretations and signifies, by verbal or non-verbal communication, to the therapist that he is safe to proceed. 'I knew I'd had it' may mean 'I knew I had been given something right from the beginning' or, alternatively, 'I knew I was finished before I had started living'. Clearly, prognosis is widely different, depending upon which intervention is received by the patient as being 'on target', but the intervention based on existential current events only 'fits' if it is based upon psychically determined premisses.

Similarly, the disclosure almost bursting from a post-graduate law student whose life seemed an endless series of academic hurdles: 'I'm getting on, but I'm not getting on!'—conveyed a complex message in epigrammatic form: 'I'm ageing but I'm not getting on ... I'm getting on but I'm not achieving success.' The appropriate therapeutic response in this existential predicament can be guided by underlying psycho-sexual dynamics and yet other connotations of 'getting on'.

It is difficult to imagine a better example of the way in which the timing of a therapeutic intervention can be 'guided' by the moment when psychodynamics and the existential predicament, in the patient's own words, coincide, than in the following incident:

(1) A piano tuner's clinical history was of impotence, against a long background of being afraid of women, uncertain of his own identity and painful awareness of his lack of assertiveness.

(2) Psychoanalytic theory and psychic determinism 'fitted' his clinical presentation.

(3) The existential disclosure in the patient's own words was made as he said to a female co-therapist:

Jane, there is something I want to straighten out with you.

I regard this as a clear-cut indication for an intervention. It cannot fail, in the sense that the question 'What are you really saying?' merely reflects the patient's own words. In this instance I would feel so certain that my intervention would 'Go home', that I would probably use a more incisive intervention if necessary. The patient is made aware that he is talking of two things at once, and he knows that he is in a group for help with his attitude to women, in general, and impotence, in particular. He is therefore relieved that the therapist has enabled him to face parts of himself he previously found difficult to face. The patient knows that 'straightening' something out might refer to many things but he has a sudden awareness of what he is saying to Jane. This reflection of the patient's disclosure is different from Rogerian reflection. It is used for a precise purpose; it will almost certainly result in an autogenous interpretation and the patient's understanding of his own resistance. The therapist uses the existential disclosure at the exact point (*kairos*) at which psychic determinism and existential predicament are 'superimposed' and reinforce each other. If the therapist is 'on target' the patient almost makes his own interpretation or it is made by 'the group'.

This incident has many characteristics of an Incipient Disclosure (see page 212).

The knowledge that the condition of human 'predicamentness' is inevitably shared with the therapist, enables the patient to tolerate an ever-increasing measure of those parts of his experience previously found to be intolerable. This, in psychoanalytic terms, occurs as the unconscious becomes conscious. This concept has been extended to include the corporate disclosure in the existential setting provided by formal group psychotherapy. This means that there is always the possibility of further openness, as the Conscious-withheld becomes the Conscious-disclosed. The fact that there is 'always further to go' (than implied by a frame of reference restricted to the process whereby the unconscious becomes conscious) implies that there are larger areas of freedom and a wider scope for joy available to the patient. It also means that there is further painful disclosure work to be done, because genuine disclosure reveals previously hidden, vulnerable parts of the self. Shared 'predicamentness' with the therapist allows the patient to endure the faultless 'guided missile' of psychic determinism to 'home in on target' and destroy previously adequate defences. The 'defence' budget is always expensive. The price is restriction and the patient's failure to thrive in the way that he feels he could, if he were a 'whole person'. Like all men (including the therapist) he is aware of the gap between 'Myself as I am' and 'Myself as I would like to be'.

The 'reassuring' fact about the human predicament is that neither the patient, nor the therapist (and the patient knows this!), are as whole as they could be. It is precisely because the patient knows that they can *both* grow, that he is less likely to hold himself back at the brink of painful disclosures. Murderousness is disclosed more easily when the discloser is aware that murderousness (whether in fact or fantasy) is part of human 'predicamentness'. The question to the therapist implicitly posited by his presence in, say, a group of murderers is not 'Do you experience murderousness?' but 'How do you cope with your murderousness?'.

What is the murderer's presence 'stating' about the human 'predicamentness' of murderousness in general and the therapist's murderousness in particular? What is the presence of the trapped, phobic, 'house-bound housewife' stating about the human 'predicamentness' of wayoutlessness in general, and the therapist's wayoutlessness in particular? What is the presence of a 'homesick' child stating about the 'predicamentness' of homesickness in general, and the school counsellor's existential home-sickness-in-the-world in particular? I suggest there are convergent considerations which at least point towards fuller understanding of the patient (and thus indicate appropriate dimensions for therapy), when the most rigorous psychoanalytic formulation (in terms of prevailing endo-psychic patterning, etc.) is made alongside the awareness of the existential 'statement'. This provides a frame of reference within which the therapist and the patient encounter each other.

Psychic determinism and the existential approach therefore equip the therapist with a flexible, but firm, instrument for structuring the therapeutic process in terms of time, depth and mutuality. They are relevant in the most difficult test-case possible and they are therefore always relevant.

It is impossible to think of the words 'existential' and 'psychotherapy' without associating them with the name of R. D. Laing. His writing is always stimulating, though the reader is frequently left in a state of uncertainty as to whether his comments are to be taken symbolically, or whether they indicate specific perspectives from which psychotherapy with the psychotic can be undertaken more fruitfully. Nevertheless, his phrase 'the effective personal world' of the patient (1959) is a *sine qua non* of the patient's experience prior to therapy, and is an attribute of therapeutic space between all therapists and their patients. 'It is the patient's life in her own interpersonal microcosmos that is the kernel of any psychiatric clinical biography.' Although this phrase comes from *The Divided Self* and refers to the clinical biography of a schizophrenic, it can never be anything less than essential in the clinical biography of any patient. Laing's latest writing, *The Facts of Life* (1976), develops the theme of the metaphorical quality of pre-natal life. It is clinically indubit-able that many patients fail to 'implant' so that every area of their life has a nomadic quality. To claim that this is something more than metaphorical is a tantalising suggestion, but one which we cannot pursue further at this point.

Laing's ideas often have an astringent quality. They counteract any myopic views of human behaviour and experience, which approach the claim of having a monopoly of 'clinical' truth. This applies equally to uncompromising proponents of views ranging from 'It's all to do with blood biochemistry' to 'It's all to do with the effects of repressed infantile sexuality'. Nevertheless, however much Laing's stance can serve as a corrective to an over-rigid orthodoxy, there are incontrovertible issues of humane containment and therapy within a secure perimeter for the patient who, say, has been a subject of a hospital restriction order on account of a sadistic murder. There is no doubt about where such a patient should be treated, irrespective of what 'anti-psychiatry' may say about 'psychiatry'.

Many of the words used by existentialists were originally coined in German, and there is frequently no exact English equivalent. The word *fragestellung* is no exception.

(b) Fragestellung

It means, literally, 'the putting of the question'. In other words, the actual manner and setting in which a question is asked influences not only the answer, but also the quality of the question itself. Tolstoy provides a classic instance of *fragestellung* in his novel *Anna Karenina*. Oblonsky, talking to himself after the realisation that, through him, his children's governess has become pregnant, says, 'Oh dear, what am I to do?' Over 770 pages further on, Anna says to the plump, placid Annushka, whose kindly little grey eyes were full of sympathy, '"Annushka, dear, what am I to do?" murmured Anna, sobbing and sinking helplessly into a chair.'

Identical questions in different situations, and with entirely different emotional para-linguistic frames of reference. A third question is linguistically similar, but existentially final (just before she threw herself under the train): '"What am I doing? Why?" She tried to get up, to throw herself back, but something huge and relentless struck her on the head and dragged her down on her back.' Literature and clinical experience abound in examples where the *fragestellung*, or the manner of putting the question, profoundly influences the appropriate answer. This is nowhere more important than in the particular emotional milieu of psychotherapy, where questions are posed and sometimes answered in shared therapeutic space.

*"Why *did* you kill your mother?' This question may be asked forcefully in an early interrogation or it may be asked with the greatest possible tact and diplomacy in a pre-trial psychiatric interview while the 'patient' is on remand. The question may be answered in several ways. The patient may be suffering from global or focal amnesia which may be organically or psychodynamically determined. He may be only too well aware of the event, but deny that he did it, or say that she was unduly provocative or that he was drunk and did not intend to do it. The same question 'Why did *you* kill your mother?', asked in the context of group psychotherapy at Broadmoor, where perhaps everyone else in the group was aware that it was a group of killers, might facilitate an entirely different answer. An identical question, but in a different setting, and with a totally different *fragestellung*. The first had the implication 'Come on, tell us, ... we know you did it', the latter was, in effect, asking the question 'Why did *you* kill your mother?...I know why *I* killed mine!' and this obviously alters the ethos pervading therapeutic space. It is this facilitating process which allows third-level disclosures to occur.

Another example is provided by the question 'There's no way out, is there?' asked by an anxious, cornered, depressed solicitor who faces bankruptcy if he gives up work. But he faces the fact that his wife has threatened to leave him, if he continues in the job which keeps him away from home, and, in her eyes, obviously means that the work is more important to him than she is. 'I am going to lose either way, aren't I? There is no way out, is there?' *Fragestellung* here is quite different from my answer to the question as I am writing this sentence. To me, at this moment, this is a hypothetical question as an example of *fragestellung*, whereas to the solicitor just described, this is no abstract illustration of *fragestellung* but a matter of ultimate concern which is causing him to lose sleep, become irritable, and be on the brink of suicide. I have described this situation in some detail because the *fragestellung* is relevant to every clinical encounter. 'Is it malignant?' This is the most obvious example where the *fragestellung* has underlined the whole tone and ethos of the question. Asked by a frightened woman with a lump in the breast, it is *not* the same question as that from a student assisting the surgeon in the operating theatre.

'There is no way out' is a factual statement made by a depressed, lonely

* This paragraph is incorporated in Rosen (1977).

widower as he thinks of his sense of being trapped by the pointlessness of life. It has its meaning altered by the addition of two words 'is there?' The fact that there is another person to whom the difficulties of way-outlessness can be ventilated, can alter the penumbra of the essence of the way-outlessness itself. In other words, the very fact that the question is asked can alter the nature of the situation and the quality of the question itself. 'There is no way out' might be the statement of a man on the brink of suicide, isolated with his alcohol and sleeping tablets in his bed-sitter. 'There is no way out ... is there?' implies a human context where he can share his way-outlessness and such sharing, *per se*, diminishes the pressure of what he needs to share.

> O gods! Who is't can say, '*I am at the worst?*'
> I am worse than e'er I was....
> And worse I may be yet; the worst is not.
> So long as we can say, '*This is the worst.*'
>
> (*King Lear*, IV. i. 24)

It is possible for a patient to describe a previous experience as 'the worst', only to discover that his experience with the therapist is 'even worse' than 'the worst' he came to describe! Fortunately, there is para-doxical hope implicit in such a predicament, which highlights the strange quality of some phases of the therapeutic process.

The optimal handling of these encounters calls for an 'effective' personal world in which the therapist can work.

CHAPTER 5

Transference and Countertransference

> ... the fix'd sentinels almost receive
> The secret whispers of each other's watch.
>> (*Henry V*, IV, chorus, 6)

> You have weaned me too soon, you must nurse me again.
>> (from *The Wanderer*, Stevie Smith)

> Now mum's not alive, I feel half missing.
>> (Anon., 1973)
>> [a demand for an impossible 'transferring'?]

> He gazed at me a long time as if I were a slot machine into which he had, without result, dropped a nickel.
>> (from *The Night the Ghost Got In*, James Thurber)

Transference and countertransference, which always influence the therapist's attempt to structure the therapeutic process, embrace both feeling and cognition. Structuring initiative is therefore a highly complex phenomenon, because it is logistic, in the sense that it is planned, but the logistics are closely linked to the emotional impact of the patient upon the therapist.

It is impossible to discuss structuring the therapeutic process and the therapist's use of time, depth and mutuality, without describing those essential prerequisites, namely, the patient's emotional impact on the therapist and the therapist's impact on the patient. Adequate emotional work cannot be done in any therapeutic situation without thoughtful consideration being given to the Siamese twins of transference and countertransference. They are born together, and for effective life must be cautiously separated, though they may subsequently live close to each other. They both occur within shared therapeutic space, and one could

119

not exist without the other. The transferring of feelings, drives and attitudes from the there-and-then to the here-and-now (and *vice versa*), invested in the therapist by the patient, constitutes transference, and, *per contra*, those invested in the patient by the therapist, constitutes countertransference.

The setting influences the way in which the therapist uses his own personality, ranging from that of formal psychoanalysis to, say, the meeting between a probation officer and his client in a prison cell. Transference in various settings needs different handling. What is appropriate in one setting may be destructive and anti-therapeutic in another. We return again and again to the fact that in order to be maximally therapeutic to *this* patient, in *this* place, at *this* time, the therapist must be sufficiently at ease within himself so that he can move from one setting to another and enter into the life of each patient in an appropriate way. This is, of course, a counsel of perfection, but the reader (probably) and the writer (undoubtedly!) will have no difficulty in recalling incidents when his personality intruded into the therapeutic situation in a way which rendered it less therapeutic because of his presence! Three important variables inevitably influence the meeting of patient and therapist: what the patient brings, what the therapist brings, and the setting in which they meet. The circumstances can be implied by such stimulus words as: analyst's couch, prison cell, group room, welfare clinic, surgery, office. In each situation, patient and therapist meet. Each views the other through the eyes of his own past, which colours present expectation. Sullivan (1940) coined the term 'parataxic distortion', by which he meant that the perception of current inter-personal relationships is distorted by previous inter-personal experiences. This implies that previous experience becomes part of us, so that when we meet a similar situation, we have pre-set expectations. For example, it is difficult for me to view with emotional neutrality a thin young man wearing a green tracksuit who sits next to me in a bus, if my previous experience with a similarly clad young man resulted in a black eye and a lost wallet!

1. TRANSFERENCE

Transference is an intensified and specific form of parataxic distortion which is modified during sequential phases of dynamic psychotherapy.

If it does not change then the therapy can scarcely be termed dynamic. The decision to work within the transference, or to work alongside it, is just as technical as the cardiac* surgeon's choice of operation. One option involves re-routing dynamic flow, the other is supportive or conservative. One leads to internal change, the other tries to preserve the *status quo*. Both may be correct in one clinical situation but not in another. Ill-judged use of this aspect of the therapist/patient relationship may, literally, have fatal consequences. In psychoanalysis, the transference is fostered, lived within, and the corrective emotional experiences and the re-routing of the patient's psychic life can be both profound and sustained. An equally skilled probation officer may deliberately opt for not using the transference. And she will do this, not because she does not know of transference, but because its use would not be in her client's interest. Similarly, the experienced GP will deliberately and strategically plan a therapeutic policy for his patient. With Mrs. Smith, he may use the transference in a formal psychotherapeutic sense, whereas with Mrs. Brown, he will deliberately not do so. The only cautionary note that must be sounded here is that for a worker to be unaware of transference and its effects, for better or worse, is to the patient's disservice. The appropriate use of transference may make the patient very much better. The inappropriate use of the transference may make the patient very much worse.

The noun *transference* has a psychoanalytic connotation. However, the verb *to transfer* and its gerund *transferring* evoke a wider set of overtones.

The restricted and precise psychoanalytic concept of transference must be clearly understood in order to minimise the chance of therapy not merely being useless, but actually harmful. Nevertheless, the less restricted use of the transference in terms of 'a transferring' as developed by Siirala, has much to commend it as far as enhancing the understanding of the relationship between the individual, the society in which he lives and the development of social psychopathology. We shall consider the wider formulation first, which provides a frame of reference within which to set the more focal psychoanalytic view.

Siirala (1969) suggests that initially a community problem may be

---

* It is interesting to note that Kahn (1972) also uses the surgical analogy. He refers to 'Opening' and 'Closing' decisions when discussing communication between doctor and family. 'The choice somewhat resembles that in acute surgery.'

imposed on a particular person (Transference I); when the community begins to listen (vicariously through the therapist or the therapeutic team), transference occurs as the problem becomes a joint responsibility of the therapeutic team and the patient (Transference II). He comments 'Hitherto only the second transference has been generally and consciously regarded as "transference", but the problem was already *transferred* on to the patient.' He indicates that a subsequent transference may occur (Transference III) as 'individuals or groups of people may gradually begin to appropriate their own share of responsibility'.

This view of transference adopted by Siirala is more all-embracing than the traditional psychoanalytic concept, and is based upon his awareness of the whole community involvement in transferring rejection and stigmatisation upon the patient. It is a useful perspective, acting as a backcloth to the more circumscribed psychoanalytic views of transference.

Greenson (1965) writes:

> Transference is the experiencing of feelings, drives, attitudes, fantasies and defences towards a person in the present which are inappropriate to that person and are a repetition, a displacement of reactions originating in regard to significant persons of early childhood. I emphasise that for a reaction to be considered transference it must have two characteristics: it must be a repetition of the past and it must be inappropriate to the present.

Thus both Siirala and Greenson help to orientate the GP and the social worker in their understanding of both individual and corporate psychopathology, which is presented to them by their individual clients and the social context in which their clients live.

However, in addition to regarding the individual as someone who may vicariously carry pathology which others have invested in him, Siirala's comments also lead naturally into the concepts of Family Therapy. Thus both the nuclear and the extended family demonstrate, in a particularly vivid way, how 'a community problem may be imposed on a particular person (Transference I)'. Family Therapy brings together psychoanalytically orientated psychotherapy, behaviour therapy, modelling and the many species of group psychotherapy; as it seeks to deal with internal conflict, re-align faulty emotional alignments and provide corrective emotional experience and new modelling opportunities. Within each of these approaches the significance of transference, in all three of Siirala's groupings, may be evident. *One Flesh; Separate Persons* (Skynner, 1976) gives an authoritative and stimulating survey of Family Therapy.

Sandler *et al.* (1973) have considered transference, countertransference and other basic psychoanalytic clinical concepts. (The reader, whatever his background, is strongly advised to read this book and to judge how far it is appropriate to his own *modus operandi*.) They write:

> [Transference could be regarded as] 'a specific illusion which develops in regard to the other person, one which, unbeknown to the subject, represents, in some of its features, a repetition of a relationship towards an important figure in the person's past. It should be emphasized that this is felt by the subject, not as a repetition of the past, but as strictly appropriate to the present and to the particular person involved.'

2. COUNTERTRANSFERENCE*

From the vast literature on countertransference I have had to cull a few selected references which are directly relevant to our basic theme, namely, the way in which awareness of transference and countertransference phenomena help the therapist to structure the therapeutic process in the interests of his patient. Sandler *et al.* (1973) write:

> Although it has not been stressed in the literature, we would suggest that the *professional attitude* of the therapist, which allows him to take a certain 'distance' from the patient and yet remain in touch with his own and the patient's feelings, is of the greatest service in the conduct of the analytic work.

This comment is particularly important because it confirms the poverty of literature upon the detailed structuring of the therapeutic process. In situations as apparently dissimilar as the medical consultation in general practice, the interview of a home-sick boy with a boarding school counsellor, and the patient attending for her 101st individual psychotherapeutic session—the therapist will be structuring the session in terms of time, depth and mutuality. Other factors come into play. For example, the GP may prescribe a drug or advise an X-ray, the school counsellor may suggest an earlier visit from the boy's parents on the ensuing weekend,

---

* The spelling of countertransference, with or without a hyphen, is not an error but in loyalty to the original sources.

and the psychotherapist may appear to be the only one who takes no overt, practical action. Nevertheless, the factors common to the emotional aspects in each situation are that the therapist will be judging the best use of time, the optimal depth of disclosure and the most helpful way of bringing his own personal experience alongside that of his patient or, alternatively, of keeping his private life firmly in the background. In the three situations just described, the therapist will be 'in the world and not of it' as far as his patient is concerned. If he is too detached and remote, he is perceived as being cold, aloof and too 'clinical', but if he over-identifies with the patient, this can be anti-therapeutic. The patient may feel that 'if Dr. Smith really felt like I do, then he would not want to hear any more about my fear of drowning, so I must talk of something else'.

Spotnitz (1969) indicates that the formulations on countertransference 'apply to *the reactions to the patient's transference attitudes and behaviour*. Other types of unconscious reactions figure in the *totality* of the practitioner's response in the analytic situation. He may develop transference to the patient, and these are often equated with countertransference.' He describes countertransference towards schizophrenic patients and discusses various types of feeling-responses which do not prevent analytic functioning if the therapist can 'sustain them comfortably. It is desirable that he behave undefensively with a schizophrenic individual and accept all kinds of personal feelings.' He then indicates that if countertransference is loosely applied to various types of feeling-responses, however, 'it is difficult to chart clearly the special right-of-way that feeling-responses to the patient's transference merit in the theory of technique'.

A negative attitude is sometimes adopted towards countertransference as a useful conceptual tool, as though there is something implicitly wrong if the therapist develops countertransference feelings. It is not the experience of countertransference feelings *per se* which has therapeutic (or anti-therapeutic) potential. This depends upon how they are used. Countertransference, in its own right, is neither good nor bad. Appropriate handling of countertransference phenomena can be beneficial to the patient. Inappropriate handling can be detrimental.

Spotnitz uses an excellent analogy where he describes 'the relationship as it moves backward or forward or grinds to a halt on the double track of transference-countertransference' in his discussion of the formidable technical problem of handling countertransference with schizophrenic patients.

Minuchin (1974) also uses the tracking analogy in family therapy. He points out that 'tracking operations are typical of the non intrusive therapist'. He has so graphically described the engagement and disengagement of the therapist as he synchronises with the oscillating rhythm of the family. Freud (1910) first coined the term when he was writing of the psychoanalyst:

> We have become aware of the 'counter-transference', which arises in him as a result of the patient's influence on his unconscious feelings, and we are almost inclined to insist that he shall recognize this counter-transference in himself and overcome it ... no psychoanalyst goes further than his own complexes and internal resistances permit.

Sandler *et al.* (1973) comment:

> While it is true that a patient may come to represent a figure of the analyst's past, counter-transference might arise simply because of the analyst's inability to deal appropriately with those aspects of the patient's communications and behaviour which impinge on inner problems of his own.

However, it is not only in formal psychoanalysis but in all psychotherapy that in addition to any current, existential, here-and-now interaction, there will be a cognitive–affective re-encounter with the introjected past. Thus, in individual dynamic psychotherapy or in group psychotherapy, the therapist will be attentively discriminating as he responds to his patient's cognitive–affective responses. Paradoxically, he will be perceived by his patient in many different ways simultaneously. For example, the regressed frightened patient vehemently expressing anger towards his father-surrogate (the therapist) during the limited time of the therapeutic session, may be almost chaotically speechless with rage and fear, yet, is able to finish the session at the appropriate time and so organise his life that he can attend punctually for the subsequent session.

One of the most difficult challenges in the therapist's early professional life is that of allowing himself to be perceived, and responded to, in several opposing ways simultaneously, depending upon the needs of the patient. This may be temporary idealisation or the exact opposite. I am aware how much I tended to withdraw from patients who idealised (or vilified) me in my early professional days, even when this was a necessary phase in the therapeutic task. Part of the disengaging, maturing process was to realise that he needed to see me in *that* way, at *that* time. It would be erroneous if this polarised perception of me persisted, as it would amount to a chronically dependent relationship in which further individuation was unlikely to occur. Nevertheless, it is equally erroneous to deny the patient the chance to free-associate and 'see' the therapist in any way he needs to. This is a particularly subtle temptation and stretches the inner reserves of the therapist.

Some impoverished personalities have never had a good early experience to fall back upon. Though all children need idealised objects which enable them to cope with an external environment which will progressively fail, as reality-testing grows, and the patient slowly and painfully develops a stable and reliable sense of self. The quality of the transference relationship with the therapist will reflect either the good experience which the patient had and subsequently lost; or the idealised therapist may, for the first time, provide the patient with trustworthy emotional evidence that the boundaries of personal space can be relied upon. This is a hazardous undertaking, and the intensified vulnerability of the patient during the sequential phases of transference will, hopefully, lead him to internalise emotional resources which he first experiences as being outside himself. It is as though several evolutionary epochs are bridged when the experience of having no skeleton at all, progressively changes to that of a strong exo-skeleton and ultimately to a reliable endo-skeleton.

In an intimate letter, written to Binswanger in 1913, Freud (see Binswanger, 1957) wrote:

> What is given to the patient should indeed never be a spontaneous affect, but always consciously allotted, and then more or less of it as the need may arise. Occasionally a great deal, but never from one's own unconscious. This I should regard as the formula. In other words, one must always recognise one's countertransference and rise above it, only then is one free oneself. To give someone too little because one loves him too much is being unjust to the patient and a technical error.

It is surely equally erroneous to give someone too much because one loves him too little.

I hope these references, which come from therapists working with the family, the schizophrenic and from Freud himself, indicate the sensitive flexibility the therapist needs as he moves in to engage with his patients in shared therapeutic space. Transference and countertransference are so closely connected, and although no analogy is perfect, they might be regarded as two sides of the same magnetic tape. Both are inextricably involved with each other and share a common fabric; nevertheless, they make different sounds and in some senses move in the opposite direction. The analogy stands on the certain fact that if dynamic movement is to occur, it will only do so mediated by transference and countertransference. Sometimes the therapist may appear to be almost passive, as though movement was occurring in his patient while the therapist waited. 'I'll be a candle-holder, and look on' (*Romeo and Juliet*, I. iv. 38). At other times 'his words were smoother than oil, and yet be they very swords' (Psalm 55. 22), and yet again, the therapist may speak to the patient as Hamlet to his mother, 'I will speak daggers to her, but use none' (Hamlet, III. ii. 402). The overriding constraint behind each approach is that the words of the therapist are used because they facilitate the therapeutic process, whether this be confrontation or support. They are part of the currency of the professional relationship. They will be dictated by the prevailing needs of the patient and not by the therapist's inner needs. It is this relative freedom from the constraints of his own inner world, so that the therapist is liberated to respond to his patient's needs and not to control the therapeutic space because of his own needs, that is the hallmark of the therapeutic process. If the therapist's needs rather than those of the patient determine events, the relationship has become skewed and an urgent reappraisal is called for. When the therapist can 'receive' the patient's transferred anger or love (his emotional need to hold or be held) and yet retain the capacity to be himself, the redefining process of psychotherapy takes place, as the patient discovers capacities within the therapeutic relationship which he did not have in the past.

Undoubtedly, the professional training of the GP, the school counsellor and the psychotherapist will differ, although there will inevitably be wide areas of overlap and congruence. Without specific therapeutic training, the 'therapist' would not have become aware of his own patterns of emotional response, and there would be risks of countertransference occurring which he may not recognise; so that he may be unusually afraid of aggressive patients, or intolerant of homosexuality, and so on. Regular psychotherapeutic sessions may deliberately foster the feelings of transference and countertransference, but they may easily develop within, say, the GP/patient relationship. If they go unrecognised, they may explain many strange emotional eruptions in general practice which initially appear inexplicable! The technical inability to deal with transference phenomena and the experiential failure to recognise countertransference phenomena are good reasons for insisting upon 'on-going, in-service' psychotherapeutic supervision of all counsellors.

A few medical examples indicating the universality of the need to structure time, depth and mutuality in the therapeutic setting may make the point. They might occur in any general practice, and it can be seen that the response of the doctor, to what the patient is telling him, varies enormously (see Kahn, 1972). The preceding comment from the patient can be implied from the doctor's response:

Time:
   (a) 'If there's nothing more you want to ask, I won't keep you any longer.' (Message received: 'Time is up.')
   (b) 'Silence seems to be frightening. Have you found this before?' (Message received: 'We are engaged in something worthwhile.')

Depth:
   (a) 'Yes, but we're here to discuss the irregularity of the meals-on-wheels service, rather than your anger towards me.' (Message received: 'We're dealing with practical matters rather than your feelings towards me, whatever they are.')
   (b) 'You're angry with me. I don't suppose it's the first time you've felt like this. When were you first aware of it?' (Message received: 'It's OK to say what you feel about me. I can take it.')

Mutuality:
   (a) 'You felt guilty because you couldn't cry at your sister's funeral?' (Message received: 'The doctor is reflecting my feelings and giving nothing of his own experience.')
   (b) 'It was just the same for me. In fact I still haven't cried about it yet ... I wish I could cry about my sister. I expect you do too.' (Message received: 'The doctor is open and shares an experience, which mirrors mine.')

Each of these responses may be appropriate in one setting but not in another. It is not a question of saying that (a) is right and (b) is wrong or *vice versa*, but rather of judging the emotional needs of the patient at the time. Neither is it a question of the 'correct' management of mourning, but of the optimal management of the way this particular patient mourns her sister's death, which might have been quite different emotionally from mourning her mother's death. The therapist must be constantly on the alert lest he neglects to

   scrutinize the reality of the actual experience between therapist and patient in its own right. This viewpoint is also inherent in Freud's original teachings. But his transference doctrine gave an opening to obviate the fact of the actual experiences between therapist and patient then and there. In practice, this at times has carried with it the danger of inducing therapists to neglect the significance of the vicissitudes of the actual doctor–patient relationship as opposed to its transference aspects.

So writes Fromm-Reichmann (1953) as a salutary reminder at the beginning of her book on psychotherapy.

The reality of the here-and-now aspect of the relationship with the therapist must be taken seriously, in addition to any transference and countertransference aspects. Using a musical analogy, these can almost lead the therapist to feel as though the relationship was transposed into another key, so that the here-and-now is implicitly diminished or construed as being of less significance than the recapitulation of earlier meetings. By the same token, the wider context in which the patient lives must also be taken seriously. It is one of the great advantages of working with offender-patients that no therapist dare risk diminishing or ignoring the significance of the environment, which might include a stabbed mother or the house of a rival girl-friend gutted by fire. Psychotherapy with such patients serves as a healthy corrective for the academic, philosophically minded therapist who may easily lose touch with the hard facts of his patient's life. Psychoanalysis without contextual awareness and, if possible, contextual analysis using collateral evidence, does the patient a great disservice by concentrating solely upon his inner world. The therapist is concerned with the responses his patient makes to various life situations. But if he is to gauge the degree of provocation, he will not only need to know as much as possible about the inner world of his patient, but also about his patient's outer world. On the other hand, contextual analysis without psychoanalysis also does the patient a disservice, and it is here that the psychotherapist has much to say that is pertinent to those evaluations of the predicament of the patient solely in terms of environmental stress. Stress is a subjective experience and cannot be discerned by a study of environmental factors alone. It is so painfully true that a change of external environment does not change the patient's internal environment.

> Grief fills the room up of my absent child,
> Lies in his bed, walks up and down with me,
> Puts on his pretty looks, repeats his words.
>
> (*King John*, III. iv. 92)

In the last analysis (a term used deliberately because of its multiple connotations), as far as any individual patient is concerned, the chaos of his inner world may be infinitely more important than the ordered cosmos of his outer world; whereas his neighbour, living in an apparently disintegrating, fragmenting and unstable environment, may retain emotional integrity.

Every textbook of dynamic psychotherapy will show many entries in the index under the headings of 'transference' and 'countertransference', and it may be justifiably asked whether there is in fact any limit to the number of possible entries, because there is nothing fixed or pre-coded about the transference phenomenon. It is a living, dynamic, developing emotional response to another person. Likewise with the countertransference. In fact, the feelings which the therapist has for the patient determine his sensitive monitoring response which allows him to gauge the texture and depth of intervention which will be appropriate *to this patient*, in *this* way, at *this* time. The therapist must be selective in communicating his response to the patient, though his freedom is complete as far as the experiencing of induced feelings is concerned. Spotnitz (1969) writes:

> A therapist who fears that he will be swept up by the patient's feelings may 'barricade' himself, consciously or unconsciously, utilising *emotional* neutrality as a defense against experiencing them... *utilised appropriately, however, objective countertransference is a diagnostic aid, an impressive source of information, and a major supplier of therapeutic leverage.*

Though Spotnitz was writing about psychoanalysis of the schizophrenic patient, his striking analogy has implications for all spheres of counselling and psychotherapy. The use of emotional neutrality as a defence is one which the therapist should constantly bear in mind. Indeed, it is a healthy reminder of one's own personal vulnerability to ask whether the therapist who describes his patient as being 'heavily defended' may be imputing characteristics of his own defence pattern. This is an extreme statement, but there is more than a grain of truth in it.

Perhaps the most frightening situation that a therapist could find himself in is with a psychotic patient whose history includes severe physical assaults against the person. Spotnitz writes:

> Considerable ego-strength is required to function comfortably and undefensively while sustaining the murderous feeling of the schizophrenic patient and utilising them

for his benefit. If the feelings are denied, it is impossible to get to understand how they are aroused in the relationship and how the patient defends himself against them. If, on the other hand, awareness of the induced feelings leads the practitioner into states of paralysing anxiety, the patient is denied the relatively secure atmosphere he requires to mature emotionally.

There are as many variations on the theme of countertransference as there are therapists and patients. Each therapeutic alliance is therefore unique and no therapist–patient relationship is ever a 'standard issue'. Shared humanity and ineradicable individuality are assured.

The therapist walks on a perennial knife-edge as he edges towards structuring the therapeutic process. He does not wish to invade his patient's personality or gate-crash into his private emotional reserve. On the other hand, he is less than therapeutic if he is too gentle and passive for the frightened young psychopath, whose defences are so strong that he can almost be seen peering over the castle walls, calling out for a battering-ram! The therapist and the other patients who are, inevitably, partial *de facto* therapists in the context of group therapy, have been likened to troops who, on occasion, needed to take a city by force, using the 'gentlest possible battering-ram', and on another occasion as needing to employ a Trojan Horse by subtle infiltration and then taking the city from inside. In an intense group, composed largely of psychopaths, the following challenge was made: 'We'll take your wall down brick by brick ... or use a sledge-hammer.' One of the pitfalls of certain types of professional training is that the trainee is so instilled with the idea that the patient is an individual, whose personality must be inviolate and sacrosanct, that it is never justifiable to force a therapeutic presence on him or, to use the previous analogy, to use any kind of emotional battering-ram. Whereas this may apply to many neurotic and inadequate, fragile personalities, I have no doubt that many aggressive psychopaths are in fact grateful for forceful, thrusting therapy. This can penetrate defences and lead to confrontation not only between them and the therapist, but between them and themselves! It is only after such confrontation has occurred that the patient can say: 'However much I needed it, I couldn't ask for it because it was too painful. But I needed it.' Judging the depth and force of confrontation depends upon the emotional needs of the patient and not upon innate aggressivity on the part of the therapist. If he does not feel in control of his ability to judge the degree of confrontation which would be therapeutically optimal for a given patient at a given time, then he needs further supervision and is not ready to work on his own. Sharing therapeutic space with aggressive psychopaths gives the therapist the greatest experience of judging that degree of confrontation which the patient needs, yet cannot ask for. The steamroller approach is inappropriate but so is that of an interpreting mouse!

The therapist tries to appraise therapeutic space and gauge the optimal point on the support–confrontation continuum for this particular patient, at this particular time. Minuchin (1974), in an interesting section entitled 'Probing within the therapeutic system', discusses the manner in which the therapist may probe certain aspects of family structure. He writes:

> One of the tasks he [the therapist] faces is to probe that structure and to locate areas of possible flexibility and change. His input highlights parts of the family structure that have become submerged. Structure alternatives that have lain quiescent become active. If the therapist then has the flexibility to disengage himself and observe the effect of his probes, they will clarify his diagnostic picture of the family.

There could scarcely be a better verb indicating the dimension of depth than the 'probing' activities of the therapist.

Attention has already been drawn to the paradox implicit in the statement that the more the therapist structures the therapeutic space, in terms of certain dimensions, the more is he liberated from constraints of the professional interview. The psychotherapist will have spent much of his training learning how to structure these subtle and intangible components in a relationship. And he probably spends the remainder of his professional life learning how to be himself, without relinquishing professional expertise, so that his patient can, in the course of therapy, become most himself.

The therapist needs to be free enough in himself, and from himself, to allow the patient to share therapeutic space here-and-now. This will demand an existential sense of immanent being so that the sudden smile or the averted gaze can be 'received' by the therapist. It needs the utmost skill to differentiate the reliving of experience which happens in the here-and-now, albeit after parataxic distortion, and the existential moment when the *kairos* coincides with the *chronos*.

Pascal* (1946) describes the sense which the patient often conveys of

---

* Blaise Pascal was a 17th-century French theologian, mathematician and savant. This quotation comes from his *Pensées*, published in 1946.

temporarily 'resting' in the here-and-now of a therapeutic situation. His questioning about how he reached the here-and-now leads him to search back and relive experiences which have, he feels, banished him from himself. 'When I consider the brief span of my life, swallowed up in the eternity before and behind it, the small space that I fill, or even see, engulfed in the infinite immensity of spaces which I know not, and which know not me, I am afraid, and wonder to see myself here rather than there; for there is no reason why I should be here rather than there, now rather than then....'

Countertransference and the offender-patient

If we imagine a father, who has battered his child, cautiously feeling his way in therapeutic space with his therapist, he will be met emotionally not by invasion or premature probing but by the symbolic welcome of shared space. In one sense the statement 'we are in this together' is true. In another sense it is not true, but the climate which may prove most effective for fostering disclosure and the painful dawning of insight is facilitated in this way. The therapist does not condone the offence, neither does he pervertedly relish it. But if he can see his patient as vicariously representing the aggressive, assaultative component of their shared experience, then it is likely that the patient will find it easier to relive the painful episodes which had been safely repressed. This would have been clinically described as 'focal amnesia' of the battering incident. I am aware that this last paragraph may be dismissed as pseudo-philosophical, far removed from the world of organic medicine or academic psychology. Nevertheless, in my experience with patients whose history includes severe assaults, many of which were fatal, the creation of the optimal climate for psychotherapy can be facilitated by the concept of shared therapeutic space: 'one of us is painfully re-living his violence.' This exemplifies a particular quality of countertransference utilisation in the service of the patient. How far does any 'murderer-patient' carry my murderousness? It is here that the strictures quoted from Spotnitz (*vide supra*), about the therapist using emotional neutrality as a defence against being swept up by the patient's feelings, are particularly apposite. It is difficult to convey the particular ethos and timbre in therapeutic situations of this kind, but it appears to be logically consistent that if the patient and therapist become close enough to genuinely sense that space is shared, then it is not inconsistent to feel that *'one of us'* has battered his child. Society has stigmatised the batterer: 'You did this.' The therapist does not condone or belittle the severity of the offence, but his therapeutic presence invites the patient to share in therapeutic space because of the unspoken awareness that 'one of us did this'. In these circumstances the patient may therefore feel as though he is *reliving the incident with himself and the therapist is alongside him* as a facilitator of disclosure. Though he is in the patient's world, yet, in another sense, he is not of it. Such an approach takes the therapist very close to the edge of his own emotional experience; yet light-hearted (though disclosure-facilitating) relief can 'break in' to even the most sombre session: 'Now you're pretending to be a hypocrite!' (A marked advance in self-awareness!) If the patient senses that the therapist is genuinely with him, and will allow him to disclose, in his own way and at his own time, events which are currently inaccessible to introspection, then there may develop an awareness of shared space and joint struggle which can overcome resistance. This enables the unconscious to become conscious and the Conscious-withheld to be disclosed. Thus the unbearable pain of battering the child is slowly rendered accessible and it takes shape within the shared space. This means that the patient senses that 'we' can therefore look at what 'one of us' has done. This is reminiscent of the idea of universally reciprocal guilt and responsibility which is widespread in the writings of Dostoevsky: 'because each is guilty for all ... for all "babes"'. 'There are only little children and big children. All are "babes".'

It is as total amnesia gives way to partial amnesia, which slowly 'lifts' like a mist, that the therapist may discern dynamics hidden from both the patient, himself, and the therapist. Sometimes a baby-batterer will be able to recall bashing the legs of his son (previously vehemently denied) but he may never fully recall the events causing a fractured skull. The therapist 'comes alongside' his patient and part of the greatest clinical skill is to make the hermeneutical jump so that the patient's disclosure, which is, technically speaking, made by patient A to Dr. B, is experienced as something 'we' have said. However, the therapist must be aware of the risks of losing emotional distance, independent reality-testing, and thus merging with his patient, who may feel invaded and overwhelmed. The hazards of all dynamic psychotherapy lie at the extremes of over-involvement and under-involvement. There are risks in misjudging the structuring of time, depth and mutuality, but these are minimised by constant reference to the homeostatic regulator provided for the therapist by his awareness of structuring the therapeutic process in the service of his compromise with his patient's chaos.

The psychotherapist's attitude towards his patient is both as technical as that of a surgeon, such as his concern with defence organisation, endopsychic patterning, transference and countertransference, and yet, simultaneously, as personal, intuitive and warm as that described by the mystic, St. John of the Cross. His maxims included a suggestion that one should 'preserve a loving attentiveness... with no desire to feel or understand any particular thing concerning... [the patient]'. The over-valuation of one at the expense of the other tends to reduce the therapeutic efficacy of the meeting of patient and therapist. The therapist who is too clinically cold may be as ineffective as the therapist who is too warm, but lacking an adequate conceptual framework, so that, despite his compassion, he is not sure of the aims of therapy. 'Therapy' may then degenerate into a haphazard, purposeless and, in the long run, frustrating exercise.

3. UNRESOLVED TRANSFERENCE

One of the most difficult complications to manage is that of unresolved transference. This occurs when the therapist/patient relationship is unavoidably broken off before transference has been fully resolved, so that the patient has not been able to work through the intense love of an idealised therapist (positive transference) or the consuming hate of a vilified therapist (negative transference). The management of an unresolved transference relationship calls for urgent reappraisal and can be a cause of great anxiety for the therapist. Unresolved transference may occur through the unexpected absence of the therapist, or by faulty management. With hindsight, this usually indicates ill-judged structuring of the therapeutic process in terms of time, depth and mutuality. These dimensions always help the process of reappraisal and realignment of the aims of psychotherapy. It is for this reason that the technical problem of unresolved transference is mentioned at this point, since it is a prime example of the value of the therapist's structuring initiative. Unresolved transference may bring the therapist an intense awareness of his personal compromise with chaos, when he finds a patient using such phrases as

> I've been thrown out ... the most important part of my life has been torn out. so I'm less than myself now ... I've been deserted.

Awareness of time, depth and mutuality and open discussion with a trusted colleague, may help the therapist to reorganise his primary and secondary structuring and so go some way towards making a compromise with this particularly disturbing form of chaos.

4. UNRESOLVED COUNTERTRANSFERENCE

It is to be hoped that this sustained and maladaptive 'complication' is a rare occurrence. Consultation with colleagues and reappraisal, agonising though it will be, is essential.

CHAPTER 6

Empathy

I see it feelingly.... Look with thine ears.

(King Lear, IV. vi. 150)

Your ignorance, which finds not, till it feels.

(Coriolanus, III. iii. 127)

He is looking at me. He don't say nothing; just looks at me with them queer eyes of hisn that makes folks talk. I always say it ain't never been what he done so much or said or anything so much as how he looks at you. It's like he had got into the inside of you, someway. Like somehow you was looking at yourself and your doings outen his eyes.

(from As I Lay Dying, William Faulkner)

For maybe we are all the same
Where no candles are.

(from The Three Bushes, W. B. Yeats)

...make passionate my sense of hearing.

(Loves' Labour's Lost, III. i. 1)

It is the disease of not listening, the malady of not marking, that I am troubled withal.

(Henry IV, **II**, I, ii. 122)

A student social worker was asked to write on a post-card what she felt about an offender-patient's disclosure in a group. 'I wrote one word ... fear'. She was *not afraid of the patient* but she *felt the patient's fear*. This *is* empathy.

(Anon., 1977)

To look at the patient; to look into the patient; to look out of the patient! The first is the basic training of the medical student. The last is perfect empathy, rarely, if ever, attained! Empathy is a *sine qua non* of counselling and psychotherapy. True empathy is always welcomed, compared with sympathy which may be rejected, because of an implicit or deliberate act of movement 'towards', rather than 'being with' and almost 'being one with'. The dictionary describes empathy as 'the power of projecting one's personality into, and so fully understanding, the object of contemplation'. Conrad, in *Heart of Darkness*, writes: 'And the girl talked, easing her pain in the certitude of my sympathy; she talked as thirsty men drink.' This was not, by definition, an example of empathy, although in this instance sympathy 'eased her pain'. The therapist's activity of facilitating the patient's confrontation with himself can only take place in an emotional climate which is generated and sustained as an empathic relationship. 'I like you enough to fight with you' implies that during the phases of negative transference patient and therapist still meet in order to proceed with the work in hand. Negative transference, or overt reality-tested hostility, cannot take place unless an empathic substrate holds the therapist and his patient together in therapeutic space. Empathy is more than listening. Dewald (1969) notes that empathy

> involves the therapist making a partial and transient identification with the patient, through which he attempts in a controlled fashion in part to experience those things the patient is describing...he...tries to gain access into the inner emotional life and experience of the patient who is facing him.

Listening and empathy are inextricably associated. There is a fascinating range of references in the literature to the idea of empathy, extending from the view that the therapist is an audience for his patient, via a subtly shaded merging with the patient, to a sense of almost vicariously being the patient. Thus Spotnitz (1969) writes: 'The type of audience that helps him talk out his painful feelings with the least strain on his vulnerable ego has been described by Michael Balint.' Balint himself (1959) writes: 'The analyst should not be an entity in his own right...in fact not a sharply contoured object at all; but should merge as completely as possible into the "friendly expanses" surrounding the patient.' And finally Kohut (1959) defines empathy as 'vicarious introspection', with its overtones of looking inside on behalf of someone else.

Training and maturation should enhance the therapist's capacity for empathic sharing the experience of the patient, without merging with him. Some therapists have greater intuitive awareness than others, but a question that teases the trainer is to know how far empathy can be both taught and learned. Muslin and Schlessinger (1971) write:

> As the residents progress over the year, the questions about each segment undergo a gradual change from 'what did you see' to 'what did you feel' to 'what was the patient experiencing'. Each question then brings up data which are essential: the first

question deals with important cognitive findings; the second with the impact the patient has on the observer as a reactive subject (i.e., the basis for countertransference reactions); and the third deals with the empathic process.

This underlines the critical conceptual jump which the trainee has to make from observation, to his subjective affective response as to what he felt, at some sexually provocative, aggressively threatening or pseudo-anhedonic sympathy-evoking behaviour, on the part of the patient. This then leads to the trainee's awareness of what the patient himself was feeling. The skill of looking inside on behalf of someone else is a consummation devoutly to be wished, and one which the therapist can never adequately master. He can always improve this ability, and many modern audio-visual techniques may enable him to do so, but in the long run it is the therapist's use of his own personality that alone sustains empathy. It is highly unlikely that the therapist himself has been, say, a murderer, an arsonist and a phobic housewife! Yet there must be some quality which enables patients who have had these experiences to feel safe enough, to risk what may amount to a further reduction of self-esteem, by emotionally exposing themselves still further. They will do this most readily if the therapist not only listens, but hears, understands and, most difficult of all, is able to convey that he understands. How is this done? Can one therapist do it for any patient? It is comforting when a patient tells me that she feels that I 'had received' what she said, yet there must be many others who felt I had not received what was to them a cardinal disclosure. However hard I might listen and even hear, they would not sense that I had 'received' what was said. The poignant fact is that if a patient is aware that what has been said has not been received, then this may be anti-therapeutic, because alienation will be exacerbated, as will the sense of having 'an unlived life' (von Weizsäcker, 1956). This concept has many implications relevant to our theme. Therapeutic space may be intensified if those within it sense that they are the 'unlived life' of 'the other'. This is felt particularly strongly in a group setting. Unlived life, corporate solidarity and empathy are closely related.

Without empathy the therapist may be an observer, but less effective than audio-visual equipment. He may reflect what his patient says, though less accurately than a tape recorder. Nevertheless, what these machines can never do is to convey to the patient that they know what it is like to stand in his shoes. Ezekiel (3.15) 'came to them of the captivity... and sat where they sat'. He was not a captive, but he remained with them seven days. It is likely that his empathic understanding of the captives was greater on the seventh than on the first. An arsonist may be able to relive his experience of setting fire to the house of his ex-'flame', who had jilted him, in the presence of therapist A (a non-arsonist); whereas therapist B (also a non-arsonist) 'would not understand'. What does this mean? It implies that there must be empathic understanding between patient and therapist A, which is not present with therapist B. There will be other occasions when therapist B will be able to receive what the patient says, whereas therapist A will not. This differential response is likely to be associated with the amalgam of personal life experience, *weltenschauung*, and professional training.

The GP knows that the establishment of empathy, often with the minimal possible time in which to do so, can make or break a potential relationship with a new patient. 'Using his own mortality as another starting point he needs to find references of hope or possibility in an almost unimaginable future' (Berger and Mohr, 1967).

Kohut's definition implies the looking inside on behalf of someone else, but it might be extended to say that empathy also implies the ability to look out on behalf of someone else. In other words, seeing the world through his eyes. This is so vividly shown in the quotation from Faulkner at the chapter heading. If it is accepted that empathy is essential for psychotherapy, and that the therapist needs to look inside on behalf of the patient and also look outside, though through his patient's eyes, he will need to know about the real contextual setting in which his patient lives. It is naïve to assume that 'reality' has been so disturbed by the patient's psychopathology that whatever the patient tells you is untrue!

This therapeutic trap is similar to that which occurs so frequently in psychotherapy with psychopaths, namely, that because a patient is known to have told many lies, therefore whatever he tells you is untrue! This leads, *reductio ad absurdam*, to stalemate. It is part of the therapist's penetrating initiative to distinguish the psychopath's pseudo-disclosure from genuine disclosures which psychopaths* inevitably make, sooner or later.

---

* Colleagues frequently show surprise when the 'disclosures' of psychopaths are discussed. 'Do such patients really make genuine disclosures? Aren't they always pseudo-disclosures?' The psychopath has often been betrayed or rejected in his early life, so that

Contextual analysis cannot be separated from psychoanalysis without incurring the danger of the analytic situation being divorced from the patient's real cosmos. The danger of taking only the patient's inner world seriously is that the reality of the outer world would be subject to no consensual validation. There can be few psychiatrists who have not been on the brink of diagnosing a patient as having a psychotic thought disorder until, at the last minute, there has been some external, corrective evidence which has shown that far from being paranoid, the patient was rationally describing an externally verifiable experience. I recall a patient who described how she had been speaking to the Pope during the preceding week, which supported my formulation of grandiose delusions; and another patient who gave many examples of paranoid ideation, such as the fact that his room in a hotel was 'bugged'. In both instances collateral evidence established beyond doubt that what the patient had told me was in fact true! The Pope had been spoken to (I saw a photograph), and the room had been 'bugged'. The patient who expressed anxiety that 'the drought might stop the clock growing', was obviously not suffering from a thought disorder when she explained that she was referring to a floral clock!

Patients often make such remarks as 'If only you could help me to understand myself' ... 'I need an interpreter; can you interpret me to me?' ... 'It's as though I'm feeling things in a foreign language, and I need an interpreter so that I can understand what I feel.' Steiner (1975) describes various stages which the translator experiences in his professional work, which are strikingly similar to the sequential stages of psychotherapy.

'The hermeneutic motion, the act of elicitation and appropriative transfer of meaning, is fourfold.' He talks of 'The radical generosity of the translator ["I grant beforehand that there must be something there"], his trust in the "other", as yet untried....'

---

his self-authenticating experience is that no one is to be trusted. Massive defences of aloofness, coldness, ubiquitous non-commitment and a pervasive ethos of suspicion and mistrust colour his relationships—including those with a psychiatrist! It is usually only after very prolonged testing in the exposed, yet facilitated, vulnerability of psychotherapy in a hospital such as Broadmoor that his 'not-yet-daring-to-trust-again' defensiveness slowly gives way to third-level disclosure. Nevertheless, when they eventually occur such disclosures have a warmth and an almost 'solid' quality, which is as unmistakable as, six months previously, it seemed unimaginable (see also page 215.) For example, 'I'm vulnerable like Hell, and frightened with it' (Anon., 1972)

This has a familiar ring to the psychotherapist, as do the four phases which he analyses. The first is initiative trust, the second is aggression. 'The second move ... is incursive and extractive.' ... 'The third movement is incorporative.' After the third stage he indicates that the 'hermeneutic motion is dangerously incomplete, that it is dangerous because it is incomplete, if it lacks its fourth stage, the piston-stroke, as it were, which completes the cycle. The a-prioristic movement of trust puts us off balance. We "lean towards" the confronting text.... We encircle and invade cognitively. We come home laden, thus again off-balance, having caused disequilibrium throughout the system by taking away from the "other" and by adding, though possibly with ambiguous consequence, to our own. The system is now off-tilt. The hermeneutic act must compensate. If it is to be authentic, it must mediate into exchange and restored parity.'

These remarkable phrases of Steiner's from the academic world of language and translation will ring bells of resonance in every therapist's ears. There is implicit the unresolved transference, the over-dependency, the 'ambiguous consequence' so that the system is 'off-tilt'. Finally, there must be 'restored parity'. These phases and phrases almost paraphrase those describing the 'Translation' of the patient to himself during the sequential phases of the therapeutic process.

Empathy is implicit in the concept of the psychotherapeutic process, and should permeate therapeutic space. If the therapist is preoccupied by events in his own personal life, say the sudden death of his wife, then it is likely that his own horizon of awareness would be so filled by his own life that he becomes inaccessible to that of his patient. The presence of empathy helps the therapist to discern why disclosure is prevented. He always tries to distinguish between what the patient *cannot say* (possibly because it is unconscious and therefore not accessible, due to repression or because of organic brain damage) and what he knows, but *will not say* (such as the man who will not 'grass' on his confederate in a bank raid), or what the patient *can say* but which he senses that those listening *'cannot hear.'**

Empathy carries a wider connotation when the frame of reference is that of the therapeutic group. Each patient brings to the group his emotional assets and liabilities and, in the complex matrix of interaction which forms the life of the group, empathy develops slowly. It is established, and then reinforced between the patient and other individual

---

* Walking over to a group session, a patient told me that her calendar had a text for each day:

'Today's text is "Beware what ye hear"!' (Mark, 4, 24)

members of the group; the patient and the group-as-a-whole; the patient and the therapist, and the group and the therapist. Nevertheless, the network of relationships is infinitely more complex than that within therapeutic space shared by an individual patient and a therapist. As in the macrocosm of social interactions outside the group, there are affective bondings of different intensity. It is this heterogeneity and the paradox of enhanced individuality within an intensified sense of corporate solidarity, that gives the therapeutic group the Janusian quality of both supporting and confronting the individual. Simultaneously, it makes members aware that there is a quality about group life as a whole which defies reductionism. When the therapist trusts the group enough to temporarily merge with it, he reinforces corporate solidarity and strengthens the sense of autonomous responsibility. There are therefore complex, interwoven empathic pathways within a group matrix. I cannot simplify what is a complex matter, except to indicate that it is the very complexity of differential empathy, which the individual experiences towards those with whom he shares therapeutic space, which so often fosters a creative redefinition of his own distorted self-image.

The empathic sharing of therapeutic space is far removed from the early narcissistic stage implicit in the statement: 'I so fill my own life that there is no room for anyone else.' This might preclude the openness which gradually develops during the course of a group. The paradoxical consequence of this narcissistic, self-preoccupied statement might be that because he was sure enough in the group to say this, there was a glimmering of emotional accessibility and reduced defensiveness which, in time, might make growth possible. If the patient had been '*so* filled with' himself he would not have embarked on group therapy in the first place.

The therapist is preoccupied with the patient as a whole person and, simultaneously, with the myriad gestures and other non-verbal declarations which say so much about him, and which guide the therapist to his inner world. Why does the patient who is rich enough to have five suits have only one pair of shoes with the uppers gaping at the toe? There are dozens of ways of holding cigarettes. Why does the patient who has held his cigarettes in a certain way for twenty group sessions suddenly hold a cigarette in a different hand, in a different way. Instead of his characteristic long, meditative, tranquil 'draw', he takes a few frenzied puffs and then forcefully stubs out the remaining few inches, so that it kinks in the middle and remains smouldering? One patient usually smokes by letting the cigarette just touch his lips but, when about to disclose something embarrassing or intimate, she puts one and a half inches into her mouth and sucks vigorously like a baby with a bottle. With another patient I had a blinding flash of the obvious when an arsonist was continually having to relight his cigarette. It became clear that he preferred 'home-rolled' cigarettes which he could almost guarantee would *not* burn, so that his pleasurable activity of setting fire to the smouldering stub was almost a full-time job! Such details may seem inconsequential, but if psychic determinism means anything, it means that behind this apparently casual behaviour there is an unconscious reservoir of feeling. The therapist may be able to discern that this frenzied puffing replaced the previously tranquil operation, as another patient in the group described a dream in which his mother had appeared as an overpowering witch.

This theme is expanded in *Coding the Therapeutic Process* (Cox, 1978), but here it must be noted how closely detailed observation, the ability to 'read between the lines' and the deepening of empathic bonding are related.

There is no patent process in the development of empathy. The therapist is concerned with the whole person, what the patient looks like, his clothes, his posture, his gestures and so on. He is concerned with what a patient feels like, and whether what the patient says he feels like, seems to tally with what the therapist intuitively senses he feels like. He is concerned with what is being said, with what is not being said, and with what is on the brink of being said.

It is not uncommon for sex-offenders and other patients with offences of violence against the person to feel that their interviewer could not 'take' what they would like to say. Therefore they either deny feelings, or else give an attenuated and diluted version of their experience, because they fear that their barely tolerable disclosures would be intolerable to others. A fundamentally different psychopathological situation exists when the patient himself is not able to take his disclosures; in other words, if his feelings for, say, killing his child, have been totally repressed, remaining inaccessible, so that he 'remembers nothing'.

For example, a patient who has killed his brother and is clinically diagnosed as being floridly psychotic may say at the earliest stage of therapy, before there is any chance to establish empathy that he needs 'time and a little support'. In this situation, the therapist's task is a bridge-building exercise and, paradoxically, the empathy is strengthened by the fact that he is not incursive and does not try to invade the patient's personality, which is already threatened by unbearable reality. There-fore a warm presence, which if possible conveys a sense of solidarity, may pave the way for more penetrating dynamic psychotherapy at a later date. At this level the patient and therapist are back at the early stage of establishing basic trust, and such trust can only be established where there is minimal fear of incursion and invasion.

Empathy involves the attempt to look intuitively through the patient's eyes with appropriately tinted spectacles. This means that the other members of the group and the therapist himself are construed as having the qualities with which the patient's earlier experiences must have led him to 'clothe' his environment. This implies massively concentrated attention to detail, and a 'hunch' as to the influences which are penum-bratic and climate-creating for the patient, although they are not overtly discernible.

The heightened aptitude for clinical observation, which all clinicians hope to acquire, can be helped by such books as *Talking Sense* (Asher, 1972). Psychotherapeutic overtones which help the therapist to pick up signs which, to the uninitiated, seem almost non-existent, can be en-couraged by Blum (1972), whose book has the stimulating title *Reading Between the Lines.*

If the therapist does not expect to see and feel, he is unlikely to see and feel anything other than that which cries aloud. Jung (1965) wrote that 'Freud's greatest achievement probably consisted in taking neurotic patients seriously and entering into their peculiar individual psychology'. It is this sense of taking the patient seriously, by providing an attentive presence and de-trivialising concern, which allows the therapist access to the inner world of his patient; a reminder of the centre of gravity, both as dynamic balance and as the core of seriousness. An isolated, withdrawn young woman who surprised the whole group by an unusually brisk response to an intervention, said: 'You've got to catch me when I'm taking myself seriously.' (How strange that she almost paraphrased what Jung had said about Freud!) Hippocrates said that 'the favourable moment is transient', and in Chapter 10 we shall study the relationship of *kairos*, which means the appropriate time, and *chronos*, which is the calculable, sequential element of the temporal process. The fact that the favourable moment is transient means that the therapist may miss *the* moment, which can be evanescent. Thus a patient might be accessible for the therapist's intervention (and let it be remembered that during the group process, the most helpful therapist may be another group member), which implies a state of vulnerability and openness which may be 'sealed off' again if the kairotic moment passes. The therapist's structuring of time, depth and mutuality is nowhere more relevant than in any discussion of empathy. What may be an empathic intervention and a reciprocally empathic disclosure at the right time on the 23rd May may be too late on the 24th, or too early on the 22nd.

Much of what has been said in this chapter has been in terms of the individual patient, but this only for the purposes of description; it will apply to all those individuals in the group who themselves constitute The Group. There will therefore be several patients smoking in their own characteristic way, or, *per contra*, not smoking. Some will make it perfectly clear that there is a stifling atmosphere and imply that the window should be opened, etc. It is as I write about the group and the individuals who constitute it that I sense this hovering and scanning attention which actually occurs in the group situation. I am aware of the group-as-a-whole, and in so doing I cannot but be aware of the un-repeatable and irreplaceably unique people who form the group.

One of the essential ingredients of developing empathy is that of show-ing by word, gesture and expression a 'de-trivialising concern'. The patient knows that what concerns him is not trivial, and he is to some extent testing out the therapist, who may be presumed to adopt a 'trivialising' attitude to the patient because that is how society has usually treated him. This, together with constitutional factors, may have influenced the fact that he has become 'a patient' and is closely allied to the labelling process. This is one of the most important sociological contributions to understanding the multi-causal nature of mental illness. I have discussed this aspect elsewhere (Cox, 1973b.)

Such words as 'solidarity', 'sharing', 'the work *we* are doing', all con-tribute to the kaleidoscopic quality of empathy which is so hard to define. Underpinning empathy must be a genuine interest in the patient.

Pseudo-empathy is not only hypocritical, but in the end will cause latent, if not manifest, disturbance in the therapist. The meeting of patient and therapist is undoubtedly 'real', and therefore the therapist is confronted by himself in the patient. Sometimes, as the patient and therapist look at each other, they seem to be looking through plain glass. On other occasions they seem to be looking in a mirror. It is perhaps the balancing of reflection and penetrating vision which is the hallmark of the therapist's initiative in trying to establish empathy. The move from vision to revision brings us close to the heart of the therapist's activity, namely, the structuring of the therapeutic process.

Vignette:
Sometimes an atmosphere of benign corporate empathy rapidly transforms a group which has hitherto been fiercely explosive.

One patient, bursting with 'so much to say' that she didn't know 'where to begin', anxious and on the brink of tears—was suddenly approached by a shy girl, from the other side of the circle, who asked 'Would you like an aniseed-ball, Mary?' Responding to this nurturing and nourishing gesture, Mary replied, 'Thanks, you're so kind, Janet'.

With a mouth totally occupied by an aniseed-ball it was then impossible to say anything, yet to remove it would be unkind!

Humour, pathos and corporate empathy made structuring superfluous!

CHAPTER 7

The Therapist Speaks

I find I am at my best when I can let the flow of my experience carry me....
(from *On Becoming a Person: A Therapist's View of Psychotherapy*, Carl Rogers, 1961)

Never allow yourself to be left in a position from which it is risky to move and in which it is risky to stay.
(Ancient Nautical Wisdom)

1. DIMENSIONS OF STRUCTURING

'Tell me what you were going to tell me—if you dared?'
'I think I do dare—now. It seems like long ago when I could tell you things.'
(from *Cyrano de Bergerac*, Edmond Rostand, 1953)

Just as the therapist tried to bring the patient to dare to be a real person, so he had to 'dare' to be a real person himself.
(Macnab, 1965)

The phrase 'if you dared' conveys the challenging, fiercely incursive 'cross-fire' of a therapeutic group in which all the members are aggressive psychopaths. It also describes the ambience of the gently evocative, almost emollient quality of therapeutic space in, say, a supportive counselling group for recently bereaved widows. In this instance the phrase 'if you dared' carries the overtone 'I know it's not easy, but when you're ready.... There'll be plenty of time. You will know when you feel able to talk a little....' The emotional climate of therapeutic space always has a point of maximal therapeutic efficacy, somewhere between the extremes of confrontation and support. This applies equally to both individual and group settings. Nevertheless, the affective thrust of the latter can provide more penetrating confrontation, from more angles, than is possible in an individual setting, however much transference may endow the therapist with added confrontational potential.

The problem arises for the therapist when there is a need for simultaneous confrontation and support; so that 'Tell me what you were going to tell me—*if you dared*' can act as a confrontational challenge to the psychopath yet, at the same time, act as a supportive invitation to the fragile, precarious vulnerability of such a patient, at that phase of therapy, when his defences have been penetrated. This also applies to patients who present with shyness and social withdrawal, possibly to the extent of retreating from painful reality into a psychogenic psychosis. The differential cognitive–affective use of himself, in modulating the cognitive–affective quality of therapeutic space, is what structuring the therapeutic process is all about. Without this discriminating response by the therapist, chaos is likely to reign. And any compromise with it is likely to be less than therapeutic.

It is not unknown for an ill-judged invitation to disclosure ('Is there anything else you want to tell me?') to be met by a volcanically eruptive retort ('Don't you dare ask me *that* sort of thing!').

Time, depth and mutuality are the dimensions of structuring and will be dealt with in turn. The point at which therapist and patient meet will vary along each of these dimensions, depending upon the stage and nature of their meeting. For example, counselling, 'brief' psychotherapy, formal psychoanalysis, a consultation in general practice or in a casework setting will be structured in different ways on each dimension. Thus the appropriate response to a dream about the therapist will be framed in an entirely different manner if the patient describes it in the course of prolonged psychotherapy, compared with a dream recounted during the patient's exit from a brief medical interview.

It may be helpful to imagine several situations and to reflect upon the use the therapist would make of time, depth and mutuality in each instance. A GP listens to an anxious young mother who has just realised that her three-year-old son seems to be going deaf. A school counsellor listens to a boy's account of the way in which a stolen radio was found in his locker, with the prior knowledge that collateral evidence established beyond doubt that the boy's account was untrue. A psychoanalyst listens to irregular breathing, increasing restlessness and watches the lighting of cigarettes which are not smoked but twisted out of recognition. He sees and hears a great deal, but no words are spoken by his patient during the fifty-minute session. A social worker listens to the dawning doubt of a father who faces the fact that his 'battered baby' might not have received the multiple fractures 'by accident'.

The GP may not formulate his emotional initiative in this way, but the example just given highlights the basic premiss.

Time. He may mishandle the situation by being too brusque and so dismiss the anxious mother too soon. He may spend too long with her, so that she gains the impression that he is perhaps even more worried than she is. He will 'instinctively' decide about timing.

Depth. He will 'instinctively' decide how penetrating his questioning should be. Will his patient consider that he is not sufficiently concerned if he adopts a casual, apparently minimising and trivialising attitude, or might the wrong kind of incursive questioning bring even worse doubts to her mind?

Mutuality. He will 'instinctively' decide how much of his own personal experience he should divulge. It may help or hinder therapeutic efficacy if he mentions that he, too, had been worried about his daughter's deafness. He had discovered that she was 'turning a deaf ear' to a commanding parent, and that full audio-metric investigation showed that there was no question of any organic disease. On the other hand, an ill-considered reference to his own child, who had subsequently died from a tumour in the middle ear would, of course, be disastrous.

A further example from general practice underlines the need for sensitive structuring of the therapeutic process. An extremely difficult situation in which to respond professionally, demanding compassion and concern without being too cold and clinical on the one hand or falsely re-assuring on the other, is that of a consultation in which a woman of 35 tells her doctor that her left breast is getting smaller. The doctor knew at a glance that it was, in fact, the right breast which had got bigger.

I have deliberately couched this discussion within the context of a consultation in general practice, because every reader will have consulted a GP, either about himself or about his relatives, and will know how he reads between the lines. I described the GP's response as 'instinctively' determined, but of course the manner in which the question is asked 'instinctively', by an inexperienced GP, is entirely different from the form of questioning adopted by a junior medical student.

Training in psychotherapy enables the therapist to be increasingly flexible so that he can act spontaneously at the existential moment of meeting with his patient, precisely because of his grasp of prevailing endopsychic patterning, fixation points, and so on. If the therapist is enabled to enter the inner world of his patient, there may be 'regression in the service of the ego'* so that he can come alongside his regressed, psychotic patient while retaining his own hold on reality. It is a further indication of the value of 'the expanding frame of reference'. A useful analogy here is that of the built-in range-finder in a camera. The therapist's initiative may be to bring what his patient is saying into focus, so that they are both operating at the same focal point. I recall an interview with a man whose baffling presentation was either psychotic or that of an hysterical pseudo-psychosis. It was difficult to meet him at any level, and I had little sense of shared therapeutic space; however, when he said 'I don't *fully* understand you', I replied 'And I don't *fully* understand you ... but could it be something like ... ?' He immediately latched on to an analogy which I floated towards him, and said quite dogmatically 'Yes, that's it'. Neither of us fully understood each other, yet we each understood a shared analogy which transformed distance into therapeutic proximity. An incident in general practice and a meeting with a psychotic patient in hospital underline the fact that the dimensions of time, depth and mutuality can provide a scaffolding upon which the negotiation of every therapeutic encounter can be based. The counselling group for widows; the meeting of inmate and probation officer in prison; the group therapy session for aggressive psychopaths; the visit to the bedridden, hemiplegic ex-bus-driver in his council flat on the twentieth floor; all make specific demands upon the therapist. Though very different from each other, they all demand optimal structuring of time, depth and mutuality.

Against the background of these clinical vignettes we may set comments which illustrate a homogeneity of practice bridging theoretical divisions. Frank (1961) reached the 'tentative conclusion that the

* See page 265.

features common to all types of psychotherapy probably contribute more to their efficacy than the characteristics that differentiate'.* Stieper and Wiener (1965), having considered several studies of 'individual differences and experience', conclude:

> Experience, then, seems to wash out the lines of demarcation among therapists of different therapeutic orientations, and to make them more alike, more sensitive to pathology, and more aware of the goals and limitations of psychotherapy.

Strupp (1955) indicated that the experience of the therapist was a more potent factor than his 'school'. Hollis (1964) writes:

> Casework has always been a psychosocial treatment method. It recognizes both internal psychological and external social causes of dysfunctioning, and endeavors to enable the individual to meet his needs more fully and to function more adequately in his social relationships.

And again:

> Casework will drastically impoverish itself if it follows the lead of Horney and Sullivan in trying to explain human behavior primarily in inter personal terms, omitting those key intrapsychic phenomena that from the start influence the child's perception of and reaction to his interpersonal experiences.

Thompson and Kahn (1970) distinguishing between Group Discussion, Group Counselling and Group Psychotherapy, which are topic-orientated, problem-orientated and personality-orientated respectively, write:

> They all have aims which include the promotion of a degree of personal change in each member; each member is prepared to expose himself to change to a greater extent than he would do in other situations, and each member relies on a leader with special skill to be the ultimate guarantor that it is safe to do so.

This safety depends upon correctly perceived dynamics and structuring appropriate to the nature, the purpose and the phase of the group. Depending upon his theoretical viewpoint, each therapist will place different weight upon the significance of these various facets of the therapeutic relationship. And it is not our purpose to examine them in detail

---

* 'When we actually participate in psychotherapy, or observe its complexities, it loses this specious simplicity … (thinking of psychotherapists as exponents of competing schools).' from Toward New Syntheses (editorial) in *Humanism and Behaviorism: Dialogue and Growth*. Wandersman. A., Poppen. P. and Ricks. D. (editors) (1976) Pergamon Press. Oxford.

here, but simply to state that the common denominator shared by psychotherapists of all schools is the significance they attach to the structuring
of time, depth and mutuality within the therapeutic encounter. The
psychoanalyst, with his emphasis on unconscious motivation and the
paramount importance of psychic determinism, here joins hands with
the existential therapist with his prime concern for the here-and-now
phenomenon of Being. They both take seriously the various aspects
of the three dimensions; time, depth and mutuality. Errors in technique;
failures in therapy; unresolved transference resulting in an unduly
'adhesive' dependency or, *per contra*, an increasingly anomic social
distance on the part of the patient, can all be traced back to dislocation within therapeutic space due to inappropriate structuring. It is not
the patient's task to structure the time–space of the therapeutic session,
but he will respond to the therapist's initiative which is initially explicit,
but always implicit in the knowledge of the 'fifty-minute hour' of individual therapy or one and a half hours of group time. There is a fundamental difference between the climate, the cosmos and the content of
the therapeutic encounter and that of a spontaneous social meeting.
Quite apart from the original reason why the encounter took place (which
in itself implies the professional referral of the patient on the one hand
and the availability of the trained therapist on the other), there will be
fundamentally different mutual expectations at the outset. A spontaneous encounter between friends is not structured but open and evolving,
whereas the therapeutic encounter between patient and therapist, however casual it may appear, has a scaffolding of structured time, depth
and mutuality. This section is written in general terms because I do not
wish to be partisan, but rather to comment on the significance of structuring itself. The reader, whether he be a psychoanalyst, a client-centred
counsellor or an eclectic therapist will be able to reflect upon the way
that structuring influences the work he does. In my experience, structuring is equally important whether psychotherapy takes place within a
hospital, a prison, an out-patient consulting room or a professional
office; and whether it is on an individual or group basis.

    In a group situation the therapist's hovering attention has the quality
of a radar scanner as he constantly scans the whole field, i.e. the group-
as-a-whole, and at the same time notices each individual. His own
personality is inevitably involved and it is to be hoped that his profes-

sional training will have taught him how to adapt the general principles of psychotherapy to his own particular style of being; with his humour, life experience, emotional assets and liabilities. Although the tape recorder may indicate that, on some occasions, conversation seems to flow and on others it is punctuated by long silences, the therapist will be responding affectively in existential openness to whatever the group wishes to disclose. He will be concentrating upon time, depth of disclosure and mutuality. The therapist's discriminating attention will be both global and focal. It may involve patient waiting and observing, it may involve penetrating confrontation within, paradoxically, a climate of concern. This is especially true with psychopaths who deflect any questions which threaten their already jealously guarded and previously threatened self-esteem, so that there is a chess 'move and counter-move' feeling about the session.

If the therapist can appropriately structure the situation, he will find that by using the dimensions of time, depth and mutuality, he can render the situation tolerable for his patient who is enabled to acquire self-awareness at a depth and pace controlled by the therapist.* The aim is to structure the therapeutic process so that the chaos which most people feel once their defences begin to crumble, is not felt to be overwhelming. Thus, structuring implies not only the perception of structure or form, but the provision of an appropriate balance of confrontation and support so that the patient is given controlled access to himself. This must be at a depth and pace which is neither too slow and gentle on the one hand, so that the patient regards psychotherapy as boring and trivial; nor, on the other hand, so rapid and penetrating that the patient regards it, at best, as a reason for opting out of an unnecessarily painful process, or, at worst, a justification for suicide.

Structuring does not limit what the therapist does, but it provides a perception of events within the therapeutic process and a style of initiative. This renders it possible for him to deal with the chaos his patient may either present, *ab initio*, or begin to experience as soon as his hitherto private inner world of fantasy and dream becomes accessible. It is one aspect of the therapeutic process which is frequently implicit in the literature on psychotherapy and counselling, but is rarely a core topic.

---

* 'As his (the patient's) endurance increases so he is given more to endure.' (Thompson & Kahn. 1970).

I hope that the ensuing discussion will be useful to workers whose training may not have included specific supervision and experience in counselling, but who find themselves involved with patients. They will know that such techniques were not part of their main-stream professional training; whether it is modifying the patient's internal environment by medication, or the social conditions of the external environment.

Structuring is also used as a description of a way of organising the patient's life outside the therapeutic session (Small, 1971). This is an entirely different concept from structuring the therapeutic process itself.

(a) Time

You were asking me to say things which I could only feel. It needed to come out but *it wasn't the right time.*

(Anon., 1977)

... ears and eyes for the time.
But hearts for the event.

(*Coriolanus*, II. i. 274)

Appoint me a set time, and remember me.

(Job 14. 13)

Ripeness is all.

(*King Lear*. V. ii. 12)

The favourable moment is transient.

(Hippocrates)

Whatever you do ... take it slowly.

(Anon., 1975)

[advice from a patient to a fellow group member who was afraid of disclosing too much too soon]

Time is always significant in therapeutic sessions. It may seem to go too fast. It may seem to drag. The duration of the session matters to both doctor and patient, as does the duration between sessions. 'Come and see me again ... if you need to', says something entirely different to the patient from 'Come and see me again in four weeks' (Kahn, 1972). The doctor will judge whether the prospect of a subsequent interview makes the patient more anxious because it is felt that the doctor 'must have been worried because he asked to see me again'. Whereas the first response given may imply that the doctor is not really interested. The significance of holidays and periods of absence from the practice also highlight the importance of time. How often the patients will 'keep' the symptom or the family problem until their own doctor returns from holiday, except in the case of an emergency. The locum, quite understandably, could not understand.

If time is important to this degree in general practice, it is infinitely more so in formal psychotherapeutic practice. Here a therapeutic alliance is established with the patient, and it is arranged that they will meet, say, for fifty minutes each week, for work to be done. The significance of the beginning and the ending of the session colour the para-linguistic overtones of the words actually uttered. Holidays and other absences become increasingly important as the sharing of therapeutic space intensifies. We have already referred to the *fragestellung*, where the manner of asking the question influences the nature of the question itself, and this is particularly pertinent to the content of psychotherapeutic sessions. The significance of words, truncated utterances, pauses, acceleration, intermittent staccato verbal fire, protracted, almost inaudible verbalised sighs are signals of interaction. There is such a close association between the use of words in therapy and the significance of words in literature that the interested reader should study *The Sense of an Ending* (Kermode, 1966). Though primarily about literary criticism, it has many illuminating passages which enable the therapist to see what he is trying to do in a new light. See also *Between Two Worlds* (Dyson, 1972). This studies experience and the form of its presentation. A pertinent theme for the therapist, though the polarity discussed is that of literature.

The significance of time as a dimension is intensified when group therapy is considered. Here the members of the group may be competing for (or trying to withdraw from) their 'share' of group time. Shared time, as well as space, gives the therapeutic group greater scope for coping with pairing and rivalry, as well as providing a 'life-raft' of cohesion on the one hand, or a 'firing-squad' of disintegration and fragmentation on the other. Such feelings may be worked through in the course of transference in the individual therapy session, but they are made much more explicit and reality-based within the context of group therapy.

A fundamental maxim stressing the importance of timing is as follows: *If the patient does not know when the end is, he cannot know when 'just before the end' is.* This links closely to the well-known experience in general practice when the patient is leaving the consulting room and, with one hand on the door-handle, says: 'There's just one more thing, Doctor....' The 'just before the end' quality is never without significance in psychotherapy. Timing is always significant. Patient and therapist must know when the end is, because only then will they know when 'just before the end' is. This truism sounds ludicrous and the ultimate platitude. But the examples of faulty time-structuring given in the next section will, I hope, underline the reasons why this basic fact cannot be overstated.

The therapist and patient are both aware of the significance of time. The therapeutic session is of a known duration, and *chronos* (time as measured by chronometer) may or may not be spent fruitfully. Another Greek word for time (*kairos*) implies time in terms of *the* moment, such as the moment of falling in love, first seeing Venice, first hearing a baby cry, etc. Kelman (1960) has written on '*Kairos* and the therapeutic process'. The therapist's aim is to enable a patient's cognitive–affective disclosure to occur in the *kairos*, i.e. at the optimal moment in the *chronos*. He never ceases to learn from his patients. No textbook could have the authenticating quality of endorsing clinical experience which the following vignette from a group of offender-patients provides (one patient is talking to another):

> '*Is it possible to ask searching questions which do not hurt?*'
> '*Yes ... when the time is right.*'

This, *par excellence*, is the *kairos*.

In other words, during the course of a session when the chronometer registers a point in time, say 15.23, *a* moment can become *the* moment. This may be when a patient is first able to say to a threatening woman in the group that he is afraid of women, or when the glamorous, attractive young woman discloses that she always chooses unsuitable men so that the relationship is guaranteed not to last. In Freudian terms, the moment of disclosure is as the unconscious becomes conscious and insight is gained. Intellectual understanding plus appropriate feeling coincide. *Kairos* coincides with *chronos*, i.e. the moment becomes THE moment. It is sometimes possible in group therapy for the entire group to share a fusion of *kairos* and *chronos*, and this is often ushered in by awareness of a shared group dream. This phenomenon occurs quite frequently in therapeutic groups and always has the effect of making the individuals, however cynical, realise that the group has in some way permeated their inner world.

There is work to be done in the therapeutic encounter and the patient and therapist meet to do it. This may involve a supportive consolidation of shattered defences, in which the patient's overwhelming grief and loss may mean that he finds it difficult to survive, let alone live with any sense of purpose. On such occasions when the 'wreckful siege of battering days' has almost demolished the patient, the therapist's task is that of facilitating the increase of defences and strengthening the patient's emotional foundations. He will not evoke areas of experience which are painful, or stimulate anxiety by withholding himself from the patient. He will allow the patient to hold on to him, and, *in extremis*, physical touch may be the only form of contact the patient can trust, and even then there is the fear of letting go.* Touching, like timing, is always important; though, for obvious reasons, its significance is different in general practice and in formal psychotherapy.

At the other extreme is the fierce confrontation with self which a psychopath experiences as he is made to face his own music. Why must he rape, kill or overpower people weaker than himself? One of the most fragile and sensitive moments in the whole field of psychotherapy is when a psychopathic offender-patient first turns to look in upon himself, in contrast to his customary manœuvre of looking out and blaming the environment for everything; or when the borderline patient becomes aware that he has been manipulating external reality so as to verify his projections. This subtle moment of self-disclosure needs the greatest caution and delicacy in handling, because it is at such painful points that self-scrutiny begins. It often follows an unexpected and inexplicable act of kindness.

'No one has ever wanted to give *me* anything.'

Long discussions occur as to what manipulative manœuvre a Christmas present might signify. Is it a bribe, a seduction or some way of gaining control? And the sheer fact that it might be a gift because someone wants to give something, can be ruled out of court, because life experience has indicated that people do not behave in this way. As Bettelheim

* This is particularly applicable to patients whose 'hold' on reality is precarious. See footnote, page 269.

(1967) says in his discussion of autistic children under the heading 'The persistence of a myth': 'This rescue will not be undertaken if we continue to believe that the autistic child's disturbance is irreversible.' The same type of myth applies to psychopaths, by which I mean that it is so often said that psychopaths do not have feelings and cannot respond to affection or understanding. I could give countless examples where even the toughest psychopath, so often presumed to be impervious, does in fact open up, provided the 'rescue', to use Bettelheim's phrase, is embarked upon. If, within a secure environment, a psychopath is not trusted, he will not become trustworthy. And if he is not given a context in which he can show warmth and the capacity to understand other people, he will not do so. The powerful thrust of an initiating therapeutic encounter with a psychopath has something of the quality of a powerful rocket, forcing a heavy craft into orbit. The therapist uses enormous initial thrust for blast-off, which must be rapidly reduced when the craft is caught up in another gravitational field. In other words, the deliberate confrontation needed to pierce the almost impregnable defences of the psychopath would be almost lethal once those defences are fractured. Therefore, the initial incursive thrust gives way to gentle evocative reflection and the warmest facilitation. So that when, for example, a baby-batterer's denial changes to cautious, precarious, frightened disclosure of events of which she was previously unaware—the penetrating, firm initiative of the therapist moderates to reinforce the shared quality of therapeutic space. As the unconscious becomes Conscious-withheld or this becomes Conscious-disclosed, the favourable moment for the optimal intervention is indeed transient.

Just when, where and at what point in the session such disclosures occur will depend on so many details that we must speak here in general terms. The therapist will be acutely aware of time-structuring, and will not allow third-level disclosures to occur too near the end of a session if there is no time for the individual or the group to 'metabolise' them. If there is a sudden surge of powerful material which erupts towards the end of the session and it would be dangerous to deflect or, even more disastrous, to reflect it, then the therapist must make rapid executive decisions. He must decide whether he should arrange for collateral and continuing support by colleagues in the ward, or, in out-patient psychotherapy, whether he should contact the family doctor. In such a situation it needs the finest balance of judgement to honour the confidentiality of the session, and at the same time, honour the patient as a person who may need help of another kind, in another place.

There are many facets of time-structuring which the therapist can only learn by experience and supervision. The texture of an appropriate intervention which may be correct in the first phase of a group may be out of place in the last phase and *vice versa*. The utmost sensitivity is needed to try to discern and read not only the obvious, manifest content of group interaction, but also the undercurrents of unconscious group phenomena which Bion (1961) describes.

(b) Depth

To start with I thought group therapy was rubbish, but *once you start going deep it keeps going deeper still.*

(Anon., 1976)

Sail forth—steer for the deep waters only.
Reckless O soul, exploring, I with thee, and thou with me,
For we are bound where mariner has not yet dared to go,
And we will risk the ship, ourselves and all.

(from *Passage to India IX*. Walt Whitman)

Asher kept by the sea coast,
dwelling at ease within his harbours.

(Judges 5. 17)

The further we got into the wreckage, the worse the wreckage became.

(Advance Rescue Team, London Underground disaster, Spring 1975)

So by too harsh intrusion
Left colourless confusion.

(from *The Author's Last Words to his Students*, Tokyo Imperial University, 1927, Edmund Blunden)

There are some things that are too personal to talk about... but the group only works when it becomes 'too personal'.

(Anon., 1976)

Any discussion of depth-structuring* must include the notion of levels. I can do no more than hint at a few interesting perspectives from which clinicians and counsellors have approached the topic. The neuro-surgeon is concerned with levels of awareness, ranging from that of the patient upon whom he operates, who may be in 'deep' coma or under a general

---

*This section indicates how closely structuring and disclosure are inter-related. Structuring cannot be considered without reference to levels of disclosure.

anaesthetic, whose level of awareness is very low, to that of his fellow-surgeon who is making executive decisions and putting them into effect, whose level of awareness will be high.

The complex interaction between the unconscious, the pre-conscious and the conscious levels of awareness has been one of the major contributions of psychoanalytic theory to the understanding of human behaviour and experience. This is closely linked to the activity of the therapist who may use interpretations and other interventions which, it is supposed, are relevant at different levels, so that an interpretation may be described as 'deep'.

This discussion of individual levels of awareness is appropriate, though incomplete, when the patient is a member of a therapeutic group which implies corporate levels of experience. I am deliberately moving back and forth between the therapeutic space of the individual patient and therapist, and that of the therapeutic group. This is so that the reader, whose experience may not necessarily embrace both, may be aware of those problems which confront his colleagues. Foulkes (1964) refers to the multiple dimensions which operate within a therapeutic group, and he asks the pertinent question 'How can we orient ourselves, and bring some semblance of order into this chaos?' and then proceeds to describe levels which can be discerned in a group 'leading from surface to hidden aspects'.

1. Current level, in which the group represents community, society, public opinion, 'forum'.
2. Transference level, in which the group represents the primary family, the present family and intimate network.
3. Projective level, in which the group represents inner objects, part-objects.
4. Body level, where the group represents the body-image.
5. Primordial level, in which the group represents archaic images, in accordance with the concept of Jung's collective unconscious.

Bernard and Huckins (1971) discuss what they call levels of discourse, and show that discourse is analogous to, and a function of, transmission, whereas communication has the connotation of communion, and implies 'doing with'. They borrow Buber's terms: 'I–it' and 'I–thou' relationships. They envisage concentric circles; level 5 is on the periphery and 'is more in the nature of psychological self-preservation and manipulation and an exploitation of others than a desire to contact them or a concern for their value'. Whereas level 1 is analogous to Maslow's 'peak experience'.

Experiences on this level are difficult to verbalise or to communicate:

> ... at these times one feels in tune; that all's right with the world and with himself. He orchestrates with reality and the scheme of things ... Words are inadequate and verbalisation is unnecessary. There is perfection in the moment and in the experience. To label or to classify these incidents and sensations as a level of discourse is a misnomer. They are to be felt, not talked about.

Bernard and Huckins then indicate ways of facilitating effective discourse, which, using their model, means moving away from level 5 towards level 1.

It has already been indicated that group psychotherapy is distinguished from group counselling by the fact that there is no control on disclosure level. Feelings towards the therapist or the authority he represents, erotic or violent fantasies, dreams about the other members and the therapist are all acceptable currency. No topic is taboo.

> The method of free association is fundamental to group psychotherapy. The expectations and anxieties of group members may often lead to requests for topics for discussion, but these must be avoided since they generally represent an attempt to avoid personal matters and so delay the development of the group to the point where it is operating at that *degree of depth* [italics added] that is the characteristic contribution of this kind of group. (Council of Europe. European Committee on Crime Problems, 1974.)

There is much of theoretical interest in the concept of depth disclosure, which is discussed in greater detail in Chapter 8. It is considered alongside 'The levels hypothesis' (Coleman, 1969) derived from psychoanalytic theory and their interrelationship with the 'depth' of interpretation. Fisher (1956) compared the depth rating of twenty judges. 'There seems little doubt, then, that experienced therapists of various orientations are employing some common cues in determining depth.' Criteria given by one depth-rater were stated thus:

> I found myself giving ratings towards the 'deep' end when: (1) interpretation was of material defended against, not of defense itself; (2) when interpretation was historical; (3) when interpretation tied past and present; (4) when interpretation was of symbolic material rather than overt behavior (e.g. dreams, phantasies).

Raush *et al.* (1956) used a working definition of the depth of interpretation as:

> a description of the relationship between the view expressed by the therapist and the patient's awareness. The greater the disparity between the view expressed by the therapist and the patient's own awareness of these emotions and motivations, the deeper the interpretation.

In the ensuing discussion, 'depth' is applied to disclosures made by the patient, facilitated by the therapist. Nevertheless, the therapeutic initiative on the therapist's part must not be confused with depth interpretation as discussed in the preceding paragraphs. The structuring of depth and mutuality in an appropriate manner for *this* patient, in *this* place, at *this* time; or for *this* group, in *this* place, at *this* time; or (much more difficult!) for *this* patient, among *these* patients in *this* group-as-a-whole, in *this* place, at *this* time, will call for the therapist's response to what is taking place within the shared therapeutic space. This may include 'deep' interpretations; but it must be made absolutely clear that appropriate activity at a particular depth of relationship with the patient, or the group, will not necessarily be that of a 'deep' interpretation. In other words, the therapist may feel it is appropriate for the individual or the group to 'rest' at a particular level. Perhaps, in the interests of fostering cohesion, or restoring poise in a group shattered by a premature disclosure by one member, he will not be pressing the patient or the group to accept a deeper interpretation than is appropriate. Being in the 'deep end' of the swimming pool may involve treading water or floating, just as much as diving down to touch the bottom.

The fostering of emotional disclosure is one of the key functions of psychotherapy. Movement is always in the direction of disclosure, from unconscious to Conscious-withheld and then to Conscious-disclosed. It is therefore useful to conceptualise the emotional 'depth' of what a patient is saying in terms of three levels. I cannot write 'three levels of speech' because actual verbalisation may only form a part of what is implied in the term 'emotional disclosure'. In other words, two patients may make the same literal, verbal statement, but for one it is a faltering, truncated utterance with averted gaze, restless posture, fiddling with cigarettes, etc., whereas for another patient it is said without 'batting an eyelid'. Therefore the idea of a level of disclosure can only be relevant for a particular patient. To say 'When I masturbate I think of ...' may be associated with extreme anxiety on the part of Patient 1, whereas Patient 2 regards it as something of a giggle, and Patient 3 is psychotic. We must therefore bear in mind that although we are considering 'levels of speech', we are not considering verbalisation on its own, but speech in a particular emotional context.

Levels of disclosure

(i) First-level: Trivial

For example: '*I thought I saw frost this morning.*'

This is trivial 'chat' such as we hear every day in a bar or a bus, and it is entirely appropriate to these situations, where the rail strike provides the verbal currency for a safe exchange with strangers. However, such speech must be appraised *in situ*. Who is saying what, where and to whom? Thus what might appear as a first-level disclosure may, in fact, have a strong emotive and affective component if it implies rebellion against the restrictions within a total institution (Goffman, 1961). The therapist is therefore on his guard against interpreting complaints about 'breakfast being cold' as automatically indicating a first-level disclosure. It may carry an investiture of hatred to all authority, 'Cold bacon ... cold feeding ... cold mother'. It may mean what it says and no more.

(ii) Second-level: Neutral-personal

For example: '*I am breeding budgies.*' ('parakeets' in U.S.A.)

This is personal in that it relates to the personal life of the patient, but it is emotionally neutral. Under this heading are numerous factual fragments of biography, 'I was born in Boston ... I support Arsenal* ... Blue in my favourite colour', and so on, though it must always be remembered that such disclosures *may* be third-level disclosures. This can only be decided for each patient individually. For example, 'I went to work in Ireland in 1916' might be presumed to be a second-level disclosure, unless it was linked with prior knowledge that the patient, complaining of pyrophobia, lived in Dublin then, the year the Post Office was burnt down.

'I am breeding budgies' would be a third-level disclosure for the devotee.

(iii) Third-level: Emotional-personal

For example: '*I never had a childhood*'.

This is personal and emotional.† It is easy for every reader to think of

* Even as he reads this, the life-long Arsenal supporter will know that this statement could never be anything other than a third-level disclosure!

† A third-level disclosure is, by definition, not easy to make. This may be because of shame or embarrassment, but it may be too 'precious' and intimate to divulge. 'I nearly cry when I see Turner's Norham Castle' could be a third-level disclosure. *The deepest third-level disclosures are not accessible to introspection; they erupt into consciousness during psychotherapy,* though they can *subsequently* be recalled.

his idiosyncratic third-level disclosures. He has only to say 'I could never talk about *that* to anyone, let alone in a group,' and he has what might be a third-level disclosure!

Each patient and all men will have their own private world, which they will not readily share with others. There is something brash and exhibitionistic about the compulsive discloser who insists on telling everyone his own most intimate experiences. It is reminiscent of certain hysterical personalities who prompted the definition of a secret as 'something which you tell one person at a time'!

It is important to remember that psychotherapy always moves in the direction of disclosure. This may be helped by dreams, group experiences, which of course include the dreams of other patients, and the analysis of the transference, which means that the patient becomes aware of that of which he was previously unaware. In other cases the patient comes already aware of disclosures which he feels he needs to make, but which are embarrassing or ego-alien in some other way. It is often only in the course of making these disclosures, which are already conscious but not yet revealed, that he becomes aware of other disclosures which, as it were, come 'out of the blue' or, more accurately, out of his buried past.

A simple way of conceptualising these three levels of disclosure is by using a heuristic device known as a disclosure profile (see *Coding the Therapeutic Process: Emblems of Encounter*, Cox, 1978). Though originally developed in relation to psychotherapy with offender-patients, it is relevant to all patients and has nothing specific to do with offender-patients. Third-level disclosures are, by definition, only so, for the patient concerned. Therefore the statement 'I killed my father', which would certainly be a third-level disclosure for me, may not necessarily be so for my patient. He might talk about the incident with comparative ease and go into any detail that was necessary, but the physiological concomitants of anxiety and embarrassment, which are so often hints that the patient is on the brink of making a third-level disclosure, may be related to some other aspect of his life, which might inadvertently be ignored by the therapist. For example, a patient may talk with ease about the details of homicide, but find that it was quite intolerable to admit that he was the only boy in his form who did not need to shave by the time he left school.

There is nothing absolute about these three levels of disclosure, and they are simply presented as a useful conceptual tool and for teaching purposes. They can indicate that dynamic movement is occurring in the patient's endopsychic patterning during psychotherapy.

Movement of a group *in toto* towards third-level disclosures, which would be in keeping with the ideas expressed by Foulkes (*vide supra*), has an extremely powerful extrusive force on the patient who is unable to reach third-level disclosures, when everyone else in the group has been able to do so. Such a patient would be safe enough in the early phases when the group was criticising the staff, the food or the political system, as tends to happen in total institutions; or medical practice or the uselessness of drugs, as tends to happen in out-patient psychotherapy. Group cohesion in the early phases may depend upon shared needs such as a shared symptom or shared enemy. However, when the other members of the group begin to make their own third-level disclosures, one individual may not be able to do so. He could join the others in blaming his GP, or 'the Governors', but less readily his father, and his impotence least of all.

Soon after the establishment of a new group, a phase of cautious testing-out begins as the individual and the group itself begin to risk the vulnerability and openness which are inevitable concomitants of disclosure. Depth structuring implies the gentle though firm presence of the therapist, who, by gesture and word, tries to help his patients to tolerate themselves. In other words, he tries to buttress them as the unconscious becomes the Conscious-withheld which, in turn, becomes the Conscious-disclosed. 'I killed my father' may be fact or fantasy, but a patient may find the realisation too much to accept. The therapist tries to modulate, translate and interpret the inner world of the patient as it reaches his outer world of shared therapeutic space.

Corporate solidarity and a sense of vicarious presence may lead an individual member to perceive the rest of the group as though it was 'carrying' the emotional stimulus previously experienced with, say, a parent. Thus the group may stand as a 'father-surrogate', and if the patient has a history of homicide, then he may re-experience the feelings of killing his father and be afraid that his own deep disclosures may in fact 'kill the group' and that in this way, history may repeat itself. This phenomenon is particularly evident with a borderline patient whose hold on reality is so transitory and tenuous. 'If I tell the group how I killed my father, then I run the risk of killing the group itself... which is so much like my father.' This means that the group is then perceived not as 'a group of patients being told of the killing', but as a father who may also be killed if it continues to exhibit father-like attributes; such as being unsympathetic, passive, carrying on as though the patient is not there, etc. It therefore becomes clear that appropriate depth structuring is of paramount importance, particularly for the patient whose reality-holding is fragile. Nevertheless, when such individuals are enabled to make 'destructive' disclosures, and find that physical destruction has not occurred, there is a reality-based validation that the environment can take their verbal attacks without disintegrating. As always, the offender-patient brings out this point most acutely, but hostility towards parents is a universal topic in group therapy. The importance of depth structuring can never be exaggerated.

In order to evoke, capture and metabolise maximal feeling in the group, in marked contradistinction to intellectualising and discussion, the therapist needs to combine the two previous sections: in other words, timing and depth both need to be structured and yet, paradoxically, the group must be allowed to be self-evolving and exhibit natural growth. This brings us back to consider the role of the therapist who is 'in the world but not of it' as far as the group is concerned. He is intensely active, observing, and discerning. His hovering attention and scanning activity lead him to make facilitating interventions at the 'favourable' moment. One of the difficulties of learning this clinical skill is that the style and emotional penumbra of his supervisor, which might indicate intervention A at point B, would seem out of place for the therapist's own particular *modus laborandi*. Furthermore, it would depend on the particular make-up of the group and its matrix. Psychopaths, psychotics, neurotics, sex-offenders and many other categories of patients who may be referred for psychotherapy, require differential structuring of time, depth and mutuality.

The therapist tries to integrate depth and time structuring into a cohesive therapeutic initiative. This leads us to consider the most con-troversial issue of all, namely, the concept of 'mutuality'.

(c) Mutuality

'All that there is of me is here ... all you can see of me, is all there is. Whereas all of you is not here. It is like American football. *Part of you is on the sidelines waiting to be called on.'*
(The penetrating reflections of a patient upon mutuality within therapeutic space. The first sentence may be saying several things, if it is read with different words italicised. This portrays, better than any words of mine, the paradoxical nature of mutuality in therapy. Can it only be therapeutic if one member of the therapeutic alliance has added reserves; so that, if the 'match' becomes critical these reserves can be called upon? The paradox is intensified when it is realised that both therapist and patient are usually confronting more than they know, with more resources than they know. Could it be that the reserves attributed to the therapist may, in fact, evoke the awareness of personal reserves in the patient, which have hitherto been denied or remained latent?)
'It does not depend on one saying to the other everything that occurs to him, but only on his letting no *seeming* creep in between himself and the other' (Buber, 1957).
'What is most personal is most general' (Carl Rogers, 1961).

Every practitioner of psychotherapy, counselling or case-work is aware of the crucial significance of the place of mutuality and reciprocity within the therapeutic alliance. In 1923, Buber battled with the question as to whether mutuality itself was the door into our existence. Is a human I–Thou relationship always reciprocal? Can it ever be in psychotherapy? After considering the I–Thou relationship of pupil and teacher, he writes:

Another no less illuminating example of the normative limitation of mutuality is presented to us in the relationship between a genuine psychotherapist and his patients ... regeneration of an atrophied personal centre ... can only be attained in the person-to-person attitude of a partner, not by the consideration and examination of an object.

With great understanding of the psychotherapeutic process, he notes how the therapist

... must stand again and again not merely at his own pole in the bipolar relationship, but also with the strength of present realisation at the other pole, and experience the effect on his own action. But again, the specific 'healing' relation would come to an end the moment the patient thought of, and succeeded in, practising 'inclusion' and experiencing the event from the doctor's pole as well. Healing, like educating, is only possible to the one who lives over and against the other, *and yet is detached.* [Italics added.]

Buber expresses this so vividly. The involvement and yet the detachment, the engagement and yet the power to disengage which the therapist must retain, so that with his fulcrum *outside* the patient, he can facilitate change *within* the patient.

Elsewhere, Buber (1947) discusses mutuality as 'a unity of unbroken, raptureless perseverance in concreteness in which the word is heard and a stammering answer dared'. And with prophetic insight he distinguishes collectivity and community. This has far-reaching implications and distinguishes between group psychotherapy in which there is genuine concern for *koinonia*, and pseudo-therapy with its ethos of package-deal, expedient collectivity. Buber writes: 'community is where community happens. Collectivity is based on an organised atrophy of personal existence, community on its increase and confirmation in life lived towards one another.' Siirala (1969) writes:

> The sick person is not an isolated phenomenon, and a truly therapeutic encounter reveals the shared common quality of the illness, not least in the therapist himself, *who must acknowledge his share*. The psychoanalytic term "countertransference" is a half-acknowledgment but does not sufficiently cover the experience. [Italics added.]

The phrase in italics is a key issue and is discussed below.

Writing of group psychotherapy with schizophrenics, Macnab (1965) says:

> It is true that this self-disclosure could be made only where there was a trustful commitment, otherwise there would be a possibility of a precipitation of a greater anxiety than if the disclosure had never occurred. Here the therapist played a crucial role, for each member of the group had to see in him the epitome of trust and commitment, and as this became more and more their experience, so it was reflected in the group. The therapist, although not disclosing himself, nevertheless had to be ready to disclose what was relevant to the relationship, and his disclosure had to be genuine at all times.

I have described the same 'preparedness' for disclosure when working with sex-offenders (Cox, 1977), in which therapeutic space is corporate and vicarious. Literally, 'one of us' is a rapist. Though mutuality, I maintain, should be restricted to responding in, and to, the existential exigency of the present moment.*

It is interesting to note that Buber used the phrase 'a genuine psychotherapist', thus heralding recent research upon the relationship between the genuineness of the therapist and the outcome of psychotherapy. The therapist asks himself what genuineness and authenticity mean in terms of the particular relationship he has with this patient, in this place, at this time. To be genuine does not imply having ambitious and unrealistic

---

* In other words, although the therapist and patient may not share life-space *outside* the therapeutic setting, the sharing of therapeutic space is as genuine as it is unavoidable.

expectations for his patient; neither excessive optimism nor excessive pessimism facilitate the therapeutic process.

It is by structuring the therapeutic process that the therapist hopes to enable the patient to come to terms with himself as he is, as he was and as he may yet become. Encouragement, but not over-zealous optimism, facilitates movement in the direction of 'himself as he may yet become'. Authenticity may imply acceptance of despair, but it also carries within it a possibility of hope, and the therapeutic space should be permeated by hope, though hope which has not degenerated into facile encouragement.

Kierkegaard (1844, 1849) elaborated this existential theme in *The Concept of Dread* and *The Sickness Unto Death*, in which he looks at the 'possibility and actuality of despair'. Authenticity is a pivotal theme in the latter book, and 'In despair at not willing to be oneself, the despair of weakness' is the title of one section. '... these caricatures of faith are part and parcel of life's wretchedness, and the infinite resignation has already consigned them to infinite contempt.' He describes those who 'tranquillise themselves with the trivial', and is reminiscent of an earlier prophetic voice: 'We looked for peace, but no good came; and for a time of healing, and behold dismay!' (Jeremiah 14. 19).

Nevertheless, the experience of dismay may well be a necessary preparation for a 'time of healing', and the therapist's activity may be to provide a temporary silent presence in the face of the patient's experience of darkness and diminishment. Acceptance of personal destructiveness and resentment cannot be bypassed, and is an integral part of the psychotherapeutic process of increasing self-awareness. Paradoxically, it is often felt more acutely by the patient who has never been involved in any violent anti-social behaviour, than by a patient with a long history of offences 'against the person'.

Without retreating into technical language which would necessitate numerous definitions and explanations, it is safe to say that in this present context, mutuality refers to how much the therapist discloses about himself in order to share with the patient the experience he is disclosing. Indeed, Jourard (1971),* who has undertaken much research on self-disclosure, writes: 'We found a correlation between what persons

* Readers who wish to follow Jourard's discussion of self-disclosure further should see the bibliography at the end of *The Transparent Self.*

were willing to disclose to other people in their life and what these other people had disclosed to them. There appeared to be a reciprocity in self-disclosure.' Jourard added that when he was faced by someone 'who behaved towards me like a client-centred counsellor or a psychoanalyst, it would almost make me vomit because it *seemed inauthentic*' (italics added). I have written the last two words in italics in order to emphasise the fact that Jourard was of course writing about *his* experience. Therefore he was saying that the sounding-board or reflecting approach, of the analyst or client-centred counsellor, seemed to *him* inauthentic. This may be because, as Jourard said earlier, this approach had not worked 'for me', i.e. when he was treating patients using either of these approaches he felt inauthentic and therefore when people responded to him in this way, he presumed that they must be inauthentic. Yet it was none other than Rogers who said: 'What is most personal is most general' which links closely with Jourard's statement: 'Disclosure begets disclosure'. After a lengthy period in a mixed therapeutic group a patient said: 'What I used to think was very personal... other people shared.' This takes us deep into the significance of corporate solidarity. Other people may 'share' the experience of the experience, but it was an 'untransferable' personal event when *my* mother died, *my* girl-friend walked out or *I* stabbed a taxidriver. The paradox of dynamic psychotherapy is that it provides the only arena in which 'untransferable' experiences of love and hate can, through transference, become negotiable.

This immediately brings us face to face with what must be the 'still point of the turning world' of psychotherapy, namely that area of professional life within therapeutic space in which the therapist feels authentic. Authenticity, one of the pillars of the existential approach when set against inauthentic existence, is one of the certain indications that the therapist is 'homing in' on the patient's radar signals.

Being authentic as a therapist implies more than having a superficially adequate technical grasp of manipulating events during an interview. It demands a coherent view of life which must include frames of reference large enough to allow his patient to free-associate and disclose anything about anything (including the therapist). He needs a sufficiently viable *weltanschauung* to give him some sense of direction and growth, so that the patient's chaos, which may be exhibited in a chaotic life-style or subsequently revealed in a chaotic inner world, can become restructured and coherent, as chaos moves towards cosmos. The place of reciprocity and mutuality within the therapeutic situation has a direct bearing upon the resemblance, if any, between the life experience of the therapist and that of the patient, prior to, or alongside, the therapeutic alliance. The therapist may, or may not, have had similar experiences to those of his patient, though in general terms he will inevitably have had certain shared experiences; most obviously birth, weaning, separation from parents, and so on. But it is one of the ground rules of psychotherapy training that *what would be third-level disclosures for the therapist are not necessarily so for the patient.* This cannot be said too often, although therapists of various schools might use different words to describe this phenomenon. It seems erroneous to assume that when a patient has spoken about sexual feelings for, say, a parent, (accompanied by appropriate affect) then this disclosure of repressed infantile sexuality is, *ipso facto*, the deepest disclosure possible. In other words, there are many other frames of reference which might have more significance for the patient than a restricted psycho-sexual one. 'Why must we always think that just because we have said something sexual we have therefore got down to basics? It often feels as though sexual things are really a cover for something else, but therapists seem to be satisfied if they reach down to the sexual level!' This particular patient had a far more pervasive sense of the threat of non-being than could be accounted for in psychoanalytic terms of castration anxiety, which, *as far as it went*, fitted the situation exactly. Therapeutic space is a particular cosmos in which it is safe to grow and explore, and therefore the patient must feel free to ask any of the ultimate existential questions of himself in the company of the therapist. It goes without saying that the therapist must be sufficiently at ease with himself to contemplate his own sexuality, violence, death, so that his patient can free-associate. I do not wish to continue to overstate the obvious, but it is so easy to give verbal approval to free-association, with an emotional cut-out switch which in effect says 'tell me anything you like except feelings about homosexuality, violence, politics, religion…'. It is to be hoped that psychotherapeutic training, integrated with our personal *weltanschauung*, will allow us to be sufficiently open so that we can catalyse the patient's disclosures which, in the long run, he makes to himself. It is part of the therapist's function to allow the patient to become progressively more able to accept the unacceptable parts of himself, and this must be carefully judged so that it occurs at a rate and depth which is neither too fast and deep to be over-threatening, nor yet too shallow and slow so that the therapeutic process is delayed. Such misjudgements are often interpreted by the patient as being due to the fact that the therapist could not take what he was saying. Every therapist must, on occasion, have felt that what the patient was about to tell him was almost more than he could bear, because it coincided with some personal event in the therapist's own life. A doctor 'could not listen' to the account of the attempts to save a drowning child, because his own daughter had just drowned. Erikson (1950) writes: 'And it seems possible to further paraphrase the relation of adult integrity and infantile trust by saying that healthy children will not fear life if their elders have integrity enough not to fear death.'

Forced mutuality is one of the perennial traps which trainee psychiatrists and social workers fall into, almost without knowing it, because they start with the fundamentally correct approach of treating patients as people! This is supported by de-stigmatising and de-labelling intentions, backed up by influential writers such as Goffman (1963), and other compassionate mentors dating back to Hippocrates! It is so easy to make the jump from assuming that because patients should be treated as people, therefore shared experience within the context of psychotherapy must be on a parity basis. In some ways Jourard points to this by showing that there is a reciprocity in self-disclosure: 'Disclosure begets disclosure.' It is perfectly true that disclosure *may* beget disclosure, so that in the early stages of a therapeutic relationship a patient may be more likely to discuss personal and hitherto undisclosed, aspects of his life if the therapist does likewise. However, I regard the risks of this approach as infinitely greater than the assets. Indeed, I would go further, and say that probably one of the fundamental abilities of the therapist is to be able to facilitate disclosures by his patient, with minimal detailed personal disclosures on his part. This could be extrapolated to the point of saying that *the capacity to 'hold' a patient with minimal personal disclosure on the therapist's part is indicative of the depth of the working relationship and has an important bearing upon the use of transference.* Minimal disclosure, paradoxically, makes the therapist more 'available'; it ensures flexibility and facilitates the patient's free-association. It thus guarantees a future for therapeutic space. If the therapist is tempted to disclose much about his own personal life, then he must ask himself why this is necessary. I find myself falling back upon basic psychodynamic principles here. If the prime aim of therapy is to facilitate the processes whereby the patient's unconscious becomes conscious, and the conscious becomes disclosed, then the therapist must keep a cautious eye on why he is disclosing personal experiences which are implicit in any idea of mutual disclosure. This brings him at once to ask whether what is happening is really for his patient's well-being, or for his own. The therapist must always have a self-regulating mechanism, whereby the therapy is really patient-centred rather than therapist-centred!

If the therapist is genuinely interested in his patient then it is entirely acceptable for a patient's question to be answered by another question. 'Doctor X is so interested in me that he wanted to know more and more details of what "happened" and how I felt about it.' Balint was referring to the questions asked by a therapist of a patient in an interview situation when he formulated his now famous aphorism 'if you ask questions, all you get is answers!' An offender-patient who did not trust psychiatrists said 'I was holding back. He asked questions and *I only gave answers*.' If, however, the question is correctly 'placed' it is received as an invitation, rather than an attack. When this happens the therapist receives more than answers; because the answer is an integral part of unfolding cognitive–affective disclosure. Concerned reflection of the patient's question or even the asking of a subsidiary or clarificatory question—'What are you saying? (asking?)…what are you really saying? (asking?)… what are you REALLY saying? (asking?)' within a penumbra of disclosure can strengthen the bond between therapist and patient, rather than the reverse. Detail and yet more detail—'What was the best/worst moment?' 'Did she struggle all the time?'—can convince the patient of the therapist's concern to know. The expanding frame of reference (*vide supra*) is useful here—'What else might he be telling me?'—however lucidly events are described and no matter how 'small print' and detailed the questions become. Tolstoy has so accurately caught the ironic duplicity of disinterested questioning in *The Death of Ivan Ilyich*.

Praskovya Fiodorovna came in well satisfied with herself but yet with a slightly guilty air. She sat down, asked how he was, as he saw, simply for the sake of asking and not in order to find out, knowing very well that there was nothing to find out…

Disinterested questioning is always disastrous and nullifies therapeutic space.

Much of the writing on reciprocal disclosure and the mutuality of disclosure refers to the response of the therapist, in which he actually recounts life experiences which may closely match those recently disclosed by his patient.* A naïve example would be the response 'so have I' to the patient's statement that he had fallen in love with the neighbour's wife! There is, however, a safer mutuality of disclosure, pertaining to the use of the existential shared therapeutic space of the current therapeutic alliance. In other words, this may refer to the therapist's response to what is happening between him and the patient in the here-and-now, and is intimately concerned with empathy, transference and counter-transference. There is safety implicit in disclosing what must be a shared experience, between the therapist and the patient in an individual session or between the members of a group in a group session. This has an entirely different frame of reference from that of the personal life experience of the therapist, which might have happened many years, and many worlds of experience, away from that disclosed by the patient. Pseudo-mutuality is a word used to describe some family relationships of schizophrenics. It would be anathema in the context of therapist–patient relationships.

Ascent from Chaos has already been mentioned (page 19), in which Sifneos (1965) describes experience with a patient who was impervious to any other forms of treatment. 'He [the therapist] must abandon temporarily his objective attitudes and attempt to encounter his patient on the patient's own level of existence and of primitive emotional functioning.' This was a risky, but successful, structuring of mutuality, and Sifneos could add 'Hope thus emerged from chaos'.

A patient of mine said 'Because of the chaos, I am coming together' (not 'in spite of').

(i) *Names and naming*

I've forgotten your name, but it's not your fault.
I think it *is* his fault, because he's not important enough!
Is it possible to feel so unimportant that you actually forget your own name?
(a fragment from a group session)

* See page 189 footnote.

There is beginning to be a person attached to my name

(Anon., 1976)

'Mrs. — —'

'Blockitt, sir,' suggested the nurse, a simpering piece of faded gentility, who did not presume to state her name as a fact, but merely offered it as a mild suggestion.

(from *Dombey and Son,* Charles Dickens)

And you do know my name, though you don't remember that I belong to it.

(from *The Hobbit,* J. R. R. Tolkien)

O horror! horror! horror! Tongue, nor heart
Cannot conceive nor name thee!

(*Macbeth,* II. iii. 63)

I am become a name....

(from *Ulysses,* Tennyson)

Let in the nameless formless power
That beats upon my door....

(from *Northumbrian Sequence,* Kathleen Raine)

The activity of naming is of vital importance in all clinical work, and is closely linked to the fostering of mutuality and empathy. The appropriate naming of people and 'the naming of parts' (see Reed's (1946) poem with this title) or pathological processes, is infinitely more significant than the dictates of tact, custom or courtesy might imply. Some patients are afraid of the unknown and unnamed, but others are afraid of the known and named.

It is the cause, it is the cause, my soul;
Let me not name it to you, you chaste stars!

(*Othello,* V. ii. 1)

The patient may also be aware that named disease carries its own stigmatic implications, such as VD. The patient has a fear of being known, just as he has a fear of not being known. At times he is afraid of knowing the 'illness' from which he is suffering, and at other times he is afraid of not knowing.

The actual process of naming can almost make or break a relationship, and there is no universal guide about names and naming which would be appropriate in every situation. A young man may feel diminished to be called John, or distanced to be called Mr. Smith or Smith, though he may sense the doctor's indecision if he is referred to as John Smith. Depending upon the inflection and the precise clinical situation, including the length of time in psychotherapy, there is much to be learned from the naming of the therapist by the patient. 'Dr. Cox, Cox, Murray, Doctor, Murray Cox', with the embellishments of the nickname or the term of abuse, all indicate different patient/therapist alignments which, like other relationships, are never static.

The significance of names and naming can never be overestimated, though each has a different timbre, depending on the setting. For example, in general practice there is frequently great relief when the doctor is able to provide a name for the complaint which is baffling the patient.

> The name may mean very little to them; they may understand nothing of what it signifies; but because it has a name, it has an independent existence from them. They can now struggle or complain *against* it. To have a complaint recognised, that is to say defined, limited and depersonalized, is to be made stronger. [Berger and Mohr, 1967]

For the patient who is afraid of feeling precarious, 'very mortal' and afraid of an unknown illness which has struck him, the fact that the doctor may write 'transient viraemia' on a certificate can be, in itself, immeasurably reassuring. The doctor knows because he is 'the familiar' of illness. At the other extreme is the suspicion or the certainty of malignant (the 'nameless') disease. I recall a patient I met as a clinical student who had cancer, 'knew' she had cancer and yet no one would confirm or refute the diagnosis because 'further investigations are being done and Doctor X, the consultant, will be seeing you next week'. She was aware that *seeing* meant that he would be *telling*. The sense of relief which flashed upon this elderly lady's face when she was actually told that she had cancer astonished me then, though I have met many similar situations since. It is obviously wrong to generalise at this point, except to say that the naming or the withholding of naming is always of profound importance in the doctor/patient relationship. Maybe John prefers to know the truth, so that he can 'get himself ready', whereas David may be overwhelmed and almost literally disintegrate at an ill-judged disclosure of the name of the malignant disease.

> When we call for a doctor, we are asking him to cure us and relieve our suffering, but, if he cannot cure us, we are also asking him to witness our dying. The value of the witness is that he has seen so many others die.... He is the living intermediary between us and the multitudinous dead. He belongs to us and he has belonged to them. And the hard but real comfort which they offer through him is still that of fraternity. [Berger and Mohr, 1967.]

The wrestling of Jacob is not dissimilar from the man wrestling with himself and with the illness which is part of him. 'And Jacob was left alone; and there wrestled a man with him until the breaking of the day. ... And Jacob asked him, and said, Tell me, I pray thee, thy name. And he said, Wherefore is it that thou dost ask after my name?' (Genesis 32. 24).

Within the context of psychotherapy, the inner chaos and sense of dislocation can be so pervasive that the patient literally feels he will disintegrate, and this is made all the more acute and unbearable because he does not know what has struck him. The man in a road accident knows what has hit him, but a 'disturbed' man with a breakdown of his defences does not know what has struck him. It is in the course of psychotherapy, when a patient may be reliving an almost unbearable, painful early experience of rejection or over-stimulation that some such phrase as the following so frequently emerges. 'As long as you know what is going on, I can bear it...what is the matter? What is my name? ... What is the name of what is happening to me?' At this point they slip so easily into a paraphrase of Kant's classical questions: 'What can I know? What ought I to do? What may I hope?' Kermode (1966) brings out the prophetic quality of naming in his discussion of Macbeth:

> Hebrew could manage with one word for "I am" and "I shall be"; Macbeth is a man of a different temporal order. The world feeds his fictions of the future. When he asks the sisters "what are you?" their answer is to tell him what he *will* be.

Shakespeare has so accurately described the 'thought disorder' of the sisters; or were they intuitively answering the question which Macbeth was 'really' asking?

A similar interaction occurred between a thought-disordered member of a therapeutic group and his questioner, a fellow member: 'What kind of things do you tell your mother when you write to her?' 'She tells me how things are at home.' In this instance a question is asked and another question is answered; but the patient's 'core concern' determines the nature of the reply: 'How things are at home' was a pervasive preoccupation and might be the answer to *any* question! His 'centre of gravity' was at home. The only question worth asking would be about home, so that all answers 'home in' on home.*

The naming of each other and the naming of the disturbance within, using the words of the patient, and sometimes the renaming and redefin-

---

* He subsequently admitted he was 'running out of answers'. A tacit implication that there was a limited repertoire of answers; they all point back to what 'Mum does'.

ing of the disturbance within the patient, may be an integral part of the therapeutic process. It is part of the structuring activity of the therapist. It is as though the patient is aware of something in code which he hopes the relationship with the therapist will help to decipher. This is similar, but not identical, to the concept of the unconscious becoming conscious. It is rather a question of restructuring what has been wrongly structured. On some occasions, names and naming colour and reinforce the empathy that permeates therapeutic space. At other stages in the psychotherapeutic process, it is a question of actually living within therapeutic space with the patient, with no attempt to probe, intervene or make any incursion into his inner life. In other words, the empathic quality of therapy is the relevant therapy itself. 'Time, and a little support.'

Such a use of the empathic process is light years away from the penetrating, incursive battering of the patient's defences, which must be broken if liberation and a wider life is to result. This is particularly so with psychopaths, whose attempts to retain self-esteem have led to almost impregnable defences, so that they shut themselves off from emotional access to or from any other person. The therapist may be the first person to break through the wall, but only when the patient will 'permit' invasion. The phrase 'to permit an invasion' may be paradoxical, but it is clinically true. Linguistic invasion is part of the therapist's initiative. A warm, empathic relationship with the psychopath may result in stalemate, whereas a warm, empathic relationship with, say, a psychotic patient who has been involved in an episode of violence may be the beginning of therapy. Names and naming; who are you? Who am I? What is the matter with me? What is the matter with you? What is the matter with us? underlie all counselling and therapeutic situations, and answers to these questions depend upon the prevailing needs of the patient. Not, I hope, upon the therapist's need to be called by his Christian name, or, *per contra*, 'Sir', or, indeed, anything particular!

(*ii*) *Clothing and investment*

> It's not what you wear—it's what you are that counts
> (a significant remark coming from a girl with '16 coat-hangers
> in the wardrobe and 4 or 5 things on each').

This brief section is interposed between 'Names and naming' and 'Gifts and giving' because it is another area of personal declaration. Clothing always indicates the degree of personal investment of energy, time and significance in maintaining 'appearance'. It is closely linked with the use of cosmetics, hair styling and other non-verbal methods of communication, by which the patient conveys important information about himself. Such matters, though important even on the occasion of an initial encounter, assume magnified significance during the course of prolonged psychotherapy.

Clothes, like cosmetics, may serve to camouflage inner blackness, so that the more depressed and lifeless a patient feels, the more she may present a colourful exterior, in the hope of convincing the world that 'all is well'. If this is so, then the sudden breakdown of this last brittle bastion, so that the patient suddenly appears with a torn dress, nail varnish peeling off, dishevelled hair and lop-sided lipstick, alerts the therapist to the fact that his patient is experiencing an anhedonic, collapse of her final vestiges of self-esteem. When this happens any reference to 'ending it all' must be taken extremely seriously.

With other patients, even a small reduction in the care of 'personal appearance' may perhaps be the first indication of some current intra-psychic change. Thus a change in physical appearance, including clothing and general 'grooming', may be either the first smallest intimation of affective change, or, *per contra*, the last, prior to total breakdown. One patient read that the ability to 'dress oneself' was evidence of sanity. She went to considerable lengths to provide such evidence.

The literature upon the sexual significance of clothing is copious, and describes such phenomena as the bachelor who studies his extensive array of attractive ties and decides which of these evocative 'partners' he will 'take out' today!

It is not by accident that clothing and investment, are, in one sense, synonymous, yet in another are complementary. I refer to the financial and the emotional investment of personal energy which is devoted to (or withheld from) the patient's sartorial presentation.

There is nothing new about the observation that the outward and visible appearance conveys information about the inner life of the patient. 'The garment of praise for the spirit of heaviness' (Isaiah 61. 3) is an ancient phrase. What is new is the use to which such information is put during the sequential phases of dynamic psychotherapy. The sartorial statement about the patient will be one, among many other factors, which reflects the patient's current self-esteem and his way of construing the world in which he lives. This influences the *timbre* of the therapist's structuring initiative. Mention has already been made (page 68) of the way in which the patient's sense of self influences the therapist's response. It will be recalled that Lord George Hell wore a mask to disguise his ugliness, in order to further his ends. The 'face' he put on is so closely related to the application of cosmetics, referred to as 'doing my face'. This in turn is part of the patient's 'investment' in the image he chooses to present to the world.

The patient will not be slow to notice the therapist's 'investment' in the image *he* chooses to present to the world! Is it for this reason that 'Clothing and investment' appears in the section on mutuality.

(iii) Gifts and giving

> It is in giving that we receive.
> (generally attributed to St. Francis of Assisi)

> 'You have to have a "gift" for giving . . . if you're not giving in response to something you've been given.'
> (a reflection about Christmas. An individual disclosure in a group which was echoed by all. Anon., 1975)

The inability to give and/or receive is rarely the presenting symptom which prompted referral to a psychotherapist in the first place, though this psychological deficit often becomes apparent in the early phases of psychotherapy. It is brought into particularly vivid focus in the context of group therapy, where there is always the problem of competition for time and attention from the therapist and other members of the group. I can do no more than hint at the various manifestations of this problem. It may relate to the giving and/or receiving of letters or other gifts; or the use of touch, which may range from a fleeting grasp and a frightened clinging to a transient but firm statement of presence. One psychotic patient found that walking away from a group arm-in-arm with Sister (a co-therapist) was a much greater evidence of being a 'member' than any 'talk', however compassionate and supportive. (See footnote page 269.)

The existential immediacy of response which, hopefully, will be in the patient's interests, highlights yet again the importance of the therapist trying to be aware of what appears to be happening, and simultaneously, what is symbolised of a deeper transaction. It is painful for the patient and unnecessarily aggressive on the part of the therapist to interpret all giving. Such a response may justifiably distance the patient, whose gift may have been a genuine expression of gratitude, that 'in spite of our battles, we are getting somewhere'. On the other hand, the therapist may deprive his patient of an important emotional 'gift' if, on other occasions, he withholds interpretation on account of his own in-experience or anxiety. Some 'giving' does not need interpretation, and says far more eloquently than words ever could, a great deal about the giver, the gift and the receiver. For example, Tom may present the group with a corporate group gift, i.e. something which can only be received by the group itself, whereas Philippa felt that she needed to give an individual gift to each member of the group. What does this mean? It is another symbolic act in which the patient's activity speaks for him at that particular stage of his relationship to his fellow-members. In such an instance, both the 'group' and the 'individual' gifts teach us all new things about ourselves and each other.

In different contexts gifts and giving may mean different things. There is the manipulative gift, the seductively persuasive gift, and it cannot be repeated too often that there is no standard way of dealing with gifts and giving which would be appropriate to all situations. The setting influences the 'meaning' of the gift, for example the bottle of gin would have com-pletely different implications in general practice and a group for chronic alcoholics!

To over-interpret can be wrong. To under-interpret can be wrong. Each case must be judged on its merits. Tournier (1964) has touched on this important topic in *The Meaning of Gifts* though the reader will inevitably think of this theme from his own particular professional perspective.

Difficulties in giving and receiving of gifts are often symbolic reifica-tions, in the realm of external objects, of difficulties which the patient has experienced with translocation or incorporation of internal objects. If the patients' endopsychic patterning changes during the course of psychotherapy, this is frequently reflected in their interpersonal world by changed patterns of giving and receiving; both symbolically and partially as gifts, and literally and totally as loving.

By definition, a gift is something given and received. It is therefore usually regarded as something highly 'personal'. I recall the annual frustra-tion of a young offender-patient whose birthday (unhappily for him) fell on 5th November. He bitterly resented the fact that his brothers and sisters all received personal gifts for their birthdays; these, depending upon their ages, were toys, books, clothing or other items 'for personal use'. 'Just because my bloody birthday falls on November the fifth, I'm always given flaming rockets. The whole damned family shares my presents. They can see the rockets just as well as me, so that my presents are really family presents, whereas theirs are their own.' This disclosure was made in a therapeutic group, and it was followed by a deafening and infectious burst of laughter, which echoed round the room, when his reply to the question 'What did you do, Fred?' was 'I went to the bloody toilet and let the rockets off in there where no one else could see them!'

2. HAZARDS OF STRUCTURING

(a) Time

(i) *Overrunning*

The enthusiastic beginner allows a group to overrun because the 'important material seemed to be coming up at the moment when we should officially stop'. This always appears so reasonable at the time and yet in any group situation, Patient A, whose disclosure encouraged the overrunning, will often be regarded as the therapist's favourite by Patient B, whose equally pressing personal needs were not met by an equal extension of time on the subsequent week. Furthermore, if a therapist is feeling well, has the time to spare and important material is being ventilated, then, once again it may seem so sensible and humane to continue... 'After all, this is a shared experience with human beings in need.' If, however, on the following week, equally significant material erupts, then the group finds it hard to accept the sudden cessation 'on the dot' which the therapist arranged because he had a heavy cold, his children were up in the night or his car had broken down. (When the original draft arrived, this sentence read 'his *care* had broken down'!) This is part of a personal world which is not part of the shared world with the patient.

(ii) *Underrunning*

The illogical or rather the para-logical utterances so often made during psychotherapy, have particular relevance to such phenomena as under-running, e.g. 'The group seems to have finished before the end'... 'What do we talk about when there's nothing left to talk about?' The error here is that of terminating the group... 'if no one has anything left to say'. It is so easy in the relaxed safety of the post-group staff discussion to see why the group should have continued until 'the end'. A patient may have been on the brink of saying many things, and silence was not because there was nothing to say, but precisely because there was. Indeed, it is one of the hallmarks of resistance in psychotherapy, whether individual or group, that the patient who arrives intending to say so much finds that 'the words just will not come'. It is the interpretation of this resistance within the transference situation that is an established part of psychoanalytic technique. Once again, premature closure is so easily construed by the patients as manifestations of the fact that the therapist has lost interest. It can never be overstated that in dynamic psychotherapy the prime concern is what the event means to the patient.

(iii) Ill-timed or faulty interventions

The therapist will never fully master the art of making the appropriately timed intervention, with the perfect balance of support and confrontation, for the individual and/or the group-as-a-whole. It is an infinitely improvable skill. The therapist uses his own personality to facilitate greater disclosure, to foster creative tension or relieve overbearing anxiety. He does this not only by speech but by posture, gesture, expression. It is as he reads the silence or deflects an overwhelmingly hurtful question that he needs to focus on what is being said, what is not being said, and what might be said.

There is no rule of thumb. The therapist is alone and must act alone in the existential moment of the group or in close collaboration with his co-therapist. His intervention may be clarificatory, confrontational, interpretive, reflective or evocative, but however systematically the therapist has been trained, when it comes to the texture and timing of his intervention, he has to make his own decision then and there. His interventions always have the appearance and immediacy of an off-the-cuff quality, but they are just as professional as, say, those of the teacher.

The trainee will always modify what he learns from his mentors and gradually develop his own professional style. Nevertheless, in no situation is the therapist so isolated as when he faces one of the limitless possible crises which can occur, *de novo*, in any therapeutic group. There is an existential here-and-now quality about this immediate call on his resources. A few examples will convey the flavour of the kind of dilemma I have in mind, though each carries implicit existential demands of judging 'optimal' structuring of time, depth and mutuality. In each of these situations it would be impossible to look up the 'correct procedure' in any index; and it is so easy to structure the therapeutic process wrongly.

How might the therapist respond when:

(a) A patient brings a birdcage into a group. The bird flies out and lands on the therapist's head!

(b) A known arsonist threatens to set fire to a locked ward.

(c) A patient starts bleeding from piles during the session.

(d) A patient has a grand-mal epileptic fit during the session.

(e) The therapist is physically threatened. He is hit hard by a man who has never been 'able' to hit anyone before.

(f) He senses he may not be able to 'take' an inevitable disclosure.

(g) The highly infectious laughter generated in a group may involve all except one member, who presumes the group must be laughing at him, even when it is not.

(h) A patient crosses the group to take the pulse of a co-therapist, during a particularly tense moment.

(i) In her first group session a female co-therapist is asked by a patient with very low self-esteem 'Do you think I am repulsive? Girls will not dance with me because they say I am!'

(j) 'Are you married?'—a reasonable question. The questioner has no means of knowing the man has killed his wife.

(k) A forty-minute silence seems to have 'gone beyond itself' and is now a matter of beating the 'record' established by another ward of forty-five minutes! When to intervene?

(l) A long silence is broken by borborygmi (gurgling guts) on one side of the circle, and is almost immediately echoed on the opposite side! The gently whispered 'Blimey ... stereo' causes convulsive laughter all round. [Anything other than shared laughter at a very funny incident would be less than human, and might easily jeopardise later fruitful disclosures which so often happen after laughter has broken through group defences. Any hint of over-interpreting such behaviour in terms of object-relations and bad internal objects would be a pseudo-therapeutic travesty. In this instance shared laughter was rewarded by greater openness within the group.]

This list of group 'incidents' calling for immediate action, whether of interpretation, intervention or other appropriate response, could be extended almost indefinitely, and every therapist will have his own list of such situations. I hope this particular selection may help the therapist who is just embarking on this voyage of discovery, to realise that he will have to act in circumstances which are in many ways always new.

Individual 'incidents' abound! I have only to mention the dilemma of a probation officer who accépted the offer of a cup of tea from the wife of a client. She had not catered for the fact that her cup would be 'swilled' (scarcely washed) in the murky depths of an old-fashioned zinc bath in the middle of the floor, in which her extremely dirty and physically uninviting client was sitting! Yet to reject the tea (after initial acceptance) would be an implicit rejection of him.

A similar situation, in a different setting, was a proffered kiss from a 'repulsive' smelly alcoholic.

Genuine spontaneous feeling, whether of anger or laughter, is so often the only way to unblock an apparently frozen group. It is almost like surf-riding. If the therapist can catch the wave of feeling and use the openness of the group immediately after such infectious laughter, patients will often say things in 'the heat of the moment', just as they will if sufficiently angered, so that the unconscious becomes conscious. Not uncommonly a patient may say 'it had almost jumped out' of him before he had time to collect himself.

On another occasion a patient said that there were painful parts of his history which he could not tell the group but he was prepared to put on a tape recorder what he wanted to say. I asked him what he would put on the tape, and he told us!

(b) Depth

(i) The prevention of depth disclosures in the interests of caution

This is a risk for people who have been trained as counsellors and are used to running discussion groups. They feel safe as long as the topic discussed relates to external problems or particular topics. It is fundamentally different from dynamic psychotherapy, in which the patient is encouraged to free-associate, as indeed is the group as a whole.* Many counsellors can be relaxed and extremely effective if their clients are discussing the faults of the social services or the possessiveness of their mothers, but they suddenly feel out of their depth if the client says: 'I

* In the group *we have to do what happens* (Anon., 1974).

had a sexual dream last night—actually, it was about you.' It is therefore sometimes erroneously assumed that a group is necessarily safer and easier to conduct if it can be maintained at first or second disclosure levels. Such groups can be effective provided there is adequate back-up psychotherapeutic support for the staff. In this instance it can be threatening and provocative to patients who, having been told to bring their problems to the group, discover there are 'problems' (like the dream about the counsellor) which are 'inappropriate'.

A hospital ward may run group discussion, group counselling and group psychotherapy sessions at different times of the week. Paradoxically, a group may be much less threatening and difficult to handle if the patients are genuinely allowed to free-associate. They can therefore say anything they like, which may include sexual fantasies about the therapist or other emotionally loaded topics. But the staff need greater training and support if free-association is to be encouraged.

The psychopath and the hysteric tend to share the capacity of making pseudo-disclosures. The former usually do this deliberately to provoke the therapist, to see how he will respond, and to test whether he can cope with the material divulged. On the other hand, the hysteric, using the defence mechanism of denial, tends to make over-dramatic, pseudo-disclosures which rivet the attention of the group on what is being said. The motivation behind a pseudo-disclosure may be to 'dominate the centre of the stage'. An ensuing genuine disclosure might prove to be something as simple as the fact that the patient could not bear silence because she was always ignored at home, and the only way to get any attention at all was to be naughty. 'A smack was the only contact I had with my parents, but it was better than having nothing at all. Because they certainly never picked me up or cuddled me.' It is not inappropriate to borrow two phrases from Goffman (1963) when he discusses disclosures which may be malicious or inadvertent. He is using the word disclosure to describe a different situation, but with our frame of reference it is quite clear what a malicious disclosure implies and an inadvertent disclosure is part and parcel of every psychotherapeutic group. By this I mean that the patient gives away the fact that he is deeply involved in the current life in the group, and this may involve feelings about another patient or a memory from his own effective (and affective) personal worlds which has been triggered off by a group phenomenon. Non-verbal communication and other psychological aspects of incipient disclosure (see page 212) may help the therapist to gauge the 'brinkness' of his patient's disclosure.

> The setting of thine eye and cheek
> Proclaim a matter from thee; and a birth, indeed,
> Which throes thee much to yield.
>
> (*The Tempest*, II. i. 237)

(*ii*) *Undue concern with depth disclosures in the interests of 'therapy'*

Here the therapist is erroneously banking on the assumption that only third-level disclosures are genuine and 'worth while'. Not only is it impossible to maintain a group perpetually at a third level, but it would not be therapeutic, even if it was possible. Patients are people and a living, developing group cannot be 'held' at a constant level of anxiety where sex, violence, death or castration are the only acceptable currency! There is rhythm, flow and almost a 'tidal' movement in the life of a group. There are amusing incidents, trivial events, which admittedly often have an important significance. Indeed, the deepest disclosures often 'happen' in the wake of 'trivia' or light-hearted abandon, rather from than as a result of deliberate 'depth charges' from the therapist.

However, a group frequently 'gravitates' to the deep end by its own interpretation of events. Thus the group-as-a-whole will be certain that one particularly aggressive knock on the door must come from the firm hand of David, when in fact it soon becomes evident that it was from the customarily gentle and timid Jean. 'What's the matter?' may be a perfectly legitimate response to the door-shaking thump from the girl who normally gives a muffled tap. In a non-therapeutic setting the 'decibels' and other vibrations of a knock on the door, though remarkable, are probably less so.

(c) Mutuality

(*i*) *Excessive reciprocity*

This has already been discussed under the headings Countertransference and Empathy, but must be briefly mentioned here. Emotional distancing, diminished reciprocity and inadequate affective bonding may be a rationalisation on the part of the therapist, though excessive reciprocity can be disastrous. The therapist's own defences may be the 'keep' within the castle walls of the patient's defences. This is not necessarily so, but the therapist must ask himself whether the patient is not 'correct' if he describes the therapist as being 'aloof' and afraid of 'being involved' (see the next section on 'Too little reciprocity').

The risks of excessive reciprocity* are brought home most forcibly with relevance to the offender-patient, where there may be not just an 'emotional' victim but a victim of a physical assault, which may have been fatal. I will cite one example which yet again illustrates the way in which offender-therapy can often highlight certain features of the psycho-therapeutic process. This underlines what has already been said about the misguided incorporation of the therapist's personal life experience into the therapeutic situation. *Let us consider a hypothetical example.* A patient had fatally stabbed a milkman. Whereas I might know few details at the beginning of the therapeutic relationship with him, during the course of therapy he would make progressively deepening disclosures about the offence and his victim. Let us imagine that he had stabbed a milkman in Epping. Then, as he free-associated about the event, he said the snow was deep 'in fact, it was the coldest Christmas Day on record'. In such a situation it is quite possible that I might recall that my own milkman had been stabbed on an icy Christmas Day and that, at the time, I had been living in Epping. I would therefore be on the brink of having not only a shared experience with the patient within the thera-peutic space, but also of knowing the details of a stabbed milkman in Epping. However well-intentioned might be my concern to treat my patient as a person, it need scarcely be underlined that free discussion of 'poor old Bert and how upset his children were!' would be entirely out of place, and anti-therapeutic as far as my patient was concerned† Such a disclosure on my part would prevent any further disclosures from my patient, who might have reached a point in therapy where he needed to relive the experiences leading up to, during and after the assault. The clock might be put back almost indefinitely if I responded in a 'man-to-man' way and revealed that Bert had been my milkman, and that I remembered the incident only too well. It had been in the local press, etc.

This may seem a dramatic example, but it is not unrealistic if the

---

* The important aspect of mutuality is shared human 'predicamentness', rather than identification with particular details of life-experience.

† The key issue is not my response as a *recipient of the disclosure* about the milkman, but how much I would be prepared, *for the sake of my patient,* to allow a similar cognitive–affective disclosure flow in the opposite direction. *This discretionary use of disclosure direction is the fulcrum upon which mutuality pivots.*

therapist works with people who have been involved with episodes of extreme violence against others. I realise this may be construed as a specialised field, but the point which it raises has a much wider application, and it is perhaps brought home by this example of the murdered milkman. Less dramatic, though equally important for other patients, might be similar types of mutual disclosure by the therapist. For example, the patient might say that she has recently become a Roman Catholic, or he has just joined the Communist Party, or the Fascists. The therapist's concern is to know why this life-event has taken place for his patient, and if he had responded by saying that he too had recently become a Roman Catholic, or, *per contra*, had renounced Roman Catholicism, then this might put up barriers for the patient and prevent fuller disclosure. It is worth repeating that successful therapy occurs most often where the therapist's personal involvement is limited to that of concentrated concern for his patient who is endeavouring to negotiate his own self-acceptance and find greater fulfilment. The therapist will have implicit attitudes and cannot exist without personal values, but they must not intrude and prevent the patient's freedom of disclosure.

Rules may exist to be broken, and there are obviously moments in psychotherapy in which disclosure of the therapist's personal experience can have a profoundly catalysing and therapeutic effect if it is used appropriately. But, as a general rule, it can be said that an *optimal therapeutic climate* is fostered by the cultivation of reciprocity felt by the patient on the basis of minimal personal detailed disclosure on the part of the therapist.* This is nevertheless perceived by the patient as the sharing of experience because there is the genuine, existential, here-and-now experience of shared therapeutic space which leads to maximising therapeutic potential. Even if it is surrounded by bars, locks and a high security wall, there is just as much shared therapeutic space with the therapist in a 'secure setting' as there is in a conventional consulting room with a readily opened door and access to the wider world.

(ii) Insufficient reciprocity

Readers from many of the 'counselling' professions (using this word in the widest sense) will recognise their own use of reciprocity and will have

---

* Sometimes therapist and patient already have prior knowledge of each other before they engage in therapeutic work. This experience can be transmuted in therapeutic space into an intensifier of encounter rather than a drawback. It implies a particularly subtle aspect of mutuality.

painful memories of occasions when manifest mutuality, which seemed so human and reasonable, delayed and even blocked therapeutic progress. There are risks in over- and under-disclosure on the therapist's part. Mutuality, paradoxically, is for the patient's benefit, and the task is made even more difficult because pseudo-mutuality is abortive for both patient and therapist.

Too little reciprocity results in the therapist being perceived as a cold, aloof, detached 'professional' who makes the patient feel that he is regarded as 'a card with bronchitis on it'. This point is self-evident and does not need elaboration.

The reader may have no personal experience of working with offender-patients, but he will easily recognise comparable situations from the hypothetical event just described about the murdered milkman. There may be events in life which he shares with his patient, such as school, hobby, knowledge of a camping site, place of birth, and so on. He will know that the core of the professional relationship with his patient depends upon his use of mutuality, and he will also be aware of the cautionary note sounded in this chapter about the risks of over-disclosure. What is meant to bring him alongside his patient may in fact have the opposite effect of distancing them from each other.

There are hazards if time, depth and mutuality are poorly structured. The other side of the coin is that optimal structuring facilitates therapeutic efficacy.

Vignette:

After months of silence, a patient who had failed to respond to invitation, confrontation, supportive encouragement—indeed every approach from fellow group members or 'other' co-therapists, who denied dreaming and had no wish to day dream—suddenly recited a poem he had written. It was about the beauty of the Alps, blue skies, forest-clad mountains, etc.—reminding me of an advert for Swiss chocolate. When the recitation ended I said warmly: 'Have you written any about people?'

My co-therapists felt the mountains (attractive but menacing) were about the patient's obstacles to be overcome and that we should 'dwell' there at the point of disclosure. Was my intervention premature or misplaced? I wanted to use the affective thrust of an almost 'inanimate' disclosure (for so it seemed to me) to reach his buried feelings about people, before the flow receded.

Who was right? This dilemma is of the essence of 'co-therapy' where each can monitor the other, and a staff-seminar must gain from sharing in such dilemmas over 'how' and 'when' the therapist speaks.

CHAPTER 8

The Patient Speaks

I don't know what there is to come out ... but something is.

(Anon., 1971)

If I brush past it, I waste the telling of it, if I don't tell it properly.

(Anon., 1976)

1. DIMENSIONS OF DISCLOSURE

(a)   This honest creature, doubtless,
Sees and knows more, much more, than he unfolds.

(Othello, III. iii. 242)

(b) Every time I come to that part of my life I can't go on, my hair stands on end, it's so terrible.

(from Dr. Zhivago, Boris Pasternak)

(c) Listen to me, do but listen,
and let that be the comfort you offer me.

(Job 21. 2)

(d)   But I have words
That would be howl'd out in the desert air,
Where hearing should not latch them.

(Macbeth, IV. iii. 193)

(e) There are minutes when one's consciousness experiences far more than during whole years.

(from The Injured and the Insulted, by Dostoevsky)

(f) It's too painful, I can't talk about it—yet.

(Anon., 1972)

Quotation (c) reminds us that sometimes ventilation only occurs in the presence of an attentive listener, whereas quotation (d) indicates that on other occasions ventilation is only possible in the solitude of 'desert air'. They speak vicariously for patients in psychotherapy who know that disclosures are avoidable no longer. But who, on the one hand, need to ventilate and disgorge the barely contained feelings which should be 'howl'd out in the desert air, where hearing should not latch them', and, on the other hand, need the 'comfort' of a listener who is invited to 'Bear with me while I have my say'.

The psychotherapeutic process may have brought the patient to the brink of disclosure. This may imply that the unconscious has become conscious, or that the Conscious-withheld, is about to be shared within therapeutic space. Sometimes the therapist brings the patient to the point of disclosure, and it is only because of his sustained presence that the patient feels able to embark upon the precarious, risky matter of trusting the therapist with part of himself which has never 'gone public' before.

In other words, having catalysed the disclosure he then 'receives' and reflects it so that the patient can see it 'objectively' for the first time. There are other times when he recedes, so that therapeutic space almost becomes 'desert air' for the affect-laden words which the patient must ventilate, providing hearing will 'not latch them'.

Following a painful disclosure, the patient frequently indicates in some idiosyncratic way that he needs time to digest and assimilate what he has 'just realised' about himself. Paradoxically, it may take time to assimilate insight! This may be done by a temporary cessation of speech, or a redirection of focus, which is always more evident in a group setting. For example, he plays for time, as though he wishes to remain with his disclosure, by diverting the attention of the group by saying: 'It reminded me of what Mary said about her brother', in the hope that Mary will take up the thread and leave him alone with himself.

It is difficult to convey in writing how the therapist tries to use himself to facilitate disclosures on some occasions and to delay premature or inappropriate disclosures on others. Such detailed analysis of the therapeutic process forms an integral part of every counselling and psychotherapy training programme, in which the trainee learns the clinical skills of judging the timing and texture of interventions, so closely linked to the facilitation of disclosures. A disclosure is not an end in itself, but it is always an important step in the therapeutic process. The patient gains insight when material which had been repressed 'dawns' upon him. He may find that he is reliving early experiences and, within therapeutic space, a corrective emotional experience allows him to restructure the frightening, buried past. It can be an alarming experience to discover that, emotionally, 'a man can enter into his mother's womb', but he is only safe enough to do so with the reinforced reality sense provided by the therapist with whom he shares therapeutic space. In *Coriolanus* (V. iv. 67) the senator cries 'Unshout the noise that banish'd Marcius'. In the depths of psychotherapy, the patient may achieve what he has always needed, but been unable to do, namely to 'unshout the noise' of rejecting parents, rival siblings, ejecting peer groups. This need to unshout or in other ways undo what the past has done is a core issue in psychotherapy.* Dostoevsky's character Lise carries much that the patient needs to work through at the centre of the therapeutic process. 'I shall love you horribly because you let me unlove you so soon' (*The Brothers Karamazov*).

Is there any particular quality or characteristic which is diagnostic of disclosures? Is there a particular content which makes a disclosure a clearly demarcated entity? Is the disclosure made by the patient to the therapist, or is the disclosure made by the patient to the patient, but reflected and perhaps intensified by the therapist? What is the relationship between individual disclosure in a group and a corporate group disclosure? Are the nature of a disclosure and the process of disclosing equally significant? Is 'disclosure potential' a more important guide to 'effective' therapy than the act of disclosing? In other words, is the ability to make disclosures (even if they are not made) of greater significance than the actual act of disclosing which might be painful and rapidly regretted? These are some of the fundamental issues we shall touch upon in the following section.

(a) Characteristics of Disclosure

The three levels of disclosure have already been discussed (page 59, 164 ff). Third-level disclosures may take many forms, depending upon the psychopathology, but there is always the somatic declaration that something important is being said. It may have the quality of surprise and convey the impression that the patient is startled by what he has said

* It's the 'irreclaimableness' of things that have happened in the past.

(Anon., 1977)

because he was not aware of such feelings; i.e. the unconscious has become conscious. The patient is often bewildered by his own disclosure. Other disclosures indicate not so much surprise but rather relief, and on these occasions it is because the patient has been aware, i.e. conscious, of an experience which he has not dared or wished to disclose. But in both types of disclosure there is always a declaration by the patient's whole body that something important is taking place.

> There's language in her eye, her cheek, her lip,
> Nay, her foot speaks!
>
> (*Troilus and Cressida*, IV. v. 55)

and the therapist does not need extensive clinical training to be aware of the more obvious manifestations: blushing, sweating, changes in the rate of respiration or customary posture. There are more focal indications such as the cessation of finger-drumming when hitherto unexpressed rivalry towards a brother became verbalised, or the 'stammering toe'! This was disclosed through the open sandal of a patient whose stammer expressed anger. She was unaware that her toes had appropriated the stammer as her speech changed to effortlessly controlled, regular and somewhat flat diction. Hand movements always 'speak', but none so indubitably as hand–mouth movements. Under stress, chin-touching can become lip-touching, and thumb-sucking may occur during a transient regression during a therapeutic session. An extreme example was when the whole hand was forced into the mouth resembling in appearance, and effect, a trumpet's 'mute'.

The patient may initially resent the fact that the therapist appears to be some kind of detective, but this becomes acceptable provided the therapist can convey that he is a detective acting on behalf of the patient, rather than on behalf of some supposed alien power. Frequently the patient's awareness that a disclosure has been made by himself 'as a person' and not just 'in words', furnishes an added emotional release and mitigates the sense of nakedness and exposure. Disclosures always occur within the context of shared therapeutic space. Third-level disclosures occurring in a therapeutic group often have a greater facilitating effect, and a heightened cathartic release, than identical disclosures made to an individual therapist. This is because the sense of group cohesion intensifies the therapeutic encouragement for the patient who has at last been able to do what, in the presence of eight witnesses, he has hitherto failed to effect.

In addition to the universal physiological concomitants of disclosure (i.e. evidence of increased or diminished anxiety) there is sometimes a primary process quality about the content (i.e. 'poetic', unpunctuated, telegrammatic, internally contradictory, partial utterances). Other authentic disclosures may be brief, trenchant and authoritative 'statements' with a forceful oracular quality. In all cases there is a 'gut' feeling that the patient is expressing, say, a profound sense of guilt rather than admitting to trivial scrupulosity; or a pervasive sense of 'way-out-lessness', lessness', rather than being vaguely 'hemmed in'.

There are other factors which are almost 'species specific' for third-level disclosures. These are as follows:

(i) Time distortion

The patient may describe an event with the intensity and detail of recent memory, together with appropriate affect which may include rage or great warmth, when, chronologically, it is clear that he is describing an event which took place in the nursery thirty-five years ago. A patient may imply he is 'older *and* younger' than his years. 'It is a *now* of long ago.'

(ii) Inter-personal distortion

'I have a son of 20, but have only just become a father,' i.e. affective qualities of parenthood and a relationship between son and father have only just 'been born', whereas biologically the man had been a father for twenty years. This might indicate that it was the first time that he had been able to express affection for his son, who had hitherto been treated as a puppet to be controlled, but not a son to be loved.

*(iii) Semantic distortion and metaphor**

Here the patient is talking in terms of double meanings but the dis-

---

* Characteristic patterning is as follows: (see also page 110).

(a) I went to work *with a vengeance* . . . (Excessive energy or retributive intent?)
(b) My husband was *single-minded*. He was more keen on his career.
(c) I'm the *middleman* (Employment status or homosexual triangle?)
(d) I was branded (brandy-ed) . . . (Stigmatised or drunk?)
(e) Our relationship was 'touch and go' . . . (Physical and brief or precarious?)
(f) He was an *idol* brother. (An *idle* brother?)

closure occurs when he becomes aware of the second meaning, alongside the more superficial, colloquial or manifest meaning. For example, a man who attacked his brother and is worried about epilepsy may be discussing the causes of epileptic attacks which, perhaps, he has had since childhood. Then, for a while, he makes remarks which are relevant both to epilepsy and physical attacks. Finally, with appropriate physiological concomitants, he becomes aware that what has been disturbing him has been the attacks which he wished to make upon his brother, rather than the 'attacks' which the epilepsy was making upon him!

Semantic distortion may have an allegorical quality. It may indicate progress in psychotherapy if a patient's perception of a 'fixed feature' changes. This implies that he has a wider range of options open to him. Not only in terms of the ways in which he construes events in his inner and outer world, but also as an indication of a wider range of options for action. He is therefore less restricted by himself, than he was prior to psychotherapy. One of the central concerns in psychotherapy is to moderate both undervaluation of self and overvaluation of self. Thus, a presumed liability may, in fact, turn out to be an emotional asset; this is a further example of psychotherapy acting as a redefining process. For example, a changed frame of reference can change an attitude of listless boredom to one of preoccupied concentration. The following vignette 'captured' from an extremely brief dialogue, in a group session, indicates that a patient is beginning to develop interest in his environment which had previously had nothing to offer him:

'The Thames—uh! . . . it flows through terrible country.'
'. . . Yes, but think of all the history it flows through.'

This recalls a passage from Conrad (1902): 'The tidal current runs to and fro in its unceasing service, crowded with memories of men and ships it had borne to the rest of home or to the battle of the sea.'

The psychotic uses semantic distortion though his disclosures are usually categorised as showing 'formal thought disorder', delusions, hallucinations, etc. *Nevertheless, they are disclosures* and 'say' something about him to us.*

* N.B. Disclosures from psychotics often have an 'inverted' threshold, compared with those of non-psychotics, e.g. Details about 'Fuck, shit, rape, kill, etc.', may be 'easy' second-level disclosures;—whereas 'I like sitting in the sun' could be a third-level disclosure. or altogether too difficult to say.

'I thought I was David *and* Goliath.'

(This so clearly expresses the internal conflict of apparently insuperable odds with the implicit fear of both victory and defeat. The patient did not say 'I was David fighting Goliath' or 'I was Goliath fighting David'. Though it should be noted that this retrospective disclosure begins with the words 'I thought . . .', whereas a disclosure made during a psychotic episode would be 'I *am* David and Goliath'.)

'There was something wrong in my make-up [personality] but I daren't show it.' (This is a further example from a borderline patient who ran her hand over her face and anxiously glanced at her fingertips to see if her 'make-up' was coming away. She was afraid that her 'make-up' might flake off and reveal facets of her personality ['make-up'] which she 'daren't show'.)

(iv) Cosmic distortion and metaphor

This is somewhat similar to semantic distortion, except that it represents a transposition, not so much in terms of words, but in terms of a patient *living out his own metaphor*. Not only does he talk of one dimension in terms of another, but his external world and his social life reciprocally reflect his internal world and his psychic life. 'My life is a metaphor of me.'

The many similarities between the sequential phases of psychotherapy and those of the translator who seeks to translate from one language to another are discussed elsewhere (page 141). A second area of congruity exists between the use of metaphor in literature and the patient's use of metaphor in both a traditional, linguistic sense and also as a means of 'living out' his own metaphor. Thus a girl at boarding school in England whose parents live in South America, and with whom she has an extremely 'distant' relationship, comments 'I am closest [compared to her relationship with relatives] to my parents but they are too far away!' Another example is provided by an offender-patient: 'When I saw what I had done, I went back to a hiding-place I knew.' In this instance the patient is not only using the metaphor of defence by describing his retreat to the safety of a known refuge (with its implications that there had been previous 'incidents' from which he needed to withdraw), but also the cognitive–affective quality of disclosure itself revealed, initially, the defence of regression. Subsequently yielding to the less secure defence of denial and, ultimately, to the 'defenceless' safety of emotional disclosure in the group setting. This, as always, coincides with an almost breathless relief; 'At last I've got it out.' The proximity between the realms of discourse of literary criticism and that of dynamic psychotherapy is evidenced by the following quotation, which would be at home in both worlds! '... "creation", as an aesthetic term, signifies, not some fantastic "creation out of nothing", but the bringing farther into consciousness of something which already exists as unconscious life ... the principal means by which this creation of meaning is achieved is—as has already been pointed out—metaphor.' This quotation comes, in fact, from *Poetic Diction: A Study in Meaning* (Barfield, 1928). Barfield quotes Shelley 'metaphorical language marks the before unapprehended relation of things and perpetuates their apprehension ...' and Barfield, himself, writes: 'Thus, from the primitive meanings assumed by the etymologist, we imagine metaphor after metaphor sprouting forth and solidifying into new meanings—vague, indeed, yet evocative of more and more subtle echoes and reactions.' He also quotes Emerson: 'As we go back in history, language becomes more picturesque, until its *infancy—when it is all poetry* ...' (italics added.) Space does not allow me to amplify this relationship between 'infancy, when it is all poetry',* primary process thought (the classical psychoanalytic concept) and the use of metaphor in which the patient creates new meanings as (to quote Barfield again) 'the bringing farther into consciousness of something which already exists as unconscious life' occurs during the free-association, leading to the affective eruption of disclosure. Smith (1933), describing Shakespeare's growth in poetic power, writes: '... his metaphors, transmuted in his imagination, interpret and in a sense *create the life he depicts*' (italics added). Here again, we see the patient living out his own metaphor. During the process of dynamic psychotherapy he also 'creates the life he depicts'. Ample evidence of this is supplied in the second part of this chapter, 'The Patient Speaks'.

Conrad has a remarkable ability to convey the ethos and penumbra of therapeutic space. He so often describes one area of experience in

---

* Many of the most 'powerful' group sessions are sparked off by 'I wrote this poem ... it's nothing really ... about ...'. *This is absolutely irrespective of education.* It is related to primitive elemental explosive feeling. 'Your illusions are not mine: so please keep your kindness.'

(Anon., 1977)

terms of another. There is a particularly vivid example in *Heart of Darkness*, where he describes the navigator's anxiety in keeping away from the banks of this rapidly narrowing African river where hungry cannibals studied his progress.

> ... just then I perceived—in a new light, as it were—how unwholesome the pilgrims [*his crew*] looked, and I hoped, yes, I positively hoped, that my aspect was not so—what shall I say?—so—unappetising: a touch of fantastic vanity which fitted well with the dream-sensation that pervaded all my days at that time. Perhaps I had a little fever, too. One can't live with one's finger everlastingly on one's pulse. I had often "a little fever," or a little touch of other things—the playful paw-strokes of the wilderness, the preliminary trifling before the more serious onslaught which came in due course.

It is interesting to read *Heart of Darkness* to see how many third-level disclosures can be recognised. I have mentioned Conrad in some detail because he manages to convey in words, what the therapist often recognises with the great advantage of non-verbal communication, namely, that the patient is on the brink of a third-level disclosure. Even the most prosaic person will say 'Funny, although I was describing a caravan, a feeling in a tube-train, how my dog looked at me, etc., *I knew I was talking about something else.*' It is the 'something else' or, in Conrad's terms, the 'little touch of other things' which almost unfalteringly leads the therapist, or rather allows the patient to lead himself over the brink of disclosure. The affective thrust of therapeutic space provides an emotional learning experience for the patient, who usually starts in psychotherapy with a false expectation that he *ought to feel* relief at disclosure. He slowly learns that what he *really feels*, however unpalatable, is what matters. He is 'put in touch' with his feelings. In a group he learns to 'Speak what we feel, not what we ought to say' (*King Lear*, V. iii. 325).

Cosmic distortion frequently implies a translocation of inner and outer world phenomena, so that the patient may describe the landscape as though it is part of his inner world.* For example, many of King Lear's disclosures occur in the chaos of hurricans and downpour on the heath, though we also know that he experienced a 'tempest in the mind', which broke and abated with lightning rapidity. The patient may also describe his inner world as though it is part of the landscape. It is hard to

---

* This is shown by a teenager whose growing fear of sexuality and 'career plans' were almost interchangeable: 'I want to control pollution and preserve wild life.'

imagine a passage in literature more crammed with psychopathological significance than the scene in *King Lear* (Act III, Scene iv) when three refugees from the storm seek shelter. King Lear, with senile dementia and dissociative phenomena due to the reality which was too much to bear, is accompanied by the fool who, in a paradoxical way, knew what was going on (though we know too little about him to confirm that his was a 'regression in the service of the ego,' he certainly reinforced the precarious defences of King Lear) and 'Poor Tom' whose pseudo-psychosis was a deliberate strategy to avoid discovery. (The stage directions are *Enter Edgar disguised as a madman.*) The complex relationship between the characters gives evidence of many kinds of disclosure. Their shared predicament in seeking shelter from the storm, irrespective of their inner world phenomena, has many of the qualities of a 'heterogeneous' therapeutic group, in which patients endeavour to come to terms with their inner and outer chaos.

I have given this single example from Shakespeare and one from Conrad as, in different ways, they have both captured the quality of disclosure which furnishes the affective *timbre* of therapeutic space. However, it is the *cognitive–affective* feature of formal psychotherapy which links emotional disclosure with enhanced understanding, and it is this amalgam which is ultimately therapeutic. Rarely, does emotional disclosure, *per se*, yield more than transient relief.

A further example of a patient talking simultaneously of two areas of experience is as follows: 'I was driving in a fog and felt I was heading for a collision, but the thing that struck me was that my relationship with my mother had become so clouded and hazy that I knew we were on a crash course.' What had started as a discussion on 'travelling conditions' imperceptibly blended with, and changed into, third-level disclosures about family relationships. The therapist's task may be to receive these disclosures when they occur 'spontaneously', and to facilitate the process by easing the patient gently into emotional engagement with himself and put him in touch with his feelings.

A similar changing frame of reference occurred when a discussion of 'security', which had started about stocks, shares and financial security, was transposed into emotional disclosures about 'being secure'.

Cosmic distortion is illustrated by a writer who buys a quiet house in a *cul-de-sac* to avoid the noise of city traffic, so that she can write in undisturbed tranquillity. However, her presenting symptoms were of increasing emotional isolation. She suddenly became aware that the house she had chosen in a quiet *cul-de-sac* was metaphorically expressing her sense of living in an emotional *cul-de-sac*, as though not only traffic but 'life itself is passing by'.

Sometimes the counsellor is confused and will feel 'although he was talking, I really didn't understand a thing he was saying ... I just didn't know what he was getting at!' But even at the most elementary level, it was clear that this was not psychotic speech with established thought disorder. This emotional response on the part of the counsellor is almost diagnostic of the fact that the client is in fact talking of two things at once. It is as though he has come to a junction in a railway line and his train continues to travel forward on both branch lines! In other words, he may be talking about an environmental situation which is readily understandable by the counsellor, but the point at which it is felt that the client becomes baffling and chaotic so that 'I didn't know what he was talking about' is when he begins to talk of himself, in addition to describing his environment.* The client gives an allegorical history so that he starts talking in one dimension and then begins to talk in terms of another. Consider the writer in her *cul-de-sac*. As she talks, the therapist will be able to facilitate disclosure if he feels that she is emotionally ready and could endure it. If, on the other hand, he feels that the disclosure the patient may be on the brink of making is, at that point, too overwhelming, he may serve her best by gently keeping the conversation in terms of the bricks and mortar. She will describe the view from the house, and how peaceful it must be and the therapist lets her do so; rather than facilitating a disclosure which might lead to an overwhelming fear of menopausal restriction and of being no longer in the main-stream of life. This deflection of disclosure might be more appropriate if it occurred towards the end of a session, when there would be no time for patient and therapist together to work through the feelings which would be released. This is an integral part of time-structuring.

---

* A patient said 'my mind feeds on badness', and proceeded to describe how he was redecorating his flat: 'I could *sense goodness coming* . . . but it's not quite yet.' The words in italics are an unusual choice for a comment on do-it-yourself decorating, but were apposite in terms of emotional growth. He could 'sense goodness coming' as he was able to tolerate badness.

Another example of cosmic distortion is provided by the son of a globe-trotting executive who had lived in so many countries that he did not know where 'home' was. When giving his history he said he wanted to 'get on with the present' because '*my past is neither here nor there!*' He was right. Dostoevsky illustrates this phenomenon superbly:

> Without a word (Kolya) threw himself into a corner, jammed himself forcefully into it, and covered his face with his hands. He felt unbearable shame, and his childlike impressionableness—as yet unaccustomed to dirt—was muddied beyond measure.
>
> (*The Idiot*)
>
> As is typical in Dostoevsky, the combined impact of "unbearable" and "beyond measure" is mimetically intensified by physical action. Both the corner and the face-covering are easily construed as symbolic of the inner recesses to which Kolya retreats.
>
> (Commentary by Rowe, 1968)

Third-level disclosures are always accompanied by appropriate physiological concomitants indicating either increased anxiety at the fear of what has been expressed or reduced anxiety at the relief of what has been expressed. Indeed, if a patient says 'I killed my father' without appropriate physiological concomitants, then, for him, this is not a third-level disclosure. Many patients whose history includes extreme violence against the person often dismiss the 'event' most coolly, and it is frequently found that such patients have other areas of third-level disclosure which may relate to events in their lives which, to the outsider, would be trivial. *The therapist must be aware that what would be a third-level disclosure for him is not necessarily so for his patient.* The emotional experience of coming to terms with this difficult 'stepping out of oneself' is a core issue in psychotherapy training. It will be seen that many of these ideas are intimately bound up with the concepts of transference, empathy and countertransference, as well as the whole theme of structuring the therapeutic process. Third-level disclosures frequently have a primary process quality about them. They may be poetic, condensed, truncated, unpunctuated, shouted, whispered, or almost indiscernible because of tears or bubbling manic explosiveness. They are frequently ushered in by a sense of augmented awareness familiar to musicians who use a pivot chord when modulating. This is a chord which is common to two keys and therefore enables transposition to be made into a different key, without the effect being intolerably jarring. Sometimes the patient is aware that he is at the point of making a third-level disclosure, and sometimes he is aware that he 'feels different ...' as though he is talking of one theme in terms of another.

For those who find musical analogies helpful, the imperfect cadence conveys a quality of disclosure facilitation. The imperfect cadence which has been said to 'push the music on and on because there is always more to come' has, for me, so accurately described the process of psychotherapy in far more eloquent terms and basic English than many highly technical psychodynamic formulations. Psychotherapy, like the imperfect cadence, with correct modulation *'pushes the patient's disclosure on and on because there is always more to come.'* Take the example of the writer in the cul-de-sac. Once she has started talking in terms, not of her house, but of herself (life passing by and so forth) the imperfect cadence provides the metaphorical language in which she goes 'on and on because there is always more to come'.

Inappropriate interventions have the same jarring, 'unacceptable' effect as badly conducted musical modulation. The similarity between therapeutic intervention and musical modulation is that of 'bridging the gap', when moving from one dimension to another. Modulation has been called 'key change without pain'. To avoid disruption it is essential to use 'a chord which the new key and the old have in common' (Jacobs, 1958).

Timing, texture and a common 'chord' of past and present experience is of the essence of therapeutic intervention. If the therapist is fortunate enough to tap this emotional reservoir with an appropriate intervention, then his patient may 'go on and on until there is *nothing* more to come'; she has then reached a tranquil point of resolution. Thereafter she will experience an increasing sense of individuation in which she finds that her symptoms become less, as her sense of being a complete person becomes more. See *The Language of Music* (Cooke, 1959) for an absorbingly stimulating analytical account of dealing with one dimension in terms of another.

Within therapeutic space I try to facilitate third-level disclosures which, in psychoanalytic terms, might be of oedipal anxiety or the earlier experience of the breast being both satisfying and frustrating, and it is as though I am helping the patients to modulate successfully in music or to interpret for themselves a relatively foreign language into their 'mother' tongue. The therapist does not always facilitate disclosure, because there may be occasions when it is wise to withhold or delay it. The patient may be frightened if he makes premature disclosures, and it is part of the merciful function of repression that a patient is allowed to become aware of himself at the depth and pace which is tolerable. Amnesia for killing can be a blessing. A retrospective view of a fatal assault, from a standpoint of clear consciousness, was:

> I didn't see it coming.
> I didn't mean to do it.
> I didn't recognise I'd done it.

Many short-cut therapeutic manœuvres, such as hypnosis or abreaction, carry great risks if they are embarked upon with a patient whose amnesia for killing his sister is perhaps the reason for him not killing himself. Timing is of the essence. 'Ripeness is all.' The intimate relationship between amnesia and disclosure is a daily concern for the therapist working with offender-patients.

The concept of disclosure in the field of psychotherapy is only a short distance removed from the philosophical concept developed by Ramsey (1957, 1965). It is interesting to speculate upon the significance of the disclosure which the patient makes in the presence of the therapist, about himself to himself. Disclosure of self to self occurs as the unconscious becomes conscious, and this is facilitated by the disclosure of self to others in a shared situation. Ramsey also used the phrase 'cosmic disclosure' for a fresh *gestalt* awareness when a new dimension breaks in upon the individual. The therapist must be sensitive to the fact that 'startling' disclosures may be made. This means that his patient's progress is not restricted by the therapist's limited horizons and the patient's increasing openness is not restricted and over-protected by the therapist's defences! This takes the therapist to the very edge of personal experience. Free-association means that the patient may disclose anything. Unless both patient and therapist are psychotic, they will not be aware that they have yet 'passed through death'! though free-association is often of death or non-being. However, the therapist must allow the patient to explore these unknown areas of life, which may frighten or invite him; 'we are to the margin come, and we expect to die' (Charles Wesley).

(b) Nuclear disclosure

I'm a large house with several rooms locked off, for safety.

(Anon., 1977)

I keep thinking of 'trailings of feeling' that come to me from the past. They don't last long, but they're never far away.

(Anon., 1977)*

A nuclear disclosure is one which carries such a concentration of meaning that it has somehow captured the quality of a relationship with such a degree of intensity and specificity, that extended amplification would only furnish more detail but not change the meaning. It is a vignette, an emotional portrait, a condensed concentrate. The therapist senses that it has captured the core pathology, so that it has something of the quality of an emotional 'identikit', by which I mean that extended inter-viewing is only likely to increase the detail of the silhouette, which was clearly predictable from the nuclear disclosure itself.

A classic example comes from a session in which a patient had free-associated with torrential urgency about her family; her uncertain sexual orientation, so that neither men nor women were satisfying sexual 'objects' and she experienced a poverty of relationship-potential; her escalating anti-social behaviour leading, ultimately, to catastrophic violence. This intense affective surge lasted fifty minutes, at the end of which I asked 'What does the phrase "Suddenly, there was nothing definite" mean to you?' Her answer conveyed that this was 'what it is all about', and, in fact, it arose as a 'give away line' during the detailed disclosures just given. '*Suddenly*': the mercurial, unpredictable, eruptive spontaneity of her experience. '*There was nothing definite*': lack of identity, depersonalisation, purposelessness, ontological insecurity. Putting these two components together as they were uttered, with the quite distinctive para-linguistic overtones of third-level disclosures, we have a nuclear disclosure. '*Suddenly, there was nothing definite.*' She knew she was talking simultaneously of two areas of experience. In my clinical experience such a nuclear disclosure reflected to the patient ('What else might this be saying?' is an implicit question repeatedly asked by gesture or even a raised eyebrow) yields infinitely greater affective material than many 'conventional' interventions. It is not surprising that psycho-sexual

---

* This affective disclosure has many characteristics of a nuclear disclosure.

deviation, oedipal fixation, etc., as well as psycho-social maladaptive experience, is disclosed.

The infinitely improvable clinical skill is of 'picking' those moments when the patient is talking of 'two things at once', 'My flat on 20th floor and my lofty, lonely aloofness.' When such a nuclear disclosure occurs in a group setting the therapeutic potential is intensified. However, it cannot be said too often that effective dynamic psychotherapy depends upon *cognitive–affective* activity, often in terms of re-encounter with the introjected past. The group frequently prevents the patient 'getting away' with a purely affective disclosure. Thus the group-as-a-whole adds the cognitive component to the equation. If, however, the patient is too 'cerebral', the group, *per contra*, evokes the affective component. Nuclear disclosures therefore always have a cognitive–affective quality and the therapeutic group itself is the custodian of this *sine qua non*.

Most therapeutic sessions contain nuclear disclosures, if only the therapist can discern them. This requires training and experience, which is well worth pursuing because the nuclear disclosure provides the therapist with an invaluable guide to the ambient dynamics and a useful 'concentrate' for his notes. The recognition of the nuclear disclosure is vitally important for the therapist if he is to make maximal use of the Chronogram. This is an almost refined essence of the dynamics of an individual session or a group (see *Coding the Therapeutic Process* (Cox, 1978). A trainee often fails to hear nuclear disclosures because he is baffled by a torrent of talk or a surging silence. During prolonged engaging and disengaging in the ground-swell of a group, or the individual session with fewer cross-currents, the therapist is likely to discover that his capacity for discerning nuclear disclosures grows.

A hypothetical example of a nuclear disclosure is furnished by a mother's escalating frustration at her inability to cope with her son's repeated defiance. She might have tried every kind of inducement, threat, reward or punishment, which appeared to be signally ineffective, to the extent that she had been forced progressively to withhold pocket money and other privileges. At last she says, with words matching the hopelessness and desperation of her expression: 'You see, doctor, *I have nothing left to withhold.*'

This is a nuclear disclosure. If she had continued talking for hours she could not have said more in essence about the stalemate of the mother/son relationship than 'I have nothing left to withhold'. If I wished to capture the emotional impact of the effect that the son was having on his mother, the phrase, which might have been a give-away line at the end of a session, would convey far more than detailed, type-written pages of formal notes. Thus the capturing of an evanescent and transient nuclear disclosure means that the therapist has fixed and pre-served an important clue to the total dynamic picture. There is an art in picking up nuclear disclosures which are always third-level disclosures but have a penetrating quality. They have the paradoxical, vivid characteristic which Chesterton described as 'a fixed flash of lightning' or Arnheim (1970), though with a different frame of reference, describes as:

> a kind of highspot within a sweep of continuous transformation. In the Japanese kabuki theatre, an actor's play suddenly petrifies into an immobile, monumental pose, the mi-e, which marks the climax of an important scene and epitomises its character. In painting or sculpture, the artist often endeavours to abstract a movement or action in a timeless image. Such a static image crystallises the nature of a more complex event in one arresting pattern;—but it also suppresses the action and *reduces the variety of phases and appearances to a single representative of them all.* [italics added] .

It is the ability to discern 'a kind of highspot within a sweep of con-tinuous transformation' which is what the therapist discerns in his patient's third-level disclosures.

Another relevant sphere of reference is provided by discernment of key items of news, such as one sentence from the news on April 30th 1975—'the war in Vietnam is over and the Vietcong flag is flying over the Presidential Palace in Saigon'. This is a concentrated essence of a vastly complex situation with implications of victory, defeat, suffering, relief, despair and many other conflicting responses. Examples taken from other areas of life may further underline the nature of the nuclear disclosure, which has a special connotation for the psychotherapist.
Arnheim continues:

> A lost wrist watch is not an abstraction of its owner, who left it behind. But the display of old-fashioned, mangled clocks and watches in the small museum at Nagasaki, on the hill over which the atomic bomb exploded, serves as an abstraction that arrests the heartbeat of the visitor. All the clocks stopped at 11:02, and this sudden concerted end of time, the death of innocent daily action, conveys an immediacy of experience, which is almost more powerful than that of the photographed horrors shown in the same museum. *An essential aspect of the event evokes the event itself.* [Italics added.]

In this last sentence Arnheim has exactly conveyed what the psychotherapist experiences as a nuclear disclosure. In retrospect it evokes for him the 'event itself' of the previous psychotherapeutic session, which, in turn, has evoked 'the event itself' for the patient, as he relives 'the event itself' from his earlier life. Pompeii seen in 1976 has similar qualities of 'captured life' from a precise moment of the past: November 23rd, A.D. 79.

Great novelists have this capacity of describing *essential aspects of events* which, in the mind of the reader, *evoke the event itself*. Thus Dickens in *Dombey and Son* conveys the different attitudes of the 'white-haired gentleman' towards the children, a boy and a girl, on the closing pages of the novel. The contrast between the following passages shows the nuclear quality of the description. 'The white-haired gentleman walks with the little boy, talks with him, helps him in his play, attends upon him, watches him, *as if he were the object of his life*' (italics added). It might be presumed that this was a description of powerful involvement and attachment, and so it is; but compare 'as if he were the object of his life' with the brief description of the 'white-haired gentleman's' affection for the girl. '*He hoards her in his heart.*' Dickens in fact elaborates and gives further details, but 'he hoards her in his heart' has the nuclear quality which shows how much more possessive, involved and almost permeated he is by the life of the girl, compared with the interest he has in the boy '*as if*' the boy meant everything to him. It can be clearly seen that the girl *is* the object of his life, whereas it was *as if* the boy were the object of his life.

Tolstoy also has the astonishing ability to describe experience so evocatively that he conveys a sense of thrusting incipience. It is as though the 'nuclear disclosure' intimates that there is much more 'behind the scenes'. He captures the affective essence of a situation which permeates the whole. Thus, in *The Cossacks* it is said of Olenin

'. . . he would surrender to his enthusiasms only in so far as they did not commit him to anything'.

The following poignant sentences come from *The Death of Ivan Ilyich*. Their descriptive penetration has such remarkable verbal economy, yet it evokes an ambience which gives the reader access into a dying marriage. It is most unlikely that the therapist will even discern what Tolstoy describes, in such an intense way and in such a small space. This is

Tolstoy's description of a marital relationship epitomised as 'stalemate', in both senses.

'There remained only those rare periods of amorousness which still came to them at times but which did not last. These were islets at which they put in for a while, only to embark again upon that ocean of concealed hostility. . . .'

Rowe* (1968) in a chapter entitled 'The child in memory' writes:

Typically Dostoevskian is Netochka Nezvanova's statement that the 'catastrophe' of her mother's death '. . . is intimately connected not only with the first impressions of my childhood, but even with my entire life.'

Having recounted her 'affair' with Katya in exceedingly vivid detail, Netochka offers the reader a somewhat specious apology: she had been 'unable to refuse herself the pleasure of being carried away to her childhood once more by means of memory'.

What is perhaps the most unusual incident involving Dostoevskian childhood memory also occurs in *Netochka. By blending a recollection and its stimulus into a strangely pervasive reality, Dostoevsky nearly succeeds in erasing the edges of time itself.* [Italics added.]

Netochka tells the reader that a 'present' experience instantly 'resurrects' in her memory 'a dark, distant childhood recollection.' She proceeds to relate the past incident, and the reader thus experiences it along with Netochka in her (also recollected) present, as a blend of both. The incidents occur in the same room and under nearly identical circumstances.

This brief selection from classical literature is manifestly a personal choice. The examples are given to underline the fact that even if an experienced counsellor could not capture the feeling of such a marriage in the way that Tolstoy did, nevertheless *in their own words his patients can, and they do so repeatedly.* Patients in psychotherapy make equally intimate, evocative and declaratory disclosures about their inner world.

I have discussed in detail the nuclear quality of disclosures taken from worlds of experience other than psychotherapy, because they serve to sharpen the therapist's appreciation of what is actually taking place in therapeutic space. The examples from Arnheim and Dickens convey the essential, nuclear aspects of detail which can imply a much wider frame of reference. But, unlike the nuclear disclosure occurring in the course of psychotherapy, they do not have the discernible physiological concomitants of disclosure described earlier. The therapist only knows for certain that nuclear disclosures are nuclear when he observes the changed

* Rowe's book *Dostoevsky—Child and Man in his Work* (New York, University Press, 1968) is compelling reading for the therapist. He deals with the Child as Adult, the Adult as Child, and the Child as Victim, among other equally interesting topics.

rate and rhythm of speaking: frequently a change of accent; the increased or diminished restlessness; the blush; the averted gaze, and other details which were described above. These physiological concomitants confirm the fact that what is being said profoundly affects the patient, thus impinging upon the therapist as an emotional stimulus rather than an emotionally flat 'item of news'. The discernment of nuclear disclosures is so often overlooked by the student because they are rarely traditional 'clinical material' and may be missed if the penumbratic nuclear quality has not been picked up. The nuclear disclosure of a floridly psychotic patient will obviously have different terms of reference from that of the phobic housewife, but it is real nevertheless. Strangely enough, the nuclear disclosure from the psychotic may not be part of his overt psychotic symptomatology, indeed the disclosure from the psychotic may be so rich in potential meaning that it is reminiscent of, say, the fool in *King Lear*. There are dangers in over-interpreting, but both the patient and the therapist know that something important has been said:

'I'm blind because I see too much, so I study by a dark lamp.'

Psychotherapeutic literature abounds with references to ego-defence mechanisms, and the understanding of such mechanisms is important for every therapist in training. Nevertheless, there is the risk that 'the trainee therapist may imbibe a negative and almost 'defensive' ethos if the most that can be said about the patient is that he is 'less defended', i.e. less regressed, exhibits less isolation of affect, and so forth. The therapist endeavours to help his patient to become less restricted, both externally and internally, and therefore to be able to love and experience life in a richer way. This highlights a poverty of relevant professional vocabulary. When the patient is able to disclose part of his hitherto private and unshared world as his unconscious becomes Conscious-withheld (which in turn becomes Conscious-disclosed), then the word 'disclosure' conveys a positive achievement. This has a more personal and perhaps warmer feel about it than such sterile words as the patient becoming more 'socialised', and it is certainly more encouraging than the double negative of being 'less defended'.

This is shown *par excellence* in the patient's nuclear disclosure, which is something positive he has made, and says far more about him than the fact that he is less defended. At the same time the nuclear disclosure provides the therapist with what is so frequently the core pathology, but it is core pathology described in the patient's own words. It has the qualities of a vignette. Even a finished vignette has the edges 'shading off into the background'.

(c) Incipient disclosure

This is closely linked to the concept of semantic distortion and cosmic distortion. It comes as a surprise to the therapist when the patient starts talking with great enthusiasm and almost falling over himself in an effort to 'get it out' when he is discussing, say, his new hobby or his proposals for a foreign journey during the next vacation. The therapist senses that behind this pressure of talk is not simply a wish to avoid the 'real' issues of psychotherapy, but, rather, a wish to ensure that the therapist understands the enthusiasm for mending clocks, visiting Skye or pruning roses. These are not discussed in a casual way as though they were 'any other business' on the agenda, but the patient indicates in no uncertain words that they are in fact *the* business. For example, the anxious teenager describes with evangelistic fervour a new-found hobby of using a particularly strong adhesive, backed up by the information that she had 'found some fantastic glue'. This glue was said to have an adhesive strength ten times that of the strongest existing known glue. Gluing was an exciting activity, not in terms of glue-sniffing but in terms of ensuring attachment. This was an incipient disclosure. I was not surprised that the patient came from a broken home. None of the family had been able to stick together, and in terms of the current professional vernacular, her early life had been sabotaged by inadequate emotional 'bonding' (see Bowlby, 1969, and Rutter, 1972). A remarkably similar 'symbolic' history is recounted by Winnicott (1960) except that 'separation' was dealt with by string rather than glue! Another patient of mine wished to devote her career to researching on glue 'to see if it will hold and [to study] how to make it even stronger'. She adopted a novel way of testing adhesive power, by applying it to the sliding doors of underground trains, just before they closed! (Inadequate maternal 'bonding' again?) An offender-patient's greatest praise for his mother was that she *stuck* by him all the time he was in prison. The point about an incipient disclosure is that it indicates to the therapist where the core pathology for the patient may lie. In this particular instance it was not so much the enthusiasm of the current hobby of using glue, but the disclosure that gluing, fixing and stability meant a great deal to the patient, who felt that there was nothing adhesive in her relationships with others. This example could be multiplied many times. 'The hands were all mangled and twisted, and the rods which should have gone through the centre had been pulled out.' This was an incipient disclosure from a young solicitor whose manifest energy was expressed in his enthusiasm for restoring broken clocks, whereas the incipient disclosure spoke of his masturbatory guilt and fear of women. This was subsequently confirmed by other third-level disclosures. The sexual symbolism underlying incipient disclosures is usually so clear and yet the patient is unaware of it. Much of the material is unconscious, but the incipient disclosure means that it is on the brink of breaking through into the patient's awareness. The therapist tries to facilitate this when the patient is ready to tolerate a previously denied part of himself, and to endure and incorporate personal events which had been rejected. It is as though the patient speaks his own lines but in some way puts his own words in italics!

Berberova (1969) called her autobiography *The Italics are Mine*. She uses Herzen's words 'The most ferocious immanence' when describing her compulsion to live in the here-and-now. It is hard to improve on these phrases because so often the patient in psychotherapy has a sense of ferocious immanence and *savagery within.**

> It was strange isolation I lived in then. The men and women around me, even speaking with me, were but figures.... In the midst of their crowded streets and assemblages, I walked solitary; and (except as it was my own heart, not another's I kept devouring) *savage* also, as the tiger in his jungle.
>
> (from *Sartor Resartus*, by Thomas Carlyle)

It is to be hoped that the therapist will only allow the inner ferocity to be experienced when it is acceptable and when the patient's own emotional resources can stand it. The disclosure of ferocity, though conveyed in words spoken by the patient, has 'the italics are mine' quality of released tension. If a patient does not reach the point of accepting the 'ferocious immanence', he may feel that one of the turning points of therapy

---

* Therapeutic space is often temporarily filled by ferocity and violence. It is usually verbal, but it can escalate into 'controlled–uncontrollability'. Anger 'now' 're-engages' with anger 'then' and work is done.

has been delayed and fear that he may never come to face himself. This experience is not confined to offender-patients who have some significant life event, say homicide, which they need to work through (ferocious immanence in a particularly literal sense), but everyone will have experienced such events which he needs to renegotiate.

Disclosure facilitation at the optimal time is an integral part of the therapist's task, and is intimately related to the structuring of the therapeutic process. It is usually a two-stage process; firstly the patient is introduced to himself as his unconscious becomes conscious, and then the patient introduces himself to the therapist or other patients with whom he shares the therapeutic space. It is as though the patient makes a definitive statement which ends with a fullstop, which the therapist transmutes into a comma. In other words, the flow of language and feeling may be furthered by gesture, expression or some other facilitation. What was originally a definitive closure statement, is transformed into the first part of something else, i.e. closure becomes disclosure. This is closely allied to the 'anticipation of a "known unknown"' and *On What There Must Be* (see page 93), and the therapist is always at the invitational edge of the patient's disclosure.

There are larger frames of reference than a purely sexual one. The existential threat of non-being may be infinitely more pervasive than a specific sexual anxiety. This may legitimately be taken seriously by the therapist and the patient, and worked through in terms of castration anxiety, the fear of being devoured or engulfed. Yet this would miss the existential predicament of the awareness of finitude that might be the key to the patient's growth and individuation. If a patient has bypassed the experience *timor mortis perturbat me* by 'hiding' behind the more restricted disclosure of castration anxiety, he may have diminished his own growth possibilities. This is a profound philosophical question because if the therapist has not been able to come to terms with the possibility, of his own non-being, he may find it difficult to allow his patient to free-associate about *homo heroica*, to use Becker's (1962) evocative words. Elsewhere, Becker (1973) comments on some risks of psychoanalysis, as follows; 'Man is thereby deprived of the absolute mystery he needs, and the only omnipotent thing that then remains is the man who explained it away.' However, it could be argued that if it really was omnipotent, it should not be possible to explain it away, in any sense that carried validating weight. Boros (1965), considering *mysterium mortis*, develops the idea that the moment of death gives man the 'opportunity of posing his first completely personal act'. Whatever may be the psychotherapist's philosophical or religious standpoint, he must be sufficiently at ease with himself to allow his patient to reflect upon the many little deaths of his emotional life hitherto, and the *mysterium mortis* which confronts everyone, including the therapist and his patient. There is a world of difference between the work of the expert on mortality statistics who knows more about death than anyone else, and the work of 'receiving' the experience of a patient who is afraid of his own death. This has nothing to do with statistics but with his patient's dread (or hope) of having a dream like that of Gerontius.

(d) Pseudo-disclosure*

This has already been discussed on pp. 27,.140 and is most commonly exhibited by the psychopath or the hysteric. It always lacks affective, somatic concomitants, and if it is perceived as a 'performance' it is usually a bad performance. Nevertheless, it is sometimes difficult to differentiate the psychopathic pseudo-disclosure from a genuine third-level disclosure, though the therapist's task is made infinitely easier when psychopaths are in a homogeneous therapeutic group. The therapist is rarely as adept at picking up the psychopath's pseudo-disclosure as seven other psychopaths intent on discerning the truth! However, it cannot be said too often that one of the greatest pitfalls for the therapist is to presume that because a patient is a known psychopath, therefore anything which appears to be a genuine third-level disclosure is, *ipso facto*, a pseudo-disclosure. The therapist, after prolonged contact with an aggressive psychopath, may be the first 'neutral' person to be entrusted with third-level disclosures. The therapeutic process is almost irrevocably sabotaged if, when the patient first tells the truth, he is disbelieved. One of the paradoxical facts about psychotherapy with psychopaths is that the opposite extreme may be equally disturbing. By this I mean that if the

---

* *A pseudo-disclosure is not a lie.* It is a true disclosure of experience, but is not related to core pathology. For example, a rapist may describe his offence, but a genuine third-level disclosure might relate to his vulnerability in female company because of a speech defect.

patient senses that the therapist takes a pseudo-disclosure as a genuine third-level disclosure, then, like so many others, the therapist is easily 'conned'. This lack of perspicacity therefore denies the patient an incursive, penetrating thrust of confrontation with self which can only be facilitated by a therapist he cannot mislead. The psychopath,* despite his overt presentation, often hopes for a therapist he cannot deceive.

The invitational edge of disclosure

The majority of disclosures at the chapter headings come from classical literature and are therefore safely universalised. The ensuing section is an unedited series of disclosures, and, though they have been taken out of context, the actual verbal statements are in the original vernacular. They follow hard upon one another and have been culled from many places over many years. To guarantee confidentiality and preserve the safety of future disclosures, any obvious identifying features have been changed, and, where relevant, permission has been obtained. Apart from this one proviso these disclosures are exactly as they were made. They indicate that the existential quality of disclosure is independent of education. They come from all social classes and all age-groups. Children from any social class can feel 'infinitely dropped' (Winnicott) as a response to maternal withdrawal. It is equally certain that a patient from social class 5 can fall in love just as deeply, and feel loss of love just as painfully, as his neighbour from social class 1. Though a prostitute may have a more restricted verbal code than the professor, her description of, say, dereliction and the sense of being used and then abandoned may be just as profound and is frequently more poignantly conveyed.

There are very few studies of wide-ranging and amassed disclosures. This chapter is headed 'The Patient Speaks', recalling *The Client Speaks* (Mayer and Timms, 1970), which revealed the disturbing fact that 'social work researchers' as well as research psychiatrists and psychologists, have rarely explored the treatment situation from the standpoint of the client. *The Client Speaks* explores, by means of free-flowing interviews, a close-up picture of the client's experience at a social work agency.

In the disclosures which follow I have made no attempt to interpret,

* Dynamic psychotherapy sometimes plays a part in hastening the maturation of the psychopath. If this was not so, the therapist would be no more effective than the gardener who looks at apple blossom and waits for autumn!

amplify or otherwise alter their impact. Though I have added comments in a few selected instances. Many, though not all, of the disclosures listed are nuclear disclosures. It is a useful exercise to see how much the reader can gain of the flavour of an emotional problem from these disclosures. Obviously, all the reader can possibly know about the 'discloser' is revealed in his truncated utterance.

Having stated that the diagnosis of a third-level disclosure is often confirmed by the simultaneous presence of the physiological con-comitants of anxiety, I am of course aware that in the list of disclosures which follows, the reader is deprived of this important non-verbal com-munication. He may well think that he recognises statements from his own clinical experience. This should not be surprising, because third-level disclosures have a quality of timelessness and ubiquity. *In extremis*, there can be no doubt of the universal experience *timor mortis perturbat me*. The gratuitous translation I was offered conveyed an identical intensity of feeling, as well as the probability of a different life-style... 'I get the shits when I think o' snuffin' out'. We are here concerned with the depth of human experience, not with the limited or elaborated language code by which a man describes his experiences. When we get below the veneer and culture-dominated first-level disclosure, and move through the less culture-bound second-level disclosure to third-level disclosures, there is an archetypal, timeless quality, because such disclosures inevit-ably impinge upon the ultimates of life, love, death and hate. The experience of Being versus non-Being is independent of education, social class and culture. Identical disclosures might be made by King Lear, Job, an East End junkie in a prison group or a suburban bank clerk.

Osler's memorable lines 'Listen to the patient, he is telling you the diagnosis', now take on a vastly deeper significance than that of organic pathology. In other words, the patient is now telling us the diagnosis, not of his liver dysfunction, but his diagnosis 'of himself'. It is not only the words he speaks but the full presentation which is coloured by posture, gesture, and is often accompanied by a slight change of dialect or accent, which may be prompted by anger or fear. During third-level disclosures a patient frequently tends to regress to the dialect of his childhood, or even his parents' dialect if he is reliving an experience from his early life, which has been hitherto hidden from him by repression. [I am not intending to change an original dictation and/or typing error in the first draft of the preceding sentence, but rather to give both versions! I had intended to write 'a patient tends to regress to the *dialect* of his childhood', whereas what 'appeared' upon the page was that the patient tended to regress to the *dialectic* of his childhood. The relationship between dialect and dialectic and the emotional cut-and-thrust of childhood carries a weight of interest!]

(2) DISCLOSURE DISCLOSED

I do but hide under these notes,
like embers, every spark of that which has consumed me.
(Edward Elgar on his 2nd Symphony, adapting Shelley)

Thomas Mann, in his essay on Freud, has spoken with good reason of the 'quotation-like life' of the men of mythological times and has illustrated this with images that could not be bettered. Archaic man, he said, stepped back a pace before doing anything, like the toreador poising himself for the death-stroke. He sought an example in the past, and into this he slipped as into a diving-bell in order to plunge, at once protected and distorted, into the problems of the present. In this way his life achieved its own expression and meaning. For him the mythology of his people was not only convincing, that is, possessed of meaning, but explanatory, that is, an assigner of meaning.
(from *Introduction to a Science of Mythology*. Jung and Kerenyi, 1951)

'Tis far off,
And rather like a dream than an assurance
That my remembrance warrants.

I, not rememb'ring how I cried out then,
Will cry it o'er again: it is a hint
That wrings mine eyes to 't.
(*The Tempest*, I. ii. 44 and 133)

The reader who finds it difficult to accept that people actually use the words of third-level disclosures is in good company. Coleridge (1884) uses the phrase 'the language of nature', and this is precisely what a third-level disclosure is. However, without the physiological concomitants of disclosure, the words, on their own, can only be accepted for what they are. For example, the novelist might easily produce a list of phrases which would not be third-level disclosures for him, but, if he was a great novelist and could take us within the personality of his characters, they might be disclosures for the people he is portraying. This is shown superbly in the example from *Dombey and Son* (see page 209).* Coleridge wrote nearly a hundred years ago and demonstrates the timelessness of emotional disclosures. I am here concerned with the linguistic and affective content of his comments rather than the questionable psychotherapeutic technique employed. (It was certainly confrontational but I suspect the structuring of depth could be improved!)

> A friend of mine had seen it stated somewhere, or had heard it said, that Shakespeare had not made Constance, in 'King John', speak the *language of nature* [italics added], when she exclaims on the loss of Arthur,
>
>> 'Grief fills the room up of my absent child,
>> Lies in his bed, walks up and down with me;
>> Puts on his pretty looks, repeats his words,
>> Remembers me of all his gracious parts,
>> Stuffs out his vacant garments with his form:
>> Then have I reason to be fond of grief.'
>
> Within three months after he had repeated the opinion (not thinking for himself) that these lines were out of nature, my friend died. I called upon his mother, an affectionate, but ignorant woman, who had scarcely heard the name of Shakespere, much less read any of his plays. Like Philip, I endeavoured to console her, and among other things I told her, in the anguish of her sorrow, that she seemed to be as fond of grief as she had been of her son. What was her reply? Almost a prose parody on the very language of Shakespere—the same thoughts in nearly the same words, but with a different arrangement. An attestation like this is worth a thousand criticisms.

It should be noted that the following disclosures are in fact the 'language of nature' which comes from 'ordinary mouths' (Pitt, 1976). They are unclassified and are not presented to indicate any particular clinical state or as manifestations of any specific constellation of endopsychic patterning. They show the wide variety of enigmatic and poignant disclosures made in the course of psychotherapy. 'Disclosers' range from the anxious undergraduate, whose self-esteem is so precarious since everyone expects him to attain a first-class degree that anything less would be equivalent to failure, to the multiple rapist legally detained 'without limit of time'. The 280 disclosures were made in many settings, over twenty years. They are therefore quite 'untraceable to source', except that precisely because they speak 'without limit of depth' they may speak vicariously for us all. The random selection which follows conveys both the existential immediacy of timeless incipience and the 'inevitable'

* In actual fact Dickens 'gets inside' his characters so vividly that *we 'know' what their disclosures would have been*. (See page 209.)

quality of psychic determinism. It is not surprising that many of these disclosures are in the first person singular because they are the words of the patient. They are gathered under the heading 'The Patient Speaks'. They may articulate various aspects of the patient's sense of self. I have already stated that I regard the recovery of lost self-esteem, or the buttressing and reinforcing of precarious self-esteem, as one of the main dynamics underlying the psychotherapeutic process. Behaviour, frequently stigmatised by society as deviant, so often has at its core the vital function of acting as a self-esteem regulator for the patient (Rosen, 1968). 'The moment I became a junkie [heroin addict] I achieved an "instant identity" because I became "one of those".' But it is not only deviant behaviour which confirms the sense of self: 'When I was a dancer I knew who I was'.

The clinician is likely to read the disclosures through diagnostic eyes, so that they are seen to suggest depersonalisation, somatisation, over-inclusive thinking, fragmentation, derealisation, splitting, paranoid ideation, etc. Of course they come from patients who usually fit into one diagnostic category or another, though not all do. It is easy to respond nosologically to the series of disclosures, though they are not given for this reason. They are presented as statements about the patient's experience and his idiosyncratic way of viewing life, and have been evoked within therapeutic space. Structuring may have facilitated disclosure, or made tolerable what was disclosed.

Disclosures always disclose aspects of the discloser, and they indicate phenomena which may be viewed from three perspectives:

1. *Nosological:* Does the discloser fall into a particular diagnostic category? Is he neurotic, psychotic or psychopathic? Could there be an organic cause? *If so, has treatable organic disease been excluded?*
2. *Psychodynamic:* What mental defence mechanism is predominant? Does the disclosure convey attitudes to authority or sexual orientation? What is implicit, or explicit, about self-esteem and its regulation?
3. *Existential:* What is 'The Voice of Illness', to use Aarne Siirala's expressive phrase, saying about the patient in terms of experience, 'illness' and the human predicament?

These disclosures were read by a theologian (Baker, 1976), whose comments I found absorbingly interesting. '*Never engaging with the present moment is a recurrent theme*...for the authentic person conditions never have to be right.' I am well aware that this sequence of 280 disclosures may well say as much about me as it does about my patients. After all, from the almost limitless range of affective material which 'erupts' during psychotherapy, I have selected these particular disclosures. Such a selection does not occur by accident. It indicates that I felt the disclosure was saying something about the patient which led me to think that he was getting nearer to the essential core of what for him, in that setting and at that time, 'it was all about'.

Quite by chance (or was it?) on the very next day after 'never engaging with the present moment' had been described as a recurrent theme, a depressed offender-patient with transient psychotic episodes said 'I only live in the present...it's one day after another...I have no past and no future...it's just today.' The juxtaposition of this depressed, anhedonic gloomy comment on life, when set against the comment 'Never engaging with the present moment is a recurrent theme', so clearly highlights the necessity of knowing the affective concomitants of these disclosures and *their significance for the discloser*. It illustrates, yet again, that the essence of disclosure is what it 'says' to the discloser and what it says about him. As his unconscious becomes conscious, he addresses himself with 'news' about himself.

Disclosures cannot be fully appreciated without knowing about the surrounding ambience. Yet, in another sense they convey what the patient feels about life, about himself and the way in which others perceive him. Some are trenchant and incisive, others express emotional nakedness and vulnerability, yet most convey some aspect of temporal progression. This may be retro-spective and retro-affective, looking back to the wonderland or dreaded past. Others are pro-spective and pro-affective, looking forward to the promised (or dreaded) land or state of being. The potentiality of becomingness and the possibility of growth can be an encouraging indication of good prognosis, providing it is not a retreat from the present. Drugs, psychogenic psychosis and 'joining the navy' are all ways of leaving the painful present. Some of these disclosures point to ways of retreat, others imply growth via a 'suffering–maturation process'. Thus disclosures made in the present often imply a comparison between the 'now and then' and the 'here and there'.

Many of the disclosures resemble the answers given by patients to Coleman's (1970) London Sentence Completion Test. The instructions for the test are as follows: 'Complete these unfinished sentences as quickly as you can. For example: If the sentence was "People in a group...", you might write "are often good friends".'

It will be seen that many of the following disclosures are statements about relationships or a comparison of time past, present and future. However, the cardinal distinction about third-level disclosures is that they often 'burst' out of the patient, because of the affective thrust of therapeutic space. The patient often surprises himself and is frightened or elated at what he has said to himself; as the unconscious became Conscious-withheld, which in turn was rendered 'public' by becoming Conscious-disclosed. There is therefore an added emotional momentum, in the setting of therapeutic space, which is not always available for introspection and 'sentence completion' in a 'test' setting.

Some examples are obviously floridly psychotic, yet all are likely to remind the reader of fragments of his own experience, because 'chaos' is not confined to 'the disturbed'. Such disclosures would not have occurred without the presence of a therapist, but the disclosures are, without doubt, of the patient's inner world. They illustrate the catalytic effect of therapy, in that the therapist enables the patient to do for himself what he cannot do on his own. 'It would be so easy to use every manipulation I've learned... it's so hard to be honest.'

While reading this concentrated series of disclosures, the reader must not forget that although they all occurred in therapeutic space, some were made during sequential individual sessions and others arose during sequential group sessions. The latter setting has the added dimension of the possibility of a corporate disclosure, i.e. it is not merely a case of crying *in* the group, but, when there is sufficient affective intensity, one patient may cry *for* the group. Thus a progressively deepening experience in group psychotherapy can lead to an awareness that one member may manifest the 'unlived life' of the others (von Weizsäcker, 1956). When this happens, both the individual and the group-as-a-whole, become aware of, on the one hand, dimensions of corporate need and corporate deficiency and, on the other, of the therapeutic possibilities of corporate nourishment and corporate integration. In a group setting there is also the advantage of consensual validation, which helps to correct transference distortion.

Attention has already been given to the constant mutually corrective, synergistic relationship between the psychoanalytic emphasis on psychic determinism and, what I regard as its necessary complement, the existential approach. It should be noted that many of the disclosures listed have a quality of existential 'predicamentness' about them. They are inevitably due to the operation of psychic determinism, in a particular social context and possibly influenced by precise, detectable organic pathology. They have been made by 'real' people in 'real' settings, and therefore their 'predicamentness' which may be that of despair at present failure, or of hope at the possibility of further emotional growth, is firmly grounded in their 'history'.

In summary, each disclosure is the product of psychic determinism. Past experience is influencing current experience in therapeutic space, at the moment the disclosure is made. It is therefore at the exact moment of disclosure that psychic determinism 'causing' the disclosure and its intrinsic existential significance become one. Thus psychic determinism links with existential significance at the precise point of both spacial location and timing when the *chronos* becomes *kairos*. It is this kairotic quality of overwhelmingly significant *now-ness* which makes the disclosure what it is, though its affective force may be due to 'then-ness' reactivated in therapeutic space. In other words, the patient, at the moment of disclosure, was forced (by psychic determinism) to make the disclosure, rather than to say something else! Although tautologous, this point needs to be made. The patient *might* have said anything else, but he did not. The disclosure was, for him, 'unavoidable'. I hope the reader will bear these facts in mind as he now emotionally engages with the people he meets at their moments of disclosure.

The archetypal, timeless, ubiquitous voice of self-esteem regulation which runs through so many of these disclosures is epitomised as follows:

I need people to want me... even if it's as a clown.
Other people were living my life... I was a puppet.

The patient speaks

1. She spoilt my prime years...she tried to buy my love and make me love her.... If I wanted a toy she'd buy it if I had a tantrum.... I accepted the cuddling because it was my ticket for what I wanted.
2. I'm terrified of discovering 'that there's nothing in me'.
3. To be lost but whole is better than being split.
4. I create an impression all the time, because there is nothing else to create.
5. I was a dead person walking about.
6. You probably only get permission from yourself to go to pieces after you've done it.
7. The gap between me as I am and me as I would like to be, is so enormous.
8. (How do you let your feelings out?) It's just a happening. There's no 'how' about it.
9. I appreciate your hope...because I haven't got any.
10. Most of me longs to go into illness.
11. I've had a son for twenty years but have only just become a father.
12. Father never forgave me for what I haven't become.
13. I'm a lodger at home.
14. I'm not joined to life. There is something going on and I'm not part of it.
15. I'm not important enough to have anything the matter with me.
16. I can't bear being on my own because there are too many of me to cope with.
17. I realised my foster parents didn't want me for myself, but because they wanted a sister for their son.
18. If we can get deep enough there is shared chaos.
19. It is being with people that keeps me in reality, and the pain of cutting myself is testing reality. Dying shows I'm alive.
20. I regard the group as a kind of bank where my real self is stored.
21. My cold aloofness was a front I put on.
22. I wanted to be part of her nightmare, her unreality was better than my real world.
23. I remember and yet I don't remember.
24. He's got no defences...he's open. I have got too many and protect myself.

25. Did mother bash you? ... She never did anything.
26. I never really had a childhood ... I shared my mother with whoever she was in service with.
27. I feel dead and still dying.
28. It wasn't just here I was running away from. It was everything. I felt like dying.
29. Was I a bugger to get attention or vice versa?
30. My past is a kind of reference book.
31. My parents gave me everything I wanted, so I had no right to feel angry.
32. You can only bury the past by looking hard at it.
33. I 'took on' this symptom and it was fabulous ... it let me out of all sorts of things.
34. We missed out in the nursery. The group is a nursery where we can go to pieces without losing face.
35. He had the baby and he unsexed me.
36. I was blamed for what I didn't do, therefore I went out and got my money's worth.
37. My body is so big I feel that I can stretch to the other side of the room.
38. I'm living on borrowed time.
39. You're out to kill everyone because they aren't what you want them to be.
40. I'm not angry with you ... you don't deserve it.
41. I've got thirty years to catch up as I'm still an adolescent (age 46).
42. [My parents said:] 'We'll make you helpless so that we can help you.'
43. If I cry, he thinks his mother's died, therefore I bottle it up and this brings chaos.
44. I'm so preoccupied with myself that I can't think of others.
45. My talk was only talk and now it's me.
46. I've been six months old all my life.
47. All is well ... I am just ill.
48. You are me ... ten years ago.
49. I'm on the edge of all edges. I can look myself in the face at last.
50. I'm manacled to me.
51. It is risky but all relationships are risks.

52. I have the insight of being an uncertain person.
53. I am a loner because I killed my friend and therefore cannot have another.
54. My grandmother is younger than my mother. More on a level with me and my brother.
55. My parents didn't have an ounce of parenthood in them.
56. I'm beginning to be able to love my dreams of myself.
57. My life is becoming so lived.
58. As long as I can love or hate, it's OK... the worse is the nothingness.
59. This is unbearable, but bearable if I can tell you.
60. I don't want to lose touch with what was my life.
61. It isn't that I can't let go of my past, but that my past won't let go of me.
62. There is a membrane between me and reality.
63. I wasn't expected to be ill, so I wasn't.
64. There was chaos before I started treatment... now there is meaningful chaos... How far I've slipped from myself.
65. I always remember tomorrow.
66. When we're in prison we can't get out, and when we do, we go to another one called society and we can't get in.
67. I couldn't have been eased gently into anything... whatever you had done would have seemed vicious, otherwise you couldn't have done anything.
68. I'm too ill to be a patient.
69. I got very involved in not being me.
70. I was his illness.
71. For me it is always Boxing Day, i.e. every day is the day after.
72. I can make you what I want because you're not real.
73. I'm trapped into being what I'm not. I was outside myself with loneliness but came back into myself.
74. If you are not careful you will start to belong.
75. There was such pain in his face that I know it isn't finished yet.
76. If the group is too polite it's like hitting your head against a feather bed.
77. I daren't risk asking for affection so I took it.
78. In my daydreams I'm in my own private group and the centre of attention, and spend the time telling others how rotten I am.

79. I shall only know it when I've wept through it.
80. Can you translate me to me, because I couldn't understand my language?
81. Everyone seemed so calm in the tube train...maybe they're dead. Perhaps it's my anxiety that keeps me alive.
82. Now I've got freedom, it's such a big space that I don't know how to fill it.... I'm trapped by my freedom.
83. The risks [of disclosure] are that you become so vulnerable that you have to walk through the world being slightly alone.
84. What you want is a gentle rapist, or someone who will slightly clobber you.
85. This is my debt to life. I make a life and need a life, and I'm afraid that I may take a life.
86. I can't trust me because I'm not there.
87. I attended the death of my own personality many years ago.
88. I said to my mother, 'Will you be here for ever?' and she said 'Yes,' and then she left me, and I've been running from her all my life. [*Note:* not towards her.]
89. You can let me be the mother I could never be.
90. I can share that. It's my ache too.
91. Perhaps psychotherapy is the only relationship in which one can still be alone.
92. I wanted to be labelled 'maladjusted' so that I always could be.
93. I'm a travesty of myself.
94. I'm sick of being a bum. My wife said 'I don't love you, I love the man I met five years ago.'
95. He thinks I'm bad, so I'm bad. He thinks I'm beautiful, so I'm beautiful. [I cannot withhold commenting on this remarkable illustration of the significance of labelling, and how a person's self-image is dependent upon how others construe him. This is an excellent example of 'The Looking Glass Self' (Cooley, 1922). It is reminiscent of Cleopatra's response to the knowledge that Antony has become aggressively masculine again.

> It is my birth-day:
> I had thought to have held it poor; but, since *my lord*
> *Is Antony again*, I will be Cleopatra.
>
> (*Antony and Cleopatra*, III. xi. 184)

In one sense Antony had been Antony all the time. It was as he became the Antony Cleopatra wanted him to be, that she became the Cleopatra she thought she should be... 'since my lord *is* Antony again, I *will be* Cleopatra'.]

96. There was a violent change in my marriage when I became a person.
97. I want to explore the extraordinary experience of waking up into a nightmare.
98. I used to come *out* of real life into here. Now I find this is real life.
99. I have crossed the dividing line for suicide and cannot take any more; no more little deaths.
100. I killed my sister because she would never show any feelings. I could not bear her silence. That's why silence makes me so frightened in the group.
101. In some ways the group is lacking teeth, it's not tough enough, so that I am waiting for the group to get the grip it wants so that I can talk about anything.
102. I am so hopeless that I can survive on the group's hope.
103. I used to ignore my children, and now they are doing it to me, and it's hell.
104. Have you noticed I've stopped being two people?
105. I just hope the hope will last, that's all. I don't want to test it too much.
106. We don't know when you want to say something because you're always talking. [c.f. I can talk until I really need to say something.]
107. It's not sympathy, it's with-ness.
108. I'm dying for the second time in my life.
109. [Re controlling mother] The moment *she* opened my mouth....
110. (Were you running back into a bolthole?) Yes, but there was such hell in the bolthole I had to get out.
111. *I know* very few things about *my secret self*, but one of them is...
112. To hell with the group, I'm going to be a member of me from now on.
113. I went too fast for myself in the group and got embarrassed, but later I could talk *when the group got to me.*
114. The feeling of breaking the shell around me. Is it me breaking out or someone else breaking in?

115. There's a space in my life where there was another person.
116. For God's sake stop cueing me in … I've got to make my own way.
117. I feel in a group a sense of a place of limbo… but I wonder if the group is shared limbo?
118. My mother was alone because she dominated everyone out of existence.
119. My father was so passive that my mother was my father.
120. The secret world was almost getting more important than the other world.
121. I exist for the group [cf. I exist in the group].
122. What I have done has not yet turned into experience. [Not yet digested, metabolished or assimilated.]
123. Often in the group we are disclosing something together, we don't need to do it separately.
124. I've got all I could wish for, except myself.
125. My eye is not just a camera, it's a projector as well.
126. I had a dream that life was a nightmare, and now I've woken up and found that it is.
127. We were shaping each other's future.
128. I'm afraid of this power that keeps me unfed.
129. (a) I come to the group both to open up and be torn apart.
    (b) I come to the group torn apart anyway, and hope to be healed.
130. What the hell do you mean by damaging my property? (… I used to damage people.)
131. I can't get back there and find what was never there… the fact that someone wanted to pick me up, because they didn't.
132. Is psychotherapy the rediscovery of something you've never discovered before? I knew it, but I didn't know I knew it.
     [A pertinent semantic and philosophical question. It is undoubtedly a common experience in psychotherapy that as far as the patient is concerned, he discovers something which is in fact a rediscovery, although 'he never knew it before'. It recalls the sense of an experience being 'eternal and yet ever new'.]
133. My symptoms have gone and nothing worse has taken their place.
134. The group is a kind of intensifier: whatever I'm feeling, depressed, isolated, happy, it makes me feel it more strongly.
135. By next winter I want to have caught up with the present.

136. That piano concerto said it for me. It would take three hundred pages of writing, and even then I wouldn't have said it!
137. Which is worse, to have had a niche where I belonged and lost it, or never having had a niche?
138. My mother's love was rationed. I wanted my mother's love and couldn't get it, *so I lost the wanting.*
139. I felt the absence of feeling and it was terrible.
140. This thing crept across and invaded my normal life.... Thoughts come in and take over. They control me.
141. It just came out...I was surprised by myself.
142. I came away from childhood not knowing I was loved for myself, but only if I was a good boy.
143. Maybe I must let it take over and terrify me, and then maybe I shall come out the other side.
144. I was separated when my parents were separated, and I'm together when they're together.
145. The group activates feelings and releases them.
146. I suppose the group is a mixture of Dunlopillo and a bed of nails ...come in and make yourself comfortable and come in and make yourself uncomfortable.
147. Nothing almost happened this morning, it was an amazing group. [Reminiscent of one of Shakespeare's most enigmatic lines: 'Nothing almost sees miracles./But misery . . .' (*King Lear*, II, ii. 165).]
148. I almost started crying and had to look away from my wife.
149. It's all over but it's got to come out.
150. It's *what isn't said* here that makes us ill.
151. I'm learning how to hug and be hugged.
152. If I make myself vulnerable and open by saying I love someone, I could be stubbed out like a cigarette. This happened once and I won't risk it again.
153. When I was battering her, I was battering everyone.
154. Living is better than any other death.
155. I could love her if I dared. [This theme is paraphrased in many ways: I'd get better if I risked loving—I'm beginning to dare to trust.]
156. Feeling comes and reasons follow it. If you've got to think out the reasons, that isn't what you thought!

157. Then the mist comes down again and I can't live in it, *but the mist is me.*
158. Have you kissed Pat? Yes.
     I mean really kissed? No.
159. When I'm not loved there is no colour.
160. Her going was a massive departure from my life.
161. I don't know if I'm seeing you or myself reflected in you.
162. Her madness invaded me.
163. When I first saw the group I said to myself 'I shall never become part *of this...'*. [The implied distancing and separation from the solidarity of a group] 'until people started talking...I then knew exactly how they felt.'
164. I had everything I wanted except what I wanted. [cf. I want to be what I was but I'm not going to.]
165. I can only talk round it ... I can't get to it ... in words!
166. The boss I hit was the one I liked...the other wasn't worth hitting.
167. This can't be unravelled, it can only be wept through.
168. Why can't I catch up with time? Time is as long as you make it. [cf. 'I wasted time, and now doth time waste me' (*Richard II*, V. v. 49.)]
169. Why do I always skate round *this family thing*? In my family it was peace at any price ... [and tears at no price?]
170. When he died, they all died.
171. I'm running away from myself every time I put my uniform on.
172. My mother protected me from too much.... I never learned to fight my own battles.
173. Part of me wanted my parents to die. There is so much cruelty in the world and there is cruelty in me.
174. [Divorced mother talking to teenage son]: 'What can I do to make you viable? [Bringing out cheque book]. 'How is your father?' 'He gives me petrol so that he can't say I have an excuse for not seeing him'. 'Why haven't you come to see me?' *'I've got nothing to see you about.'* [A 'disclosure' overheard in a train. The last phrase is a 'spontaneous' nuclear disclosure.]
175. He lied to his own mother and father till they died.
176. I'm clinging on to the past ... or is the past clinging on to me?

[Either a foundation on which to build or a restriction to relinquish.]

177. I'm looking for excuses to ruin myself.
178. It takes me time to climb into myself.
179. Chaos was on the brink of ruling me again.
180. Am I getting out of my depth or into his?
181. I am terrified of the overwhelming force of chaos.
182. I've been boomeranging around and never coming back to the place I was meant to. I'm a boomerang that no one can throw away, but a faulty boomerang which does not come back as it should.
183. I am a battlefield, but I am fighting on both sides at once, and this is why I feel so tired. It takes all my energy. [cf. I was arguing with myself and you kept butting in.]
184. I'm overloaded by my past.
185. It's easier to talk in individual therapy ... you've got to fight for space in the group.
186. When I'm on my own there's nothing there.
187. My sister escaped from Mother.
188. I can't take any more separation.
189. When I was married I had a perfect relationship with my wife ... for a few hours per day!
190. I wanted to retrace the journey a bit, to make the experience my own, instead of it just happening to me. Because although it was hell, it brought curious enrichments.
191. With-ness heals.
192. I've been able to *feel it all at last*, instead of feeling bits that were so painful that I couldn't feel anymore. [A classic example of a third-level disclosure.]
193. This was a destruction I wanted, a demolition I needed prior to rebuilding.
194. I feel that the group has an arm round me so that I can collapse in company.
195. Why have my protective arms—human—turned into wings ... angels?
196. I am beginning to be able to trust my nightmares.
197. I feel as though I'm carrying a huge hole around.

198. Every group is my first one ... they're isolated events, there's no sequence.
199. It's strange looking at your mother when she isn't your mother any more.
200. I've never been me.
201. Without my past I'm not a real person.
202. I stayed away from home whenever I went home!
203. Can I get behind my mask?
204. There is always my not-worth-bothering-about-me-ness!
205. There was no real end to it, it just stopped.
206. I'm outside everything, even myself but I'm trying to get back in.
207. I don't trust myself enough to be able to send out an SOS. I need something regular.
208. I am terrified of being dependent on anything, because whatever you depend on always fails in the end.
209. I feel angry but I can't get at the feelings behind the feeling of anger.
210. I was pulled into a nightmare.
211. I was in deep water.
212. Chaos sometimes finds me.
213. I need people to want me, even if it's as a clown. I'd rather be wanted as a fool than not wanted at all ... then I met someone who accepted me and I couldn't take it.
214. I've never really lived my life.
215. I wish I had never had a home so I would have a real identity.
216. Learning to live *with* my past was the most difficult thing. [A patient who had previously denied the past and then 'lived' *in* the past and was at last able to live *with* the past.]
217. He asked me to forgive him again but I'm running out of 'agains'.
218. There's a raging chaos in me like lava in a volcano, and occasionally it erupts.
219. The chaos is outside me and inside me ... but it depends on how I'm feeling whether I notice it outside.
220. I can't stand this need of love ... I'd rather hate.
221. I am chaos when my mother is in it.
222. I'm not near enough my chaos to get through it.
223. To be in chaos, to have it round me and to bear it, is to grow.

224. Chaos is part of me.
225. Chaos destroys me.
226. I am chaos.
227. My past was chaos.
228. I'm cut off from my past. It weighs on me.
229. I had to distort myself to achieve a relationship with him.
230. I cause chaos.
231. I had a lift of happiness from chaos.
232. Instead of love, I experience chaos. This is the Catherine wheel that goes round and round in my head. It is chaos because love is not there on demand.
233. I had to imagine a family. This is a big part of my chaos.
234. I am me. And they wanted me.
235. You are more than like me...you are part of me. [cf. 'You *are* me' of the psychotic.] [This remark made by one group member to a fellow-patient is pregnant with significance. It may imply identification, fusion, a demonstration of corporate concern or vicarious experiencing 'for' another, rather than 'with' another. The therapist's structuring initiative, appropriate to the situation, would depend upon the connotation which this phrase held for the group-as-a-whole, as well as the individuals concerned. In situations such as these, a premature intervention might seem trivial and inappropriate. It illustrates the therapist's task of endeavouring to gauge the texture of his intervention, which matches both the semantic and the affective circumstances.]
236. There is something distant, far away inside me, that has got to come out.... I'm wasting a lot of usefulness on anxiety.
237. The knife is a sharp reminder.
238. We've never had a cross word in our lives, and it wouldn't be safe to do so now.
239. I'm not ready to feel it yet.
240. I can't blame anyone else ... home, school, wife ... I know it's me and this is so hard to talk about, because it changes the way people see me.
241. In my dream I was in a boxing ring and I knew I was fighting myself. I knew I had lost. [When a patient is in a boxing ring fighting himself and knows he has lost, he is giving such a clear

presentation of low self-esteem; in contrast to the reply 'I knew I had won'.]

242. It stains your soul. [A third-level disclosure or a frivolous give-away line? The distinction depends upon physiological concomitants and other non-verbal communication].

243. There are some things I can't show, so I have to be partly here and there.

244. If only I could love someone a little more than myself, without being destroyed in the process.

245. It seems safe to love (or hate) when I'm in the group. [This shows the safety of therapeutic space. It is a preserve in which feelings, usually hidden, can be safely expressed and explored. It also illustrates the legitimating and authenticating function of psychotherapy. The patient is 'allowed' to have feelings. They are taken seriously.]

246. I remembered the facts all the time ... but *I hardened myself* to the feelings. [An interesting statement of 'affective amnesia' for a painful event, which could nevertheless be 'remembered' as a 'fact'].

247. I have the burden of having no burden.

248. I can't get what I love, so I hate it.

249. I've mellowed inside ... but it's up to others to notice I've mellowed.

250. Tom's loss is everybody's losses. [A reminder of each individual's loss, as well as everybody's loss, i.e. a corporate diminishment.]

251. I haven't taken a word in.... [The response of a patient who may not have taken 'a *word* in', but had responded to the affective flow in a group session. The *feeling* had been 'taken in', to a greater extent than by any other member of the group, though the patient was impervious to 'words'.]

252. I have to be what I'm not really.

253. I was my own undoing in my past.

254. I want to be myself in my own way ... not a mirror image of someone else.

255. We can't just die, we've got to have history.

256. Life has got to amount to something.

257. It's breaking with the non-ness of my past that's the difficulty.

258. I can't run away any more, there are no more defences, I can't turn the 'off' switch.

259. I was less secure than I cared to admit.
260. It started with sexual chaos, which led to emotional chaos, then everything became chaotic.
261. *She* was in my arms when she died ... *it* was grey and horrible.
262. I'm Number Two in Mum's eyes.
263. I know I won't steal again but I am worried that whatever this is might come out and in a different direction. I'm afraid of not getting it cleared up.
264. So many bits of me were in other places.
265. I don't have thoughts, they have me.
266. I'm afraid of learning who I really am.
267. When you're upset you won't let yourself get disturbed.
268. You're safe nowhere.
269. I want to do something ... but I've got no one to do it for.
270. You are a nut-cracker and have cracked my outer shell. So I don't need a shell because my confidence is the same.
271. My trouble is that I can't break down.
272. Friends are more frightening than strangers.
273. Life has gone liquid.
274. If I'm walking on my own, music keeps bursting in, and I can usually get past it, because I think of something stronger.
275. I need someone who is patient and continuously there.
276. I don't linger long [in the traumatic past] but the feeling comes back with me and lasts quite a long time. It's very strong and tails off.
277. I live in a world of flash-backs. They may be triggered by a song ('This nearly was mine') or a film and remind me of what was ... and what could have been. I live a lot in the past.
278. I'm not me yet.
279. I'm divorced from me.
280. I can't keep up with what is happening to me.

Any psychotherapeutic session contains disclosures such as these. To the reader they may appear to be a list of random comments and fragmentary phrases, but to me and to the patients to whom they came, they were important because they marked a changing level of disclosure. Any one of the examples just given would have been 'different' if the patients had, as it were, always said them. The dynamic behind them was that they indicated that the patient had reached a deeper level of disclosure. Therefore it should be imagined that in brackets after each disclosure is the comment: 'I never thought I could say that … either to you personally or in the presence of the other members of the group.' There is nothing absolute and diagnostic about a third-level disclosure taken on its own, but there is when viewed from the contextual analysis of the patient's history leading to the point of disclosure. The therapist will match this with any change in endopsychic patterning which becomes evident. The reader will have his own memories of occasions when patients have made third-level disclosures in his presence, and he will know that his handling of disclosure, for better or worse, will have had a profound effect on the further course of the therapeutic process. Formal assessment of the patient's mental state and the search for, say, thought disorder, must not cloud the therapist's awareness that his patient is on the brink of disclosure. However, alongside this scanning attentiveness there must be a rigorous on-going reappraisal of traditional clinical phenomena, such as appropriate diagnostic classification or the changing need for medication, admission to hospital, etc.

Sensitivity to disclosure and rigorous clinical awareness are inseparably linked, so that the *expanding frame of reference* implicit in the question 'What else might the patient be telling me?'—is always embedded in a conventional clinical context.

Third-level disclosures tend to 'cling' to the patient, as though he needs time to 'digest' his expanded awareness:

It can occur in a flash and hold my attention for many days.

CHAPTER 9

Boundaries of Therapeutic Space

> *I* feel secure in here.
> (Security experienced by a patient in a secure hospital)
> He brought me forth ... into a large place.
> (Psalm 18. 19)
>
> I will put you in a cleft of the rock.
> (Exodus 33. 22)

The term 'therapeutic space' has already been discussed. It refers to both the hypothetical epiphenomenon of the intra-psychic 'space' of the therapist and patient as individuals, and also to the shared space in which their work is done. It also refers to the literal physical context in which therapist and patient meet. It is to this latter reality that this chapter relates. The relationship between patient and therapist is inevitably influenced by the context in which they meet. My reason for stating what appears to be self-evident is that this axiomatic fact is often overlooked by those who attempt to transpose therapeutic techniques and skills from one context to another. Adequate attention must be paid to the influence which a new *locus operandi* will have upon the *modus operandi*, however successful it may have been in a previous context. Thus the startlingly original and stimulating discoveries Freud made, about the significance of the transference relationship and the place of interpretation, were formulated in the professional setting of Viennese private practice. These would be at best ineffective and, at worst, positively harmful if incorporated, without modification, into the incredibly complex life of a total institution such as Broadmoor Hospital, where staff of all disciplines and mentally abnormal offender-patients are exposed to each other's presence 'without limit of time'. I have deliberately chosen this extreme example because it makes the point so clearly. Psychoanalytic insights are of inestimable value in helping us to understand the offender-patient and also to 'treat' him. Nevertheless, they need to be adapted to the particular setting in which patient and therapist meet. In this chapter we are concerned with the influence which changing boundaries have upon the way in which the therapist structures the therapeutic process, and in the following chapter the influence of numbers who share therapeutic space will be discussed.

Boundary delineation must be established before it is possible to be aware that a boundary has been crossed. Psychotherapy is a boundary discipline in several senses. Much of this book relates to the creative potential of using the boundary between self and others as a 'zone' for risk-taking and growth. Boundaries may be emotional and/or physical.

There are many ways in which both therapist and patient are aware of the physical boundaries around them. This may be the door of the consulting room in which they meet; it may be the reminder of bars at the window of a prison cell and the shared knowledge that only one of them has the key to the outside world; it may be that the paraplegic patient feels equally restricted, though there are no locked doors or barred windows; it may be that the client officially 'reporting' to his probation officer knows that there is the risk of a possible return to custody if further sessions are ignored. The reader will be able to furnish from his own experience further examples in which counselling and psychotherapy are influenced by the context and the boundaries of therapeutic space. The cramped cells beneath a law court are literally and metaphorically far removed from the carpeted comfort of a consulting room, yet, in both, dynamic confrontation and third-level disclosure may occur. And each will demand, within human limits, the appropriate response from the therapist. The total privacy of, say, a GP's consulting room, encloses therapeutic space; and at the other extreme is the intense whirlpool of life within a total institution. The encounter between patient and therapist is permeated by their shared knowledge of the likely duration and frequency of their meeting, and the setting in which it takes place. Time-structuring takes on an added significance if there is also a change in the setting; in other words, changing physical boundaries and simultaneously changing temporal boundaries also add to the complexity of the therapist's task. He must judge the optimal balance of support-confrontation appropriate to his patient, seen, let us say, in a cell preceding a trial. He must also try to gauge what the patient needs which can be of use subsequently in the post-trial period, when the boundaries around the therapeutic space may be either those of the prison or, say, those of a probation officer's office or a hospital out-patient department.

The nature of the physical boundaries range from open access to total custody, and of the temporal boundaries from intensive, regular psychotherapy to 'occasional' reporting on a 'drop-in-when-you-like' basis. Flexible adaptability to changing circumstances colours the therapist's best use of himself in his patient's immediate and long-term interests. The work of the probation officer who works 'inside' and 'outside' a Total Institution exemplifies this *par excellence*. My own experience does not permit to write from first hand about many professional disciplines where such counselling and psychotherapeutic strategies are important. However, in view of the enriching experience of sharing regularly in staff groups with probation officers and school counsellors, I decided to take these two areas of expertise as representing many other professional disciplines involved in social work or one of the many counselling professions.

The probation officer

After his generic social-work training, there will be a period of field-work placements where the probation officer learns at first hand what a professional relationship with a client implies. Parsloe (1967) discusses 'particular role satisfactions and stresses for the probation officer' and these become evident in his initiation into field-work. What he has been taught in theory he now tries to put into practice. At this stage he will be under the close supervision of an experienced senior probation officer, and as his confidence increases, so does his desire for autonomy. It is comparatively easy to teach administrative matters, such as how to write a social enquiry report or what to do if a client on statutory after-care or parole fails to report at the appointed time. However, it is much more difficult to teach exactly how an individual probation officer* should learn to use himself in his client's best interest. If the probation officer is

---

* There is a specialised expertise demanded from a probation officer who works with clients 'on remand in custody'. Here the skills of responding to 'deep' needs in a crisis setting have to be balanced by the common knowledge that neither the probation officer, nor his client, know the 'future' of the relationship. Each session *might* be the last.

able to structure the 'space' which he shares with his client, in terms of time, depth and mutuality, he will discover that he becomes freer and more spontaneous with his clients. Probation officers who have shared in the facilitating experience of a peer-group where such concepts as structuring and disclosure are discussed, not infrequently discover that they are better able to use their warmth, assertiveness, masculinity or femininity, as the case may be, with greater ease. They thus feel growing discretionary judgement in providing supportive or confrontational counselling, depending on the needs of the client. A few examples now convey this professional discretion:

A client having served a prison sentence for increasingly severe offences 'against the person', with simultaneously decreasing care in avoiding detection, admits that he really wanted to be caught. He felt guilty about feelings of wanting to assault women. Does his female probation officer transfer him to a male probation officer, and thus risk confirming the fact that he is frightening to women? Does she change her response in any way by structuring time, depth or mutuality in a way better-suited to her client's emotional needs?

Case-load allocation could mean that a female probation officer may be involved in a professional relationship with, say, a client on parole who is a multiple rapist. A psychotherapist might have decided on theoretical grounds that such a patient with a long-standing personality disorder might not be 'suitable' for 'therapy'. Nevertheless the probation officer has a statutory obligation to see the multiple rapist regularly, and often the setting for their meeting is far removed from the protected clinical atmosphere of an out-patient department. The probation officer, and all social workers, not only have a difficult job to do, but often have a difficult place to do it in. A noisy office with minimal privacy or, *per contra*, an isolated office, almost alone in a building on a 'reporting evening', may have a cut-and-thrust ethos from which the members of other professions are more protected.

It is in situations like this that the crucial importance of adequately structuring the therapeutic process is self-evident. Thus the probation officer may deliberately opt for minimal personal involvement, so that the multiple rapist on statutory after-care merely 'reports' showing that he is in no further trouble and working steadily. If, in the example just given, the probation officer decides to be more professionally involved than simply allowing her client to 'clock in', then what is she supposed to do? Her client has profound psychopathology resulting in multiple rape. He may tell her that he always attacks women from behind; always attacks young women; always attacks young women in jeans; always attacks women who don't talk to him; always attacks women whose figure resembles that of his sister. Does the probation officer embark upon supportive or confrontational counselling? What does she do if the multiple rapist begins to describe his dreams, and to indicate that he has recently begun to dream about her? What does she do if he says 'You're the only person I've ever been able to talk to, Miss ——. I could never talk like this to the head-shrinker at the hospital, I'd certainly never see one of them again'? This apocryphal incident with fragments from many genuine experiences could be multiplied many times. If the probation officer does nothing except allow her clients to 'clock in', she may feel she is not doing what is required of her, yet her client refuses to see a psychiatrist. She is therefore left in an extremely exposed position, seeing, on her own, a client who is beginning to trust her; and who, perhaps for the first time, has begun to experience the mobilising acceptance which occurs when it is realised that therapeutic space is shared. What the probation officer does in these circumstances is no parochial, trivialised counselling, and the idea that such a client is 'just talking' to a probation officer, when seen against the deep interpretive work of the psychotherapist, is not true. The probation officer herself is aware of transference phenomena, and the professional use which she makes of herself in the therapeutic space she shares with her client, may make all the difference to her client's subsequent deviant career. It might come to an end or it might escalate. It is for this reason that the paramount significance of the 'therapeutic' work of the probation officer cannot be overestimated. It is hoped that the concept of structuring the therapeutic process, together with participation in the shared experience of a support group, may enable the probation officer to exercise her complex role in a more relaxed manner, yet with greater precision.

Pursuing this hypothetical history a little further, it can be seen that the significance of structuring and the importance of boundaries surrounding therapeutic space need to be continually borne in mind and reappraised as the situation changes. For example, the probation officer and her client will agree on the frequency and probable duration of their sessions.

Though, as in general medical practice, there may be the need for *crisis intervention* when the client wishes to pop in at the end of the evening. Such a request must be judged in the light of ambient circumstances. Does the client appear to be genuinely distressed? Is he drunk? Does he appear over-threatening or unduly seductive? These and many other questions will be going through her mind as the probation officer decides exactly how to respond to this SOS. This means that the regular sustained sessions may have many of the qualities of formal psychotherapy. They will be timed, and the depth of disclosure and the place of interpretation and the quality of other interventions cautiously assessed. What may be appropriate in the regular setting, may be out of place if the temporal boundary (the SOS), as well as the physical boundary (possibly on the pavement between the office door and the probation officer's car) changes. It is this degree of vigilance and awareness that makes the work of the probation officer so demanding, yet dynamic. She never knows exactly what is going to happen, and, like all other professionals, she will know there are certain risks inherent in the situation, depending upon her response. The client who says 'You've got a marvellous pair of legs' may be saying many things, depending upon the temporal boundary of therapeutic space (is this the first, the last or part-way through a long series of sessions?) and the physical boundary (a prison cell, the probation officer's office, the home visit, the local pub or queuing outside the cinema!).

A final example of the need to structure the therapeutic process is furnished by the following history: During the course of a reporting session in a probation office a man on probation for repeated larceny begins to talk about what thieving really means to him. He says that the crime which worries him most was not the taking of money but of ladies' underwear; and, with downcast eyes, falteringly describes increasing awareness of being a transvestite. He was relieved that he was on probation for larceny and had a chance to talk to a probation officer, and, indeed, he was compelled by law to do so. The probation officer finds that whereas the interview started with a client convicted of larceny, he is now involved with counselling a transvestite who has, for the first time in his life, been able to disclose this. The probation officer is experienced in discussing larceny. He may have no experience of psychotherapy with transvestites. Does he carry on? Does he refer the client to a psychotherapist and risk the fact that this may be construed that he could not emotionally 'take' what he had been told?

There is a perennial debate about the prime task of the probation officer. Is he a counsellor? Is he a 'servant' of the court? Is he a crime preventer? Writing of the work of American probation officers, Klockars (1972) succinctly describes the role confusion and genuine dilemma in which a probation officer often finds himself. 'Our observations yield a typology of probation officer which falls roughly between the thesis, "Probation is not Casework", and the antithesis, "Probation is Casework".' What Klockars calls a 'typology of probation officer' implies that the many roles expected of a single probation officer, though always complex, may be clarified and disentangled by adequately structuring the therapeutic process.

The relationship between the probation officer and her client does not take place *in vacuo*. She will be involved with colleagues from her own and other discipline.* She may be one of a team of professionals in touch with her client while he is in an institution, or she may be his only professional contact, particularly if he is of 'no fixed abode', a recidivist and unemployed.

I hope this brief account of the potential depth of a relationship between probation officer and client, with its many opportunities for cultivating disclosures or 'playing it cool', may convey something of the complex nature of the psychotherapeutic challenge presented by each client in a case-load. The concept of structuring the therapeutic process with which the probation officer is inevitably and inextricably involved allows him a greater sense of freedom, providing he has adequate supervision from an experienced senior or 'outside' expert psychotherapeutic cover. 'I am really learning how to use myself better' is almost a tune in unison from the probation officer, the GP, and many others who are beginning to tackle psychotherapeutic aspects of their work which they had previously found daunting.

One of the important areas of current debate, within the Probation and After-Care Service, centres around the question: 'How far is "group work"

---

* There is a finely poised balance between preserves of professional autonomy and the relationship between disciplines; especially when the senior post is held by a member of a different discipline, e.g. Prison Governor and Probation Officer; Headmaster and School Counsellor.

appropriate?' The outcome of these deliberations will have far-reaching implications in terms of the organisation of training and the provision of continuing support for those officers who undertake 'group work'. Subsidiary questions are: Is group work an optional extra ... a further imposition upon an officer with a heavy case-load? Are there intrinsic merits in group work? Is the expediency argument tenable, i.e. *is more rather than less time involved*? Is a relatively isolated work setting appropriate for group techniques? How far can concepts derived from group psychotherapy, where there are usually motivated patients who can sustain and endure ego-dystonic dynamics, be transferred *in toto* to the probation setting, where there are usually clients whose rebellion towards authority and lack of sustained motivation is an inherent part of the reason why they became clients in the first place?! How necessary is consultant supervision from a colleague experienced in group work, who is not involved in the day-to-day (and minute-by-minute!) crises of a local office? Will there be specialist group workers within the service?... This debate will continue.

The school counsellor

In recent years there has been a surge of interest in the work of counselling in schools (Hamblin, 1974). Training courses multiply, new journals are born, and some would argue that new species are born! Maguire (1975) has written on the important subject 'The school counsellor as therapist'. The aims of original pioneer work in this field was to give extra training to professionally qualified teachers, so that they could act as counsellors within the schools where they already taught. However, the position is changing so that there are now specialist school counsellors employed by education authorities, alongside traditional academic and other appointees. This is still relatively virgin soil, and problems of territorial rights and the guarding of preserves are hotly debated, as is the role of the specialist psychotherapist in the psychiatric hospital. 'Every teacher is a counsellor and the best counsellor is the practising teacher' has a reminiscent ring to those who heard 'every psychiatrist is a psychotherapist and the best psychotherapist is a practising psychiatrist'. I am sure other disciplines could echo these phrases.

Exactly where counselling differs from those peripheral areas of experience which all teachers know, which are not directly didactic but concerned with helping the pupil 'as a person rather than helping him to learn French', is difficult to define. But there is undoubtedly a growing need for 'counselling' in schools. This applies right across the board, including the independent and the maintained sector, and at all levels, i.e. primary, secondary and higher education. It then leads naturally into the counselling services for students in both branches of the binary system of higher education. Here again there is the problem of defining boundaries. Does the university health service have a direct link with curricular advisers, student counselling services and local adolescent psychotherapeutic facilities? This debate is currently taking place in many centres of higher education. (See *British Medical Journal,* 1976a, Meeks, 1971.)

In each of these situations the precise role of the counsellor and therapist impinges upon the community and inevitably sets up eddies and cross-currents. The physical and temporal boundaries of therapeutic space have the same general implications already considered for the work of the probation officer, and it is unnecessary to repeat these. I will merely indicate that the scope of the counsellor is obviously considerably influenced by such facts as whether he is working in a day school or a boarding school; whether it is a boarding school with normal 'terms' or whether it is a special school for handicapped children without parents so that they live at the school 'without limit of time', although there may be no custodial wall to contain them; whether the traditional boarding school is miles away from the nearest town or whether it is in the centre of population; whether the school is co-educational. (This makes a fundamental difference to one aspect of a counsellor's work, namely, that in a one-sex school any feelings of warmth and affection towards other individuals must be towards those of the same sex. Therefore the anxiety that the client may be homosexual is intensified. The adolescent likes to feel a hand on his shoulder. The only possible hand on his shoulder is, say, a masculine hand. Does this mean he is destined for a life-long homosexual orientation?)

In this discussion the probation officer and the school counsellor have vicariously represented all those professionals who are involved in counselling as an integral part of another discipline. (I am aware that the full-time school counsellor is relatively immune, though he has other conflicts to face.) They are frequently acutely conscious of role conflict, when their allegiance to 'authority' clashes with their loyalty to their client.

This applies with less force to members of the medical and nursing profession, though those who work in total institutions cannot avoid the conflict between acting for the good of the individual and that of the community. It is a simplistic escape to say that the individual must come first when, for example, the consultant or the headmaster is, in fact, also equally responsible for the well being of the whole community.

In varying ways and with differing degrees of intensity, all counsellors and therapists face the dilemmas of confidentiality, and the issues of differential alignments of confidence between those with staff colleagues of different disciplines, and those with their clients/patients. I suggest that the dimensions of structuring the therapeutic process, which we have discussed at length, frequently help to clarify the role conflict when difficult decisions are called for by the counsellor's responsibility to, say, the school as a whole, and his individual client. Therefore, the dimensions of time, depth and mutuality not only facilitate the therapeutic process in 'safe' unambiguous settings, but they can also help to steer the counsellor through the difficult waters where loyalties pull in opposing directions. However expert may have been his preparatory training and self-scrutiny at depth, there is always a first time when, in contrast to the parliamentarian, the counsellor makes his own 'maiden silence' in the presence of his client. It has been my privilege for many years to share in staff groups with counsellors and therapists whose work-settings range from the total institution to the GP's consulting room. As stated earlier, it was as I listened again and again to problems presented in different ways that I began to discern a common theme: whenever a patient or client with whom a colleague was having 'difficulty' was discussed, the 'lesion' would almost invariably be placed along one of the three dimensions.

'Listen to the patient, he is telling you the diagnosis.'

In shared experience with colleagues, we can say 'Listen to the probation officer, the GP ... he is telling you the diagnosis', not only in terms of the technical 'diagnosis' of his patient, but in terms of the dynamic formulation of his relationship with his patient. In other words, as he presents his patient in a *staff-support group*, he is presenting himself.

It has been exciting sharing this experience with colleagues from different disciplines, because we have come to realise that whether the consultant psychotherapist or the most junior nurse is presenting 'a difficult patient', it is likely to be that consideration of time, depth or mutuality will throw into sharp relief the precise difficulty that is blocking progress. It may be a defence to say 'if only I knew more theory I could be more effective', or 'if only I was a man I could deal with this indecent exposure', or 'if only I didn't work in the same hospital as the patient and therefore was not involved with him in group therapy and in the day-to-day life of the hospital—then I could be more effective!' It has been our experience that as we hold up the structuring dimensions of time, depth and mutuality against our relationships with our patients, we come to see where the difficulty lies. If this awareness can be followed by emotional sharing and 'unbinding' within a staff-support group, then the patient/client may be liberated from his restrictions, which may have been intensified by the therapist's own restrictions imposed upon him.

Staff of all levels can be supported in a support group! The pooling of experience helps everyone; because staff-support groups are not academic, prestige, out-quoting-each-other, I-know-the-literature sessions. They are about the sharing of response to being hit, threatened, frightened, etc. These are predicaments in which we all find ourselves and seniority does not confer immunity.

CHAPTER 10

Numbers within Therapeutic Space

The group is *empty* without Bill.

(Anon., 1973)

The inward thought of every one of them, and the heart, is deep.

(Psalm 64. 6)

What is the use of them, but together? Keep them together.

(Turner's advice to Ruskin about exhibiting his pictures, and requested in his will)

You do like the chairs arranged in a vicious circle, don't you?

(A perceptive question from a member of the domestic staff who 'stage-managed'
the group room)

Can one of us cry for us all, or must we all do our own crying?

(Anon., 1973)

A vicarious release of bottled-up feeling for the
group-as-a-whole, or an asylum (a place of safety) where
the individual can 'go to pieces without losing face'?

I want individual group therapy!

(Anon., 1972)

I'm your greatest threat because you are what I used to be.

(Anon., 1976)

Talking about the past or the future or the present upsets me. I regard the group as
a *pastime* or like a job ... something you go to.

(Anon., 1975)

(This disclosure reveals someone who is too precarious, vulnerable and is only 'just
together', so that participation in a group would be destructive; unless a group can
be guaranteed to be entirely supportive and involve no confrontation with self or with
others. The effective affective thrust of a formal therapeutic group is precisely because
this immunity from confrontation is impossible. Nevertheless, the therapeutic effects of
'group work', such as occupational therapy, are doubly necessary for such a frightened
patient. This disclosure conveys the brittle hold on reality of the psychotic, who is
constantly on the brink of living in two worlds at once. The group was regarded as
both a diverting 'pastime' yet a potentially painful reminder of 'past time'.)

249

When she spoke. it triggered off a fund of other things that have happened.

(Anon.. 1977)

The group is a kind of intensifier...whatever I'm feeling. it makes me feel it more strongly.

(Anon.. 1975)

No other variable influences the nature of the therapeutic space as pervasively as the number of those who share it. There may be one therapist and one patient; one or more therapists and approximately eight patients (small group psychotherapy); or one or more therapists and eight plus *x* patients, materialising in the form of large group therapy (Kreeger, 1975), a ward meeting, or a marathon, which implies a 'capacity crowd' with almost 'timeless time'. Dynamic psychotherapy can be on an individual or a group basis, and each may be supportive or confrontational. A group may be construed as an aggregation of individuals or as *sui generis*, with an irreducible autonomous life.

This conceptual approach always studies the group-as-a-whole, though it is inevitably composed of individuals who initially must have been referred, as individuals, for psychotherapy. The referring GP or psychiatric colleague is obviously concerned to know how his patient, John Smith, is doing, and has no particular wish to know of the current dynamics of the group-as-a-whole. Therefore, however much the literature may imply that the group therapist is solely concerned with the group-as-a-whole, this is misleading. The therapist is inevitably aware that his patients have been referred from different sources, to which they will ultimately return. The group therapist therefore maintains a Janusian perspective. He may work with the group-as-a-whole yet, simultaneously, he must never minimise the ultimate significance of each individual member.

The development of Family Therapy brings many therapeutic initiatives together, in a particularly intricate and fascinating way. It calls for the therapist's reappraisal of previously established techniques, and raises questions about structuring and his use of himself in relationship to his patients. This applies to time, depth and mutuality, though mutuality perhaps needs the greatest reappraisal. Family Therapy bridges the traditional division between individual and group psychotherapy; though the GP who customarily thinks in terms of families rather than individual patients, is probably less surprised than the therapist trained on traditional individual psychoanalytic lines. It is in such therapy that the relationship between the individual, who has been described as a 'nodal point in a system', and the group-as-a-whole needs to be rigorously thought through (Skynner, 1976): '... the family is an interface where youth meets age and birth and death are juxtaposed, linking the inner with the outer world, the individual with the group.'

Using the structuring dimensions already described, it becomes clear that the different ways in which the therapist uses himself when involved with group discussion, group counselling and group psychotherapy (Thompson and Kahn, 1970) depends upon differential structuring in each situation. For example, the therapist's use of mutuality would be quite different in group discussion where, say, common hobbies were being discussed, from his use of mutuality in psychotherapy involving dreams, transference and interpretation. This point is perhaps best illustrated by indicating that the appropriate response of the therapist to the statement 'I had a dream about you last night' is quite different, depending upon the ambient circumstances. The daily life of any psychiatric hospital will involve staff and patients in many interactions which will, it is hoped, all be therapeutic. There will be occasions for group discussion (topic-orientated),* where a local football referee has come to talk to the patients about changes in, say, a new off-side rule. There will also be group counselling (problem-orientated). This frequently takes the form of ward meetings, where various items of domestic concern can be raised; ranging from the difficulty in finding sufficient partners for the Christmas dance or the continued delay in renewing out-dated plumbing, to personal problems such as the impending visit from a relative which is not welcomed but is something which the patient does not 'dare' to postpone. There will also be group psychotherapy ('personality'-orientated).† Psychiatric hospitals vary in the extent to which group psychotherapy is an intrinsic part of their daily programme. It may be 'essential' or an 'optional extra'. Availability of trained staff is obviously a key issue. Some large hospitals employ no consultant psychotherapist, whereas other smaller hospitals are run exclusively on

---

* Is this a debating-society or group therapy?

(Anon., 1976)

† Is this individual therapy with an 'audience'—or is it group therapy?

(Anon., 1974)

psychotherapeutic lines with several group therapy sessions per day. There is also the total life of the hospital, lasting twenty-four hours per day, which in the widest sense, attempts to be therapeutic. The pioneer work of Maxwell Jones (1968) in establishing the concept of the therapeutic community has now permeated many hospitals, where staff are increasingly encouraged to look at their own roles and the presence or absence of authoritarian, hierarchic structures. Clark (1964) has made a special study of staff hierarchies and roles in *Administrative Therapy*.

The literature on group psychotherapy is vast, but no source is as important as that of the pioneer work of Foulkes (1948, 1964 and 1975, and Foulkes and Anthony 1957) to whom the Institute of Group Analysis, the Group-Analytic Society and the concept of group-analytic psychotherapy itself owes its birth. Foulkes (1975) wrote:

> It grew out of and is inspired by my experiences as a psychoanalyst, but is *not* a psychoanalysis of individuals in a group. Nor is it the psychological treatment of a group by a psychoanalyst. It is a form of psychotherapy *by* the group, *of* the group, including its conductor.

He makes it clear that group-analytic psychotherapy is a form of psychotherapy of the group, and this is a marked change from the early pioneers of group psychotherapy who regarded group therapy as offering psychotherapy of individuals in a group. Obviously the individual patient receives psychotherapy otherwise it would be a pointless exercise, but the group-as-a-whole is the frame of reference. In an earlier book Foulkes (1948) wrote:

> The deepest reason why our patients can reinforce their normal reactions and correct their neurotic reactions in such a therapeutic group is that *collectively they constitute the very norm from which, individually, they deviate.*

The italics were in the original, but clearly this remark would depend upon the population from which the group came. For example, in Broadmoor Hospital, where most of the patients are offender-patients and many are guilty of manslaughter, this interesting statement would not apply. Nevertheless, there is the corrective emotional experience of participation in a mixed group taken from the population at large, that enables patients to redefine their faulty self-definitions which they have gained through previous stigmatising experiences. This means that a group can offer a redefining process with a corrective consensual validation, which individual psychotherapy cannot afford.

Events impinge upon, and are interpreted by, the individual from his moment of birth and, in part, determine 'who' he is. If the group is the original primary milieu in which an individual's self-definition takes place, then, *ipso facto*, the group will also be the place in which re-definitions occur.

> Self-definition is a continuous existential process, and modification and redefinition can occur spontaneously in every human encounter, but within the more restricted context of a formal, professionally organised therapeutic group, redefinition is, *inter alia*, an inevitable consequence. [Cox, 1973b.]

> 'If only you could see yourself with the values we see in you.'
> 'People look at me *now*, as they *used* to see me.'

In addition to the 'negative' momentum which group psychotherapy derived from the shortage of individual analysts and from the 'positive' momentum due to the development of group-analytic psychotherapy (with increasingly clear-cut theoretical premises, as well as the professional skills described by Foulkes) there has been another source of momentum which comes from a completely different direction. I am referring to the increasing interest among, say, junior prison officers* who are aware that there is much more potential in their role than that restricted to a purely custodial, 'lock-them-up' approach. Such prison officers may not have read Freud or Foulkes, but their interest in group methods, group counselling and the potential for group corporate activity, arises from the realisation that there are many encouraging and enriching experiences which can occur between those who are locked up and those who do the locking. The growing interest in group counselling within the prison service is not merely because it has been part of top-level prison policy, reflected in the increasing number of visiting psychotherapists employed in the Prison Medical Service. But also, because at grass-roots level, where man with key meets man without key, there is a realisation that counselling has much to offer prison staff, prison inmates and the quality of life itself within the prison. This is particularly important in prisons which house inmates with relatively long sentences. Such an exercise involves intense collaboration between discipline staff, hospital staff and other workers within the prison such as psychologists and probation officers, still usually referred to by inmates as 'the welfare'. The increased momentum for establishing group counselling in the

---

* These are personal views and do not necessarily reflect those of the Home Office.

Social Services, in the National Health Service, in the Prison Medical Service, the Probation and After-Care Service and in many branches of the educational system, has been matched by an avalanche of books covering both the theory and practice of groups which are, in the widest sense, intended to be therapeutic.

No book, in itself, is ever going to produce an experienced therapist, because all psychotherapy training must involve the suffering–maturational process of monitored introspection and supervised psychotherapy, with gradually increasing autonomy. Nevertheless, there are many professional workers who are at the front line of clinical involvement who simply cannot leave their place of work for further professional training, even on a part-time basis, so that they could return equipped to run a group. They are in a ward of chronic schizophrenics; they meet a group of relatives of patients who are on kidney machines; they are involved with a group of recently bereaved widows; they are in a boarding-school with a group of children who suffer from homesickness ... and so on. Such colleagues need guidelines and reading material of a depth to match their existential executive responsibilities. There are many short books on how to run a group in a social work department or in medical out-patients. But there seems to be a gap between 'heavyweight' theoretical formulations and simple logistic descriptions of the 'arrange eight chairs in a circle, let the patients choose the topics ... etc.', variety. Such writings are excellent when combined with the accessibility of local facilities for supervision and personal training in group psychotherapy methods.

There are many 'ground-rules' to conducting group sessions and they are only learned under supervision. *Discretional flexibility is a key concept* and is exemplified when a member of a group asks for an 'extra' individual session. This may be manipulative, because the *exact* reason why an individual session is requested may be the *exact* reason why the issue must be faced in the group. But it may *not* be manipulative.

If the therapeutic process can be structured in such a way that the therapist can see more clearly what is happening at a given time, then he will be free from unnecessary anxiety which might divert him from enabling the therapeutic process to continue. There are therapeutic bonuses which accrue from working in groups, because it is not a question of one 'sick' patient seeing a so-called 'healthy' therapist, but rather of the coming together of people who have strengths and weaknesses. And there is usually a paradoxical effect in that the pathology of one patient reinforces the non-pathology of another. (Though if the group members are wrongly selected, the pathology of one may intensify the pathology of the others.) Obviously the prevailing dynamics depend upon the reason why the group was established in the first place, the population from which it was drawn, the duration and frequency of the sessions, and also the immediate existential contingent happenings which affect everyone.

Fortunately, no individual or group session is immune from the incursive, abrupt exigency of 'significant' life-events. This means that the complicated network of relationships in any therapeutic setting in which reality and fantasy merge, or grow apart, may be shattered by the forceful incipience of the statement 'My father died last night ...' or 'My son committed suicide and left this note which says ...'. Such sombre events are startling in any situation. But they frequently have a paradoxically reality-reinforcing quality when they impinge upon the affective life of a therapeutic group. It reminds the group that all events are not illusions. Although there are so many conflicting emotional responses to the death of a parent, there is frequently a corporate sense of relief at this reminder that all problems are not internal. The patients are recalled to the fact that a substantial part of the compromise which they make with chaos may, in fact, relate to coping with chaos in the outside world. One of the risks of prolonged psychotherapy is that the patient may come near to believing that all conflicts, and all chaos, are part of his inner world, and that 'healthy, normal people' do not experience conflict or need to cope with emotional chaos. The death of a relative of a group member is always significant, though not as profoundly disturbing as the death of a group member himself. The significance of coping with the reality, as well as the pervasive symbolic significance, of the death of the therapist during the on-going life of a group where murderousness has been expressed, can never be exaggerated. The death of a parent, the failed exam, the successful interview, are all events which will be reported in the group and bring reality-testing and concensual validation to the group, in a way which is absent in individual therapy unless the individual therapist takes the unorthodox line of saying 'Yes, that was how I felt when my mother died'. The patient on the brink of paranoid ideation, who describes how he regarded the fact that his postman walked past his house one morning as a form of passive attack, is likely to have seven fellow-patients who are not caught up in his paranoid perceptual perspective. One patient may confront him by saying that there were strong chances that there might not have been a letter for him anyway. The group therefore gradually changes from seeing itself as composed of eight patients and one therapist (or two if there are co-therapists) into becoming a group of therapists and then, with luck, realising that the group is in fact a group of human beings!* The enhanced self-awareness, the ability to accept one's liabilities as well as rejoice in one's assets, begins to take on the character of the 'unlived life', though lived vicariously through other members of the group. The members really do learn to weep with those that weep and rejoice with those that rejoice. As the patients are able to tolerate their own third-level disclosures, so they can tolerate and indeed facilitate the third-level disclosures of others which, previously, may have seemed abhorrent and horrific. There is a sense in which reality breaks through, when impotence, homosexuality, the fear of success, the guilt at being praised and the enjoyment of failure can be openly expressed; and this leads to an increased sense not only of individual self-acceptance but of the group accepting itself. This then spills over into either the wider life of the hospital or the local community.

The presence of co-therapists is as essential as any luxury can be! Even their silent presence in, say, a mixed group of sex-offenders provides an added stimulus to the group; not only in terms of how the group responds to the therapists, but how the group perceives the relationship between the therapists. This in turn is compared with the group's previous experiences and expectations of the way in which men and women 'should' relate, as far as dominance–submission, activity–passivity, as well as the overt sexuality of the situation, is concerned. Many of the patients in such a group may need to negotiate the difficult task of disclosing that their offences were intimately connected with the misinterpretation of cues in an incipient male–female 'encounter'. Prolonged working as a co-therapist in a mixed group must be one of

---

* Non-psychotic patients often feel that the psychotic member of a group 'knows' what they are experiencing. The psychotic sometimes has an enhanced capacity for vicarious experience, which has more resonance and duration than a transient transference phenomenon. For this reason, the psychotic often makes an invaluable 'co-therapist'. However baffling and turbulent a session may be, he 'knows' the group is 'afraid of Tim's fear'.

the most rewarding experiences open to the psychotherapist. I have learned more about 'the use of self' in such work than in any other professional activity. Even the most brief reflection will indicate that such a partnership, in such a setting, demands reciprocal sensitivity of a high order.

Depending upon his training and experience, the therapist knows that his professional weak spot is that he either tends to intervene too early or too late. The group-as-a-whole, including the therapist, learns from his errors. The remark 'Why the hell did you have to cue me in?... I've got to make my own way' was an apposite stricture. This was an error in structuring on my part, and it is by such technical errors that we continue to learn. This being so, it is essential that therapists and co-therapists should meet, once per week if possible, to share experience; though this weekly staff group should never take the place of the pre- and post- 'group therapy' staff session. Working with a co-therapist is not only a training exercise for a junior co-therapist, but it also provides quadreceptive eyes and ears for the pair of co-therapists. In *Coding the Therapeutic Process* the chronogram is described as a method of recording group psychotherapy, and it is a fascinating exercise in selective perception where two therapists independently complete a chronogram for the same group and then compare notes!

Some of the questions raised in a staff group of co-therapists are as follows:

1. How can we distinguish the deeper meaning beneath the 'ordinary conversation' in the group?
2. How does the therapist use himself to structure the therapeutic process? Is it what he says, how he says it, or when he says it?
3. Is it said to the group-as-a-whole, or is it 'beamed' at one member?
4. Why do we respond in different ways to apparently identical situations involving different members?
5. Even if overt psychopathology is 'crying aloud', why is it ignored on one occasion and fostered, extended and amplified on another?
6. What theoretical concepts govern the therapist's changing style of involvement?
7. What kind of theoretical model do you have of the group, against which to carry out structuring activities?

I am not attempting to answer these questions here. I offer them as an indication of the kind of questions which student co-therapists quite properly and inevitably ask. And all therapists, however experienced, should go on asking! Is this a teacher-taught relationship or that of an apprentice-senior, or are we co-workers each working in our own way? How do the patients perceive what we are doing? I suggest that dimensions of time, depth and mutuality can stimulate every co-therapist into trying to grapple with these questions.

The profound influence of Foulkes and the establishment of the Group-Analytic Society and Institute has provided a much-needed frame of reference for the psychotherapist involved with groups. His theoretical views and practical approach may differ from the Foulksian group-analytic model, though it is now so well known that the therapist can take this theoretical perspective as a reference point. He will become aware of shared symbolic meanings, the expanding lattice of interactions and the possibility of facilitating (or delaying) disclosures not only of the individual to the group, but of the group to itself. There is an existential *koinonia* of corporate group life in which the therapist is inextricably involved. The unlived life of one member of the group, being lived vicariously by a fellow-member or the group-as-a-whole on his behalf, adds to the philosophical, metapsychological and transpersonal frames of reference which the therapist must think through. There is a resemblance between corporate, shared *koinonia* of cohesive group life and many Catholic equivalents; and also between the intensely individual psychoanalytic emphasis upon personal experience, and Protestant equivalents. The group is inevitably made up of individuals who were originally referred for therapy by their general practitioners or other consultants. Frequently this is because the lack of an adequately nourishing earlier corporate life has meant that the patient needs a corrective corporate emotional experience, which group participation can provide.

The therapist needs a poised balance of science and art as he tries to catalyse group interactions in the direction of integration via disclosure. I am reminded of a seminar for GPs where the group was divided as follows: half the members thought they used the science of medicine to reach diagnosis and then the art of medicine to treat their patients, whereas the other half thought they used the art of medicine to diagnose and the science in treatment! I suspect that the therapist involved with groups needs both all the time! Precisely because the science and art of the psychotherapist are infinitely improvable, it is hoped that both the teacher and the trainee will experience a sense of learning together. An unavoidable question confronting the therapist takes the following form: 'How can I share in therapeutic space which is primarily for my patient's benefit, not mine, so that he can feel it is a painful risk worth taking?'

The patient so often has a splendid way of cutting the therapist down to size! In a mixed group of offender-patients, in which several showed 'borderline' personality organisation and others had complex disorders of sexual identity which added up to an extraordinarily intricate group matrix within which useful (I hope) psychotherapeutic work was done, I asked a patient 'Could you say, in one word, what you would most like to receive from the group?' I received the reply which I have every reason to think was honest. It so accurately expressed the need of that patient, in that place, at that time. It was infinitely more important than any profound analytic interpretation. The answer I received was 'A handshake!'*

Wrongly selected patients may find that group therapy is not therapeutic:

> The cares I give I have, though given away.
> *(Richard II.* IV. i. 198)

Fortunately, correctly selected patients can find therapy therapeutic:

> And in this thought they find a kind of ease,
> Bearing their own misfortune on the back
> Of such as have before endur'd the like.
> *(Richard II,* V. v. 28)

With psychopaths, group therapy may hasten the advance towards 'elder days':

> As dissolute as desperate; yet through both,
> I see some sparkles of a better hope,
> Which elder days may happily bring forth.
> *(Richard II,* V. iii. 20)

---

* A further example of cutting the therapist down to size is afforded by a silent 'preoccupied' patient in a group. I explained to a staff seminar that the silence might be due to psychotic intrusion, pseudo-psychotic manipulation, increased medication, etc. I was then informed that the patient was awaiting new batteries for his deaf-aid!

CHAPTER 11

Compromise with Chaos
(borderline, psychotic and offender-patients)*

> How shall your houseless heads and unfed sides,
> Your loop'd and window'd raggedness, defend you
> From seasons such as these?
>
> (King Lear, III. iv. 30)

> Do not adjust your mind, reality is at fault.
>
> (Graffiti)

> NURSE: Forgive me, Mr Adolf, forgive me. I had to stop you from killing your child.
> CAPTAIN: Why not let me kill the child? Life's a hell, and death is the Kingdom of Heaven; children belong to Heaven.
>
> (from The Father, August Strindberg, 1887)

> 'I felt that to bring out its deeper significance which was quite apparent to me, something other, something more was required; a leading motive that would harmonize all these violent noises, and a point of view that would put all that elemental fury into its proper place.'
>
> (from Conrad's author's note on Typhoon, 1919: italics added)

> 'Do you want to know what I did?'
> 'Yes.'
> 'Why?'
>
> (Anon., 1975)
>
> (This intense vignette comes from a Broadmoor group. The questioner, with penetrating precision, forces the distinction between voyeuristic inquisitiveness and the evocative empathy of corporate concern. The former freezes disclosure, the latter promotes it.)

No group of patients poses a greater challenge to the therapist, either in terms of basic clinical 'management' or in the more specific task of

---

* The effective 'management' of such patients demands an integrated total therapeutic policy. This may include medication, appropriate physical treatment, and is likely to involve a period in hospital. When the patient is a mentally abnormal offender-patient, it may necessitate treatment in a secure hospital, such as Broadmoor, 'without limit of

structuring the therapeutic process, than the triad forming the sub-title of this chapter. When, however, the three groups assume the trinitarian form of 'three in one', the therapist experiences the need for the utmost rigour and assiduity in the clinical precision with which he structures time, depth and mutuality. Such patients exhibit borderline personality organisation and have a history of transient psychotic episodes, during which there may be catastrophically violent assaults against the person, perhaps with fatal consequences.

There is always an optimal point along the support-confrontation therapeutic continuum for each patient, ranging from the chronic psychotic's need for support to the narcissistic psychopath's need for fierce confrontation with self.

The criteria of 'success', when judging the efficacy of psychotherapy with such patients, are so complex that space does not permit a detailed analysis now. However, when psychotherapy is conducted within a total institution, such as Broadmoor Hospital, it may be considered under three headings:

1. *Conventional.* Attention is focussed upon changes in endopsychic patterning, relinquishment of primitive defences, enhancement of impoverished self-esteem, increased object constancy, ability to identify with explicit and implicit needs of others in a group setting, crystallisation of intensity and direction of libidinal orientation, etc.

2. *Monitoring.* By which I mean that the therapist has the chance to see at very close quarters, and at a depth of vulnerability impossible in

---

time'. Nevertheless, it is self-evident that in addition to the necessary therapeutic initiatives such as the prescription of medication and, maybe, the containment of such patients in hospital, the prime significance of the staff/patient relationship can never be exaggerated. This is the *via therapeutica*, upon which all else hangs. The psychodynamic therapeutic initiative of structuring the therapeutic process in terms of time, depth and mutuality, is inextricably involved with the way the patient is 'treated'. This may involve receiving drugs and/or dancing lessons and/or participating in formal psychotherapeutic sessions. This chapter concentrates upon the structuring aspects of treating Borderline, Psychotic and Offender-patients. It is divorced from other therapeutic modalities solely for the purposes of description. This may appear to be stating the obvious, but it needs to be underlined because descriptions in the literature sometimes give the impression that dynamic psychotherapy is a form of treatment totally encapsulated, and segregated from the complex therapeutic thrust of the rest of hospital 'life'.

other settings, exactly how the patient reacts in the presence of the other members of a group (including the co-therapists).

This is often in marked contrast to the way he *says* he reacts to girls, older women, homosexual men, authority figures, etc.

3. *Endorsement.* At its simplest level this facet of psychotherapy endorses the human value of the patient, by providing a matrix from which something is 'missing' if he is not there. This may be the acid thrust of the psychopath, or the absence of Barbara's silence. If Barbara is a withdrawn schizoid 'loner', she can scarcely believe that she would be noticed by her absence, let 'alone' missed! Precarious self-esteem can be enhanced in this way, but only very slowly and over a very long time.

This final chapter has been given the title 'Compromise with Chaos' because the therapist's most profound confrontation with the chaos within the patient may re-ignite his previous personal experience of inner chaos. There is also the well-documented evidence of chaos in the outer world, where property or another person has been drawn into the path of the disorganised chaotic destructiveness of the patient. The first chapter made the point that if the therapist's structuring initiative, to be subsequently discussed, was only appropriate in conventional counselling or traditional group psychotherapy with neurotic patients, then the reader (whose experience might include work with the psychopath or the psychotic patient in such settings as a prison, a conventional psychiatric hospital or other total institution) might infer that the dimensions of time, depth and mutuality and the concepts of primary and secondary structuring would not apply to him. It was for this reason that I adopted the heterodox approach of 'starting in the deep end' by mentioning the borderline, the psychotic and the offender-patient at the outset.

Compromise with Chaos therefore ends where it began, though with a more detailed consideration of the patient showing borderline personality organisation, who posits the ultimate challenge to the therapist, in terms of structuring the therapeutic process.* It must be repeated that I am here solely concerned with the dynamics of the inter-personal relationship between the individual patient and the therapist, or that within the therapeutic group. Other facets of global therapeutic policy, such as the use of appropriate medication or other physical treatments, the need for

* See footnotes page 23.

containment within the safety of a secure environment, are outside our present frame of reference.

Stern (1938) wrote the original paper describing patients showing borderline personality organisation, and Grinker's (1968) monograph followed thirty years later. The first comprehensive book on this important topic is a recent publication: *The Borderline Patient* by Wolberg (1973).* Borderline personality organisation furnishes a good example of a psychodynamic concept providing 'shorthand' for what might otherwise take a lengthy descriptive sentence. Such patients are neither neurotic nor psychotic, nor do they suffer from a personality disorder, *per se*. They frequently defy accurate nosological description; unless the description is so inclusive as to be almost meaningless. For example 'this patient suffers from a long-standing hysterical personality disorder, together with episodes of reactive depression and transient psychotic phases'. Compare this with the brevity of the statement 'this patient shows borderline personality organisation', with the implication which captures so accurately the clinical experience of working within the therapeutic alliance, 'this patient shows defensive fluidity'. This defensive fluidity is the hallmark of the borderline patient. Pines (1975a) writes: 'Great turmoil, anxiety and pain often enter into the therapy situation, and much unsatisfactory treatment results from contact with these patients. Most of us know what it is like to have had such experiences, which leave us hurt and confused, and seeking clarification so that we may be better equipped the next time we enter into the arena.'

The borderline patient demands constant reappraisal in view of the rapidly changing endopsychic patterning. Splitting and other primitive defences appear to change in an almost capricious and unpredictable way, so that at one moment the therapist is intensely aware that he is sharing therapeutic space with a patient who presents as a florid psychotic, whereas within minutes the entire psychopathology seems transformed. The patient then appears to have become in firm touch with reality and exhibit none of the primitive defences which were almost caricature proportions of the 'textbook' psychotic only minutes before. It must be noted that the borderline patient is not a histrionic hysteric or a psychopath who can put on 'a good performance' of a psychotic. The borderline syndrome is a clinical presentation *sui generis* and not a

* See also *Borderline Conditions and Pathological Narcissism*, Kernberg, 1975.

presentation *manqué* of some other condition. When such a patient is also an offender-patient with a known history of a severe offence, it is not difficult to see why such a patient presents as the North Face of the Eiger, as far as the therapist's activity of structuring the therapeutic process and his personal compromise with both internal and external chaos is concerned. *The patient not only experiences chaos, he causes it.* Chaos is explicit in such a patient's catastrophic and destructive behaviour. It is implicit in the hyper-fluidity of his endopsychic patterning, and may be experienced by the therapist as calling for the utmost caution and clinical precision as he endeavours to structure time, depth and mutuality to make optimal use of therapeutic space. These comments are intensified and multiplied when such a patient is a member of a peer group of others with similar histories and similarly rapidly fluctuating defences. There are few clinical settings where it is possible for group therapy with such patients to be undertaken. For obvious reasons it is unlikely that group therapy with psychotic patients is likely to occur in an out-patient setting, although this is to some extent influenced by cultural attitudes to mental illness. It can occur more readily in other countries than is at present possible in England.

A different quality of structuring the therapeutic process is called for, when the therapist is involved in the complex task of working with the psychotic patient; though the dimensions of time, depth and mutuality are even more important than in conventional psychotherapy, with neurotic patients. It is only when the therapist is as certain as it is humanly possible to be, that he is aware of what is 'going on' in terms of time, depth and mutuality (both as perceived by the therapist, himself and his patient) that he dares to risk the abandonment of enlarging his ego boundaries and venturing upon a 'para-regression'. This is a loosening of his own controls so that through the agency of primary process thinking, and a fluid affective response, he may 'come alongside' his patient and be 'welcomed', precisely because he has risked this loosening of conventional ties. There now follows a sentence which will be repeated because it cannot be over-stressed. This particular aspect of structuring the therapeutic process with psychotic patients must always be partial, transient and reversible, at the therapist's discretion. If the therapist senses that he is even approaching the brink of losing this 'discretion' he will cease to be a therapist, and will soon be looking for one himself!

Rothenberg (1971) discusses the place of 'regression in the service of the ego' (Kris, 1952) in 'The process of Janusian thinking in creativity':

Psychotherapy, a major modality of psychiatric treatment, is clearly more an art than it is a science at the current stage of our knowledge. Although interest in creativity began with poets, philosophers and theologians, it now seems crucially important for psychiatrists to understand and delineate the psychological factors in creativity, particularly artistic creativity, since such understanding should have direct application to the basic theory and everyday practice of psychotherapy in all its forms.

In my view, this links closely with the expanding frame of reference, because creativity in the therapist is implicit in his ability to allow his patient the creative liberty to free-associate; this is needed *a fortiori* with the psychotic. This means that blocks to free-association arise within the patient (a classical psychoanalytical perspective) and not within the therapist. Flexibility, openness and the alertness of creativity should be a hallmark of the therapist who not only allows, but actually fosters, disclosure. When the patient is psychotic, extra demands are made upon the therapist. He may then temporarily need to expand his ego boundaries (Rose, 1964) so as to try to see the perceptual field of the psychotic as he does, but also (and here the lack of appropriate vocabulary is so apparent) partially to 'sink into' his patient's social construction of reality. It is almost a partial regression in the service of his patient's regression. *This must always be partial, transient and always reversible, at the therapist's discretion.* The executive aspects of the therapist's personality retain a firm hold (and I would add an extra firm hold) on reality, while simultaneously engaging with his 'disturbed' patient in a way which is acceptable to him. The ability to share the perceptual perspective and affective thrust of his patient's world and, at the same time, to retain executive, stabilising autonomy is an important aspect of the skill of structuring the therapeutic process (*vide infra*). The patient's compromise with chaos is furthered by a therapeutic presence which eases the frightening task of free-association, the recalling of painful memories and it may stimulate the evocation of 'The Guided Day Dream', which is so popular in Europe at the moment. This means that a patient may find enlarged possibilities for introspection, because he is not merely remembering forgotten dreams but he is also free-associating about dreams he would like to have. Therefore he is daydreaming in the presence of his therapist. This technique often 'unfreezes' the patient whose statement 'I don't dream' or 'I can't remember dreams' blocks conventional interviewing. 'What would you like to dream about?' usually brings about an atmosphere of safe expansiveness. Thus a patient was enabled to disclose for a 'group interpretation' (interpretation *by* the group not *to* the group) the fantasy-fact of crossing a deep fast-flowing river on stepping stones, only to discover that three were missing in the deepest, most dangerous spot. He did not know exactly how deep the river was and might be 'up to the neck' (or higher) if he risked walking on the river bed. The river may only be an analogy for the non-psychotic, but for the psychotic the river is 'real'. The expanding frame of reference, implying the therapist's ability to briefly expand his ego boundaries and (if necessary for his patient) to regress *partially* in the service of his patient's ego, may sound a tall order. It is, however, 'teachable' though it requires an amalgam of flexibility and rigour. This somewhat specialised facet of psychotherapy has been discussed in some detail, because the psychotic presents the greatest challenge to the therapist's structuring initiative.

There are many facets common to this undertaking with the schizophrenic and the borderline patient, who often presents as an ephemeral psychotic. Arieti (1976) discusses psychotherapy with schizophrenics and his penetrating comment that 'It is just as nourishing as it is interpretative' applies with even greater weight to the borderline patient. Nevertheless, it is more difficult to structure the therapeutic process with the borderline patient because of the capricious, quicksand quality of affective instability. The psychotic patient may have a sustained delusional system which allows the therapist greater time to judge his structuring initiative, so that he may enter the orbit of the patient's experience along an appropriate trajectory. It is the mercurial, flash-point of the borderline patient that makes this undertaking so hazardous. Yet, if it is not undertaken, the borderline patient may defy any psychotherapeutic initiative, so that a total management strategy is restricted to medication or containment. When the borderline patient is also an offender-patient, then it may be only within the security of a total institution that the therapist is enabled to enter the patient's inner world. This is closely allied to the opening comments in the chapter on empathy, where it was indicated that the therapist's greatest challenge, and occasional achievement, may be to reach the point of 'looking out of' the patient. This is therefore perceived by the patient as though the therapist sees the environment as he does. Only then will the patient risk seeing the therapist as a trustworthy ally, so that therapeutic space can be shared. The expanding frame of reference, described in Chapter 1, facilitates this. A caveat must be inserted here. If the therapist so loses his touch with reality that he *only* sees the environment as his patient does, then he has ceased to be a therapist and is poised at the brink of chaos. The borderline patient therefore brings out most clearly the therapist's need to be firmly rooted in reality and yet, simultaneously, accepted into the psychotic patient's social construction of reality. In such circumstances the therapist is aware that his own reality-testing is stretched, sometimes almost to the limit. I find that the heuristic device of structuring the therapeutic process in terms of time, depth and mutuality, together with the 'expanding frame of reference', can sometimes permit the therapist to gain entry to the psychotic's world without being perceived as threatening and intrusive. At the same time, this provides firm boundaries to the therapeutic space within which he and his patient meet.

> I killed the dog I loved 'for attention'. but it was dark and no one saw. I didn't realise this until afterwards.
>> (A psychotic's misjudged 'cry for help': No one heard and no one saw.)

The psychotic may present with formal thought disorder, delusions and hallucinations, or retreat into the safety-zone of emotional distance, where he is inaccessible to fellow-patients and therapist alike. Whereas the offender-patient will have been involved in disturbed and disturbing social relationships, ranging from committing petty offences to such a catastrophic out-cropping of violence as the savage dismemberment of a homosexual partner. The borderline patient bridges both groups, and therefore poses a great challenge to the therapist. The transient absence of chaos in such a patient's presentation may imply a massive defence, especially if he leaves a 'wake' of chaotic destruction behind him. He then shelters behind a barrier of symptoms, or a bland denial of any suggestion that he might be involved with, say, the battered baby, the burning barn or the murdered man.

The absence of a sense of 'almost chaos' within the therapist himself, may imply that he is too detached from his patients and shelters behind a barrier of administration, research or 'doing-things-to' the patient, rather than 'being-with' him. (NB—These comments apply solely to the specialised work of the psychotherapist and obviously *do not* apply to the consultant psychiatrist who is the responsible medical officer, or other colleagues, doing essential administrative work.)

The therapist walks a tightrope, because he is dismissed by a patient if he is seen as too 'clinical' and intrusive, so that the patient is aware that he is being studied as a specimen rather than met as a person. On the other hand, if the patient senses that the chaos which almost overwhelms him may have a similar effect on the therapist, his precarious vulnerability will be hidden rather than running the risk of destroying the therapist too. Or it may again lead to catastrophic destructiveness.

The finely poised balance of being in the world of his offender-patient but not of it, is seen with particular intensity in the probation officer's response to the question 'Would you like to see photographs of my victim?' In such an existential encounter the emotional reserves of the probation officer are stretched to the limit, because he is intensely aware that faulty structuring at this moment could start a chain reaction which might be difficult to control. A borderline patient asking such a question poses a doubly difficult problem.

I hope this discussion illustrates that the basic premisses of structuring the therapeutic process is of clinical relevance in this most testing situation. (Barker and Mason [1968] have caught the core conflict of offender-therapy in the evocative title of their paper 'Buber behind bars'.)

The self-fulfilling prophecy of escalating, stigmatising experiences described by the offender-patient shows the basic similarity between the conditioning qualities of experience, whether viewed from a Freudian or Pavlovian standpoint. Thus, a sequence of relationships may be epitomised as follows in the words of such a patient: 'See a man, fear a man, hate a man, kill a man.' Presumably, other early experience might lead to a different sequence: 'See a man, trust a man, love a man, share life with a man.' Many of the complexities of offender-therapy can be simplified by saying that the aim of such therapeutic work is to convert the former sequence of experiences, by the process of redefinition, into the latter. Nevertheless, although it is easy to describe the aims of the process and the techniques whereby it is attempted, it is one which makes constant demands upon the therapist's reserves and 'stretches' therapeutic space.

The Fourth International Symposium on the Psychotherapy of Schizophrenia was held in Finland in 1972 (Rubinstein and Alanen, 1972) and the Fifth in Oslo in 1975. They represented a far cry from Freud's remark, recounted by Federn (1952) 'Psychotics are a nuisance to psychoanalysis!'* The changing attitude towards the psychodynamics and psychotherapeutic management of the psychotic is brought out most vividly by comparing Freud's dictum with the work of Spotnitz (1969, *Modern Psychoanalysis of the Schizophrenic Patient*). The growing interest in the borderline patient demands the fullest possible co-operation between the 'helping professions'. Wolberg (1973), Leibovich (1975), Pines (1975b) all offer valuable insights into this baffling problem.

Spotnitz (1957) asks the question about 'structuring' which permeates this book, though it is an inquiry relating to the schizophrenic patient and his response to psychotherapy. It is interesting that he, too, uses the word 'nourishing' as Arieti (1976) does, with its connotations of early feeding, sustaining, life giving. It recalls my patient, described earlier, who said 'I knew I had had it, right from the start'.

> This approach is not designed to overcome the resistances, as psychoanalysis overcomes them, but to master them in a different way: first, they are reinforced, until they have become so firmly secured that the patient no longer finds it essential to use these resistances and can subsequently outgrow them. Let me stress this goal to which treatment is directed: the resistances are not *overcome* but *outgrown*. [Spotnitz, 1957: italics in original]

and again:

> *Will the therapist be able to structure sessions and situations so that the patient obtains the exact amount of psychological nourishment he needs, at the exact moment that he needs it?* [Italics added]

These references reinforce the growing awareness that conventional psychoanalysis with the schizophrenic may be the wrong sort of attack.† Rostand (1953) described the futility of an inappropriate approach:

> What a war,
> When the besieger starves to death!

*Though it was in 1977 that I was asked to say what happens 'when psychotics come in and *ruin your groups*'. There is still strong opposition to the idea that, *with optimal selection*, a psychotic can enhance and intensify group life. (See Cox, 1977b).

† A psychotic who had been silent for weeks responded to an invitation to 'do a mime' with more alacrity than any other member of the group. There was one condition. I had to do one first. I 'became' a teapot!

Another patient found that walking silently back to the ward, arm-in-arm with a nurse, 'said' more about security and warmth than any words could.

'Starving, besieging, defences, nourishment' have many overtones of attempts to engage with the schizophrenic in therapy. *Without appropriate medication for the patient the therapist may not even be allowed 'within range'.*

The borderline patient is also the one most likely to highlight deficiencies in the therapist's personal training. Many psychoanalysts have inadequate experience of working with psychotic patients, and it is possible to have full psychoanalytic training without working on a ward in a psychiatric hospital. Alternatively, the psychiatrist who has spent nearly all his professional life with chronic psychotics may have inadequate experience in dealing with problems posed by the transference relationship in intensive psychotherapy. The heart of the matter is that the clinical presentations of the borderline patient are legion. He may present as a suitable patient for out-patient psychotherapy, though he may enter a floridly psychotic phase during the course of ensuing treatment. Unless the therapist is experienced in dealing with psychotics, he may over-respond and might, for example, admit the patient to hospital when in fact the most appropriate treatment might be more frequent therapeutic sessions which would hold the patient within a relationship. Every therapist will have areas in his own professional experience which are weak compared with others, but unless the therapist has first-hand experience of working with transference in 'traditional' psychotherapy, and also experience of working with florid psychotics in an in-patient situation, he is likely to be 'thrown' and therefore to over-react to a borderline patient who does not fit neatly into either camp.

I suggest that the borderline patient poses the greatest test of adequate reality-testing on the therapist's part. Greater than that of, say, a phobic neurotic patient, who is negotiating an intense transference relationship with the therapist, or, on the other hand, a psychotic whose delusional system includes the therapist who 'controls' him through the street lights. The borderline patient tests the therapist's understanding to the limits, because of the rapidly fluctuating defensive pattern evident in his interpersonal relationships. Such patients have a passive–aggressive personality organisation, so that at one moment they are importunate, pleading and passive, and yet, often with mercurial speed, they can change to exhibiting aggressively threatening behaviour with the attendant risks of acting-out. Hock and Polatin (1949) worked with pseudo neurotic schizophrenics and described their mobility of defensive patterning.

There is no more exacting therapeutic task than that of conducting group psychotherapy with borderline patients. Many offender-patients with histories involving serious crimes of violence fall into this category, and it is not uncommon to find that the offence is committed during a psychotic phase. Tuovinen (1973) has written a seminal monograph *Crime as an Attempt at Intrapsychic Adaptation* which enlarges upon these issues. During the official psychiatric interview some days after the offence, there may be no evidence of such psychosis, and yet during subsequent treatment in a hospital such as Broadmoor, further psychotic phases help to establish the intermittent or cyclical pattern. Sometimes these phases in which defence organisation changes rapidly can be monitored and perhaps fully understood for the first time, while the patient is in a therapeutic group. The particular challenge to the therapist is that the defence pattern changes so rapidly. Though much anger may appear to be confined to a transference relationship, there is factual evidence in such patients that they have literally assaulted another person, perhaps with fatal consequences, and there is no cast-iron rule why this should not occur again.

Each reader will have his own personal battlefield where he feels most exposed and vulnerable because of the relative poverty of his training, but structuring the therapeutic process should facilitate his own compromise with chaos. Nelson (1968) refers to the

> uncovering of psychotic processes or the development of psychotic ideation during the course of classical analysis of seemingly neurotic patients. It is therefore essential that the psychotherapist be familiar with the overt and covert signs of psychosis through direct experience with institutionalised patients and through the writings of clinicians prominent in this area. He will also wish to develop techniques for maintaining an atmosphere of treatment which facilitates the study of patients' patterns of defense and resistance without inducing unmanageable regression in those who harbor significant elements of psychotic ideation beneath outwardly rational behavior.

It is my hope that the maintenance of such an 'atmosphere of treatment'* may be helped by this discussion of borderline states, which are of compelling interest to the therapist. He may seem to go through the

---

* When a borderline patient has developed sufficient corporate awareness to say 'If I broke a window, I thought I was letting the group down,' an 'atmosphere of treatment' is no misplaced description.

entire range of emotional responses with such patients, with the solitary exception of boredom! The offender-patient brings forcefully home to the therapist the importance of trying to understand both the inner and the outer world of his patient. If he concentrates on one to the exclusion of the other, he is likely to do a disservice not only to his patient but to the wider community. Sometimes the chaos of disturbed social interactions can be seen to preoccupy the attention of the patient, because it distracts his attention from the chaos within him. Bernheim (see Cox, 1978) develops the theme of the Offence as a Defence.

During the early stages of his life in the group the offender-patient may hide beneath the label of formal mental illness...'a psychiatrist said I was a paranoid schizophrenic'...'I was told I was a manic-depressive psychotic'. It is one of the rare moments in psychotherapy when the patient begins to resent not the formal diagnosis as such, but his use of it as a shield against the feelings of having stabbed, raped or poisoned. This progression is in keeping with the hypothesis that progressive disclosure of hitherto ego-alien material is facilitated during the course of psychotherapy. At the beginning of therapy the patient is glad to have his own defences reinforced by the defence provided by the label of mental illness. However, during the affective flow and sequential progression towards deeper disclosure, which inevitably occurs during psychotherapy (though it occurs with intensified momentum in a group setting), there is a subtle shift from the statement 'I did it...but I was mentally ill' to the acknowledgement of responsibility 'I did it though I was said to be mentally ill at the time', leading ultimately to the sombre existential statement 'I did it...whether I was mentally ill or not!'...'I did it'. Development of retrospective responsibility is intimately linked with development of insight and the capacity to sustain emotional disclosure. From a technical point of view, this frequently runs parallel to the gradual demisting of focal amnesia for the traumatic episode when 'it' was done.

Barker and Mason (1969) describe drug-induced 'Defence-disrupting therapy' which was requested by their patients. I prefer to use the defence disruption developing in conventional dynamic psychotherapy, when the patient is able to 'take' it. 'You are only in the hot-seat when you put yourself there.'

This specialised field of psychotherapy underlines the crucial significance of structuring the therapeutic process in the therapist's compromise with chaos. I have discussed this elsewhere. (Cox, 1974, 1976, 1977; Macphail and Cox, 1975).

Within the security of a custodial setting, an offender-patient said: 'I'm shielded, in here.' The defence of a 'secure setting' allowed his personal dynamic defences to be slowly and safely relinquished. Changed defences and an opening of latent capacities followed his deepening awareness of corporate life and this was commensurate with enhanced self-esteem.

In the opening pages it was suggested that the student can begin to learn how to respond to disclosures from psychotic patients, in such a way that they feel sufficiently safe to entrust the nurse with further parts of themselves. The example given was that of the patient who said 'I'm blind because I see too much, so I study by a dark lamp' to which the nurse responded by saying 'has it always been as dark as this?' The patient was then safely able to talk of other kinds of darkness which perturbed him.

However, skills of relating successfully to all psychotic patients require more than a lifetime of professional experience. Such therapy makes particular demands upon the therapist who has to be free enough to allow himself to 'split' to the extent of being able to give a tangential comment or commentary upon a process in which he, himself, is involved. It requires participation and concurrent appraisal and reflection, as though the therapist was not a participant. Sometimes the affective flow of the psychotic resembles that of a boat moored in an estuary. There is a surging thrust of energy in one direction, which is later reversed to that of equally intense movement in the opposite direction. The therapist may then be called upon to engage with the patient at a silent point of almost imperceptible movement, which, with hindsight, is seen to be the moment when feelings of great dynamic force are changing direction. Primitive elemental forces, such as tides and tempests, are apposite symbols to carry psychotic turbulence.

It seems appropriate that King Lear should close this chapter because he opened it. He was in no doubt that the chaos without, distracted him from the chaos within:

> This tempest will not give me leave to ponder
> On things would hurt me more....   (*King Lear*, III. iv. 24)

Terminating the Therapeutic Process

I want to get the time right ... I can have too much of this.

(Anon., 1977)

Too long is more than enough

(Anon., 1973)

Unless the psychotherapeutic relationship has a predetermined duration, the adequate negotiation of the ending of 'open-ended' psychotherapy demands finesse in the appropriate structuring of time, depth
and mutuality. 'Ripeness is all.' But for many patients in whom separation
anxiety is a prominent feature, the prospect of the termination of formal,
sustained therapeutic sessions is menacing.* However, when rightly
judged, there can be a sense of completion and the experience that work,
often extremely exhausting work, has been done. This experience is shared
by both therapist and patient who have been working on a joint project
(indeed, 'project-ion' will almost certainly have occurred at some stage
during the vicissitudes of transference and countertransference).

It is probably no accident, though it was not originally intended, that
the quotation at the head of Chapter 1 was from *The Sense of an Ending*
(Kermode, 1966) and that the last pages of the book discuss the implications of structuring time, depth and mutuality to achieve the sense of an
ending. Tolstoy has caught the atmosphere that sometimes surrounds
termination of psychotherapy. It is not the dreaded anticipated end, but
it is rather a state of mellow completion when separation anxiety has
been finally overcome, so that the experience is more that of 'The End
of Ending', rather than 'The End'.

I live because I've ceased to die.

(St. John of the Cross)

* N.B. Separation anxiety may be the core pathology, but *all* patients in psychotherapy find separation a crucial concern. Transference will intensify the desire for, or
the dread of, separation. Transference resolution enables separation to be safely
negotiated.

274

What we think is going to be an end, isn't when
it comes. It's just development.

(Anon., 1975)

'It is all over!' said someone near him.
He caught the words and repeated them in his soul.
'Death is over,' he said to himself.
'It is no more.'

(from *The Death of Ivan Ilyich*, Tolstoy)

Relinquishment occurs as autonomy grows. One of the most rewarding moments at sea is when the auxiliary engine, however necessary it
was for earlier progress to be made, is relinquished. Slow but 'autonomous' movement begins as the sails fill; though this depends upon a facilitating environment. If this fails, the engine may need to be started again.

It is sometimes implied that prolonged, intensive psychotherapy or
formal psychoanalysis can so reconstruct the personality that further
'therapy' will never be needed. In some ways, this would be a caricature
of the fully integrated personality. He would be a strange, anomalous,
almost 'affectless character', if he was guaranteed to be able to withstand
the 'thousand natural shocks that flesh is heir to' (*Hamlet*, III. i. 62). To
be immune and impervious to bereavement or other emotional losses,
never to run the risk of being rejected or anxious about dwindling
emotional and physical resources, seem to describe a person who is less
than human. One of the prime aims of psychotherapy is to put a patient
'in touch with his feelings'. The vulnerability implicit in the need to love
and, its corollary, the sense of diminishment at the loss of love, means
that there will always be a possibility of an inner experience of chaos,
with which a man must come to terms. If, by a devious route, a patient
has somehow reached the stage where there is no risk of needing to
Compromise with Chaos, therapy has gone 'too far'. I hope psychotherapy
will never enable a patient to get 'beyond' the need of loving relationships with individuals and the ability to find corporate solidarity enriching. '...when I love thee not, chaos is come again' (*Othello*, III. iii. 91)
[ignoring the context of the original quotation] is a positive statement of
an affective attribute, rather than a 'symptom' which needs 'treatment'.
It is how a man copes with the chaos of lost love, rather than the
experience *per se*, which is the overriding issue.

When the intensity of a transference relationship has been safely negotiated, it is possible for the following essential human exchange to take place, without 'reading between the lines':

'It's good to see you.'
'And its good to see you.'

Berberova (1969) lucidly describes the existential relaxed acceptance of life to which psychotherapy may ultimately lead; if anything more than symptom reduction is attempted. To achieve a 'history of receiving and being received' and an ability to be thankful, in contrast to an aloof autonomy, has the ring of Buber about it. However, this goal may require rigorous, painful, prolonged, personal self-scrutiny which psychic determinism calls for, as a counterpoint to existential preoccupation with 'encounter' here-and-now. Both approaches may be useless if medication, admission to hospital, surgery, etc., are withheld when they are indicated.

The Italics Are Mine (Berberova) as a description of 'being in touch with myself... this is my experience... these are my words' cannot be bettered.

In this last birth I will live in *expectation of the unknown*, because life for me has no more unlived sides, everything has been lived through, save ONE thing. This unknown today lies in a sphere still closed, but it is not extrinsic to me, it is a part of myself and of my whole existence. *It always was*. And thus I will get ready for that last thing to which I long ago gave my whole consent, and which is not frightening, simply because it is unavoidable. [Italics in original.]

Closure

We have considered ways in which the therapist structures the therapeutic process in terms of time, depth and mutuality, so that he may maximise the therapeutic potential of the space he shares with his patients. The therapist's response to patients both individually, and as a group, led us to consider the nature of disclosures. Reading the wide range of third-level disclosures in 'The Patient Speaks' we probably became aware that we were reading about ourselves! This should not be surprising, because third-level disclosures get beneath the veneer of social class, custom and superficial manifestations of behaviour to the core experiences of life which relate to being, loving, hating, sharing and separating.

'The weakness I have in myself is what is in you ... it's loneliness* and desertion'.
(Anon., 1976)

This book has attempted to provide a conceptual framework which can ease the therapist's difficult task of growing in two directions at once. Increased rigour and precision in discerning dynamics, together with a simultaneous personal growth and a willingness to 'receive' the presence of his patient, can be fostered by structuring the therapeutic process. If this has occurred to even the slightest degree, this closure may optimistically be termed therapeutic.

Because of the chaos, I am coming together.
(Anon., but widespread)

---

* A psychotic discloser (out of touch with reality?) yet exactly sensing the 'reality' of universal experience. See Hobson. R. F. (1974) "Loneliness". *Journal of Analytical Psychology*. **19**. (1), 71–89.

Postscript

Compromise with Chaos opened with the statement 'We can't just die...
we've got to have history', an experience echoed in another disclosure
'I'm not me without my past'. This postscript draws attention to the fact
that though the therapist 'takes' and 'receives' his patient's history in the
early phases of psychotherapy, he gradually becomes part of the unfolding
history he is 'taking and receiving'. This process applies in any clinical
encounter but the special nature of the transference relationship, with its
particularly vivid and pervasive cognitive–affective intensity, means that
the therapist is invested with constantly changing sequential attributes,
so that he is incorporated into the patient's history in an almost kaleidoscopic way. When psychotherapy ends and no lingering vestiges of
transference remain, then both patient and therapist are aware that they
have each become part of the other's history, in a substantial and literal
sense.

Psychotherapy can provide the patient with a corrective emotional
experience and a second chance to face previously daunting experience,
so that he can respond differently to 'significant others' who hitherto
were frightening to the point of chaos, or caused a specific symptom
such as impotence. This means that the therapeutic process can go some
way towards facing the dilemma voiced by T. S. Eliot: 'We had the
experience but missed the meaning.' The shared life of therapeutic space
may enable the 'missed meaning' to be realigned and integrated with 'the
experience'. This implies that the statement 'I've never been me' or 'I'm
not me yet' can be filled with meaning; though the meaning may be the
painful reminder of the state of 'predicamentness' from which no one is
immune. Clinebell (1966) writes:

> There are no psychological or psychotherapeutic answers to existential anxiety. It
> is 'existential' in that it is inherent in man's very existence as a self-aware creature.
> But *its impact on the individual can be either creative or destructive, depending on how
> it is handled.* [Clinebell's italics.]

It is the acceptance of the ubiquity of ontological insecurity, as distinct from neurotic maladaptive insecurity, which may be the *ne plus ultra* of psychotherapy. The confirming, validating experience of individual psychotherapy, or the consensual validation of experience in a group, ensure that the patient not only has a clinical history to 'give', but is in fact 'part of history'.

This is a painful and sometimes risky business for both patient and therapist. The following vignette has caught the inevitability of both components of that suffering-maturation process which the enhanced vulnerability within therapeutic space brings:

> 'Whenever I come to the group there's always the bet of bitterness.'
> 'Did you say "the bit of betterness"?'

Creative chaos

In the long run everyone has to come to terms with the chaos within him. Chaos does not cease to exist because its presence is denied. Passive tolerance of chaos is not enough. Once the chaos within has been fully integrated, creative energy is released. As each man makes his own personal compromise with chaos, so it is transmuted into creative chaos, the evidence for which is found in more productive living. This may take the form of greater energy to live, laugh, or love. It may take the form of more intense overt activity or in a greater capacity to tolerate solitude, stillness and silence.

> 'Gather up the fragments that remain, that nothing be lost.'

This injunction expresses a deep, archaic and universal human need. It is precisely because of its ubiquity that it is frequently implied, or paraphrased explicitly, in therapeutic space. The patient indicates that he will only trust the therapist if there is an assurance that all the broken, buried, disowned, incomplete fragments of himself can be gathered up, that nothing be lost; because, without them, he would not be complete. The individual says 'I'm not together...I'm shattered... I'm fragmented ... I've gone to bits ... I'm all over the place.'

Such statements of fragmentation are not the prerogative of the individual. Fragmentation also has corporate significance. This is shown by members of a therapeutic group who experience that the group-as-a-whole demands that the fragments of the group-as-a-whole may be gathered up so that nothing be lost ... 'We are not together ... we are shattered ... we are fragmented ... we have gone to bits ... we are all over the place.' 'Gather up the fragments that nothing be lost' has perennial relevance to both individual and corporate experience and it does not need to be localised to that particular corporate setting in which it was said (John, 6. 12). (See footnote, page 103).

Compromise with the chaos within is a universal human task. The more precise task of the therapist is to try to liberate those who are restricted by an overwhelming sense of inner chaos; and to introduce a tolerable level of chaos to those who are impoverished by having no sense of chaos which demands such a compromise. Too little chaos denies full humanness. Too much chaos likewise precludes it. It is for this reason that the therapist's intention is to so structure the therapeutic process that the patient is edged towards those parts of himself which may border upon chaos. Only then can archaic, primal energy be used optimally, and malignant chaos be transformed into creative chaos. Williams (1977)* has so accurately caught the essence of the paradox of psychotherapy in *Becoming What I Am*. This must be the experience of both patient and therapist alike. Both are in the process of becoming and, though they may have had widely differing life experience, they each know that neither has yet experienced personal physical death. The resources available to them then will depend upon their capacity to become what they are. It is only when death and separation is an existential *Now-Event* that it can be engaged with: prior to this it can only endorse anticipatory activity.

Sometimes the patient needs to be shielded from his own chaos and on these occasions supportive psychotherapy is indicated. Sometimes the patient needs to be introduced to the chaotic expanses of his inner world so that ventilatory, 'uncovering' psychotherapy is indicated. The therapist will only be sufficiently free from himself, so that he has both executive energy and affective freedom to engage with his patient in therapeutic space, if he, too, has made his own personal compromise with chaos through a suffering-maturation process.

Winnicott (1974),† introducing his paper entitled *Fear of Breakdown*, wrote: 'Naturally, if what I say has truth in it, this will already have been dealt with by the world's poets, but the flashes of insight that

* Williams. H. A. (1977) *Becoming What I Am* Darton. Longman & Todd. London.
† International Review of Psycho-Analysis (1974) **1**, 103-7.

come in poetry cannot absolve us from our painful task of getting step by step away from ignorance towards our goal.' I hope the concepts conveyed in this book, particularly the dimensions of structuring the therapeutic process and the levels of disclosure, facilitate this 'painful task'. In many ways it has already been 'dealt with by the world's poets' yet it still demands a 'step by step' progression within therapeutic space.

> Not in the outward reach
> Where speech encounters speech
> Lies understanding. When the mind is stilled.
> Beneath the ordered clear
> Sharp thoughts there may appear
> Levels with unfamiliar chaos filled.

(from a poem hitherto unpublished. by kind permission of Sasha Orley)

Suggested Further Reading

This brief bibliography has involved an almost impossible task of selection, and is inevitably limited by my experience and reading. Nevertheless, I hope the reader will discover that the invitational edge of his experience is stimulated, so that he wishes to explore further. I am well aware that some readers will have read all the references and more, whereas for others *Compromise with Chaos* may be breaking new ground. These references have been chosen on the basis that they underline certain cardinal aspects of the therapist's response to the individual and the group.

I. Orientation

Crown, S. (1970) *Essential Principles of Psychiatry*, Pitman Medical and Scientific, London. This is highly recommended to both medical and non-medical readers. It shows how psychoanalysis and psychotherapy are related to each other and, via the wider practice of general psychiatry, to medicine as a whole.

Guntrip, H. (1961) *Personality Structure and Human Interaction: The Developing Synthesis of Psychodynamic Theory*. Hogarth Press, London. An excellent survey. Especially good on 'Theory and Therapy'.

Khan, M. M. R. (1974) *The Privacy of the Self*, Hogarth Press, London. This brings together in one volume many papers on different aspects of psychoanalytic practice and is a stimulating and provocative point of entry into psychoanalytic literature.

May, R. (1958) Contributions of existential psychotherapy, in *Existence: a New Dimension in Psychiatry and Psychology* (May, R., Angel, E. and Ellenberger, H. F., editors), Basic Books, New York. This shows how the existential contribution leads towards a global awareness of the patient's need and indicates a particular therapeutic perspective. See also: Macnab, F. A. (1965) *Estrangement and Relationship: Experience with Schizophrenics*, Tavistock Publications, London. Though primarily about psychotherapy with chronic schizophrenics, it also gives a lucid exposition of existential psychotherapy.

Roth, M. (1969) Seeking common ground in contemporary psychiatry, *Proceedings of the Royal Society of Medicine* 62, 765–72. This was a presidential address to the section of psychiatry, the Royal Society of Medicine. He strongly reminds the 'open-minded psychodynamicist' that he does not have a monopoly of truth (but neither does any single theoretical perspective or therapeutic modality).

Varma, V. (editor) (1974) *Psychotherapy Today*, Constable, London. An excellent survey, particularly for the non-medical reader.

Winnicott, D. W. (1965) *The Maturational Processes and the Facilitating Environment*, Hogarth Press, London. A modern 'classic'. Particularly important for the general clinician, the family doctor and the paediatrician who may, as yet, have relatively little psychoanalytic experience.

282

Although this reading list is relatively short, the various publications listed will open up appropriate areas of interest to the reader. Each has its own bibliography, which will locate more precisely topics of special concern. As there are many references to individual psychotherapy and counselling in the text, I am not suggesting separate bibliographic references, except in specialised 'areas'.

II. Group Psychotherapy

Bion, W. R. (1961) *Experiences in Groups*, Tavistock Publications, London.

Foulkes. S. H. (1964) *Therapeutic Group Analysis*. George Allen & Unwin. London.

Foulkes. S. H. (1975) *Group-Analytic Psychotherapy. Methods and Principles*. Gordon & Breach. London.

Foulkes. S. H. and Anthony. E. J. (1957) *Group Psychotherapy: The Psychoanalytic Approach*, Penguin Books. London.

Kaplan. H. I. and Sadock, B. J. (editors) (1971) *Comprehensive Group Psychotherapy*. Williams & Wilkins, Baltimore.

Kreeger, L. C. (editor) (1975) *The Large Group: Dynamics and Therapy*, Constable, London.

Maré, P. B. de and Kreeger, L. C. (1974) *Introduction to Group Treatments in Psychiatry*. Butterworth Press, London.

Skynner, A. C. R. (1976) *One Flesh: Separate Persons. Principles of Family and Marital Psychotherapy*, Constable, London.

Stock Whitaker, D. and Lieberman, M. A. (1965) *Psychotherapy Through the Group Process*, Tavistock Publications, London.

Thompson, S. and Kahn, J. H. (1970) *The Group Process as a Helping Technique*, Pergamon Press, Oxford.

Walton. H. (editor) (1971) *Small Group Psychotherapy*. Penguin Books. London.

Yalom, I. D. (1970) *The Theory and Practice of Group Psychotherapy*, Basic Books, New York.

III. Probation and After-Care, and Other Social Work

Barr, H. (1966) *A Survey of Group Work in the Probation Service*, Probation Research No. 9, HMSO, London.

Biestek. F. P. (1957) *The Casework Relationship*. Loyola University Press and George Allen & Unwin. London.

Ferard, M. L. and Hunnybun, N. K. (1962) *The Caseworker's Use of Relationships*, Tavistock Publications, London.

Foren, R. and Bailey, R. (1968) *Authority in Social Case-Work*, Pergamon Press, Oxford.

Klockars, C. B., jr. (1972) A theory of probation supervision. *Journal of Criminal Law. Criminology and Police Science* 63 (4) 550-7.

Konopka, G. (1954) *Group Work in the Institution*, Association Press, New York.

Konopka, G. (1963) *Social Group Work: A Helping Process*, Prentice-Hall Inc., New Jersey.

McCullough, M. K. and Ely, P. J. (1968) *Social Work with Groups*, Routledge and Kegan Paul. London. (Probably the most useful book to start with. It briefly surveys the field both in terms of practical experience and underlying dynamic theory.)

Monger, M. (1967) *Case Work in After-Care*, Butterworth Press, London.

Parsloe, P. (1967) *The Work of the Probation and After-Care Officer*, Routledge and Kegan Paul, London.
Salzberger-Wittenberg, I. (1970) *Psycho-Analytic Insight and Relationships. A Kleinian Approach*, Routledge and Kegan Paul, London.

IV. The Teacher and Counselling

Daws, P. P. (1973) Mental health and education: counselling as prophylaxis, *British Journal of Guidance and Counselling* I (2) 2–10.
Daws, P. P. (1975) Common errors in counselling, *The Counsellor* **21**, 3–5.
Fullmer, D. W. and Bernard, H. W. (1972) *The School Counselor-Consultant*, Houghton Mifflin, Boston. (Includes Huckins' (1971) Levels of Discourse.)
Hamblin, D. (1974a) *The Teacher and Counselling*, Blackwell, Oxford. (This book has an extensive bibliography.)
Hamblin, D. (1974b) The counsellor and alienated youth, *British Journal of Guidance and Counselling* **II** (1) 87–95.
Maguire, U. (1975) The school counsellor as a therapist, *British Journal of Guidance and Counselling* **III** (2) 160–71.
Richardson, E. (1967) *Group Study for Teachers*, Routledge and Kegan Paul, London.
Shertzer, B. and Stone, S. C. (1966) *Fundamentals of Guidance*, Houghton Mifflin, Boston. (This discusses problems of adequate notation for the counsellor's cumulative records. It therefore has affinities with *Coding the Therapeutic Process* (Cox, M. 1977a, Pergamon Press, Oxford.)

V. Counselling the Adolescent

Berkovitz, I. H. (editor) (1972) *Adolescents Grow in Groups: Experiences in Adolescent Group Psychotherapy*, Brunner-Mazel Inc., New York.
Coleman, J. C. (1974) *Relationships in Adolescence*, Routledge and Kegan Paul, London.
Meeks, J. E. (1971) *The Fragile Alliance: An Orientation to the Out-patient Psychotherapy of the Adolescent*, Williams & Wilkins, Baltimore.
Meyerson, S. (editor) (1975) *Adolescent: The Crises of Adjustment*, George Allen & Unwin, London.
Shields, R. W. (1962) *A Cure of Delinquents: The Treatment of Maladjustment*, Heinemann, London.

VI. Pastoral Counselling
(See the Constitutional Papers of The Association for Pastoral Care and Counselling for a recent (1976) statement of 'the broad areas of concern'.)

Clinebell, H. J. (jr.) (1966) *Basic Types of Pastoral Counseling*, Abingdon Press, New York.
Hiltner, S. (1949) *Pastoral Counseling*, Abingdon Press, New York. (A classic.)

VII. General Medical Practice and Nursing

The structuring of the therapeutic process is inextricably involved in every clinical encounter where doctors, nurses and patients meet; ranging from the anaesthetic room prior to an operation, to the home visit of the district nurse. It is therefore implicit on almost every page of the present volume. Nevertheless a brief selected reading list follows:

Altschul, A. T. (1972) *Patient–Nurse Interaction*, Churchill Livingstone, Edinburgh.
Altschul, A. T. (1973, 4th edition) *Psychiatric Nursing*, Baillière Tindall, London.
Balint, M. (1957) *The Doctor, His Patient and the Illness*, Pitman Medical, London.
Balint, M. and Balint, E. (1959) *Psychotherapeutic Techniques in Medicine*, Tavistock Publications, London.
Browne, K. and Freeling, P. (1967) *The Doctor–Patient Relationship*, E. & S. Livingstone, London. (Originally published as a series of articles in *The Practitioner*.)
Burr, J. (1970) (2nd edition) *Nursing the Psychiatric Patient*, Baillière Tindall and Cassell, London.
The Future General Practitioner: Learning and Teaching (1972). Published for the Royal College of General Practitioners by the *British Medical Journal*, London.
Hopkins, P. (1972) *Patient-centred Medicine*, Regional Doctor Publications, London.
Nurse, G. (1975) *Counselling and the Nurse*, HM & M Publishers, Aylesbury.
Tallett, E. R. and Walker, K. A. (1972) *Methods of Treatment in Psychiatry* (Nursing in Depth Series), Butterworths, London.

VIII. Sexual Deviation and Offender-therapy

Crown, S. (editor) (1976) *Psychosexual Problems*, Academic Press, London.
Glover, E. (1960) *The Roots of Crime*, Imago Publishing Company, London.
Rosen, I. (editor) (1977, in preparation) *Sexual Deviation*, Oxford University Press, London.
Tuovinen, M. (1973) *Crime as an Attempt at Intrapsychic Adaptation*, University of Oulu, Finland.

Other specific topics referred to in the main text, such as the place of structuring in the psychotherapy of the psychoses, will be found in the References.

Shakespeare should be added to every bibliography concerned with each man's 'compromise with chaos'; no matter whether it is the chaos of his inner world or the chaos of his outer world which confronts him.

References

(NB—This bibliography refers only to references in the text. Some books included in Suggested Further Reading are therefore not listed here)

Arieti, S. (1976) The psychotherapeutic approach to schizophrenia, in *Schizophrenia Today* (Kemali, D., Bartholini, G., Richter, D., editors), Pergamon Press, Oxford.
Arnheim, R. (1970) *Visual Thinking*, Faber & Faber, London.
Asher, R. (1972) *Talking Sense*, Pitman Medical, London.
Baker, J. Austin (1976) Personal communication, London.
Balint, M. (1957) *The Doctor, His Patient and the Illness*, Pitman Medical, London.
Balint, M. (1959) Regression in the analytic situation, in *Thrills and Regression*, International Universities Press, New York.
Balint, M. (1968) *The Basic Fault: Therapeutic Aspects of Regression*, Tavistock Publications, London.
Balint, M. and Balint, E. (1959) *Psychotherapeutic Techniques in Medicine*, Tavistock Publications, London.
Bally, G. (1956) Translated and included in Siirala, M. (1963) *Gedanken zur Psychoanolytisch Orientierten Begegnuag mit Geisteskranken*, Psyche Heft 7/x, Ernst Klett, Stuttgart.
Barfield, O. (1928) *Poetic Diction: A Study in Meaning*, Faber & Gwyer, London.
Barker, E. T. and Mason, M. H. (1968) Buber behind bars, *Canadian Psychiatric Association Journal* 13, 61–72.
Barker, E. T., Mason, M. H. and Wilson, J. (1969) Defence-disrupting therapy, *Canadian Psychiatric Association Journal* 14, 355–9.
Becker, E. (1962) *The Birth and Death of Meaning*, The Free Press, New York.
Becker, E. (1973) *The Denial of Death*, The Free Press, New York.
Beerbohm, M. (1967) *The Happy Hypocrite: A Fairy-tale for Tired Men*, John Lane, New York and London.
Berberova, N. (1969) *The Italics are Mine* (translated by Radley, P.), Longmans, London.
Berger, J. and Mohr, J. (1967) *A Fortunate Man: The Story of a Country Doctor*, Allen Lane, Penguin Press, London.
Bernard, H. W. and Huckins, W. C. (1971) *Dynamics of Personal Adjustment*, Holbrook Press, Boston.
Bettelheim, B. (1967) *The Empty Fortress*, Free Press, New York.
Biestek, F. P. (1957) *The Casework Relationship*, Loyola University Press and George Allen & Unwin, London.
Binswanger, L. (1957) *Sigmund Freud: Reminiscences of a Friendship*, Grune & Stratton, New York.
Binswanger, L. (1963) In *Being-in-the-World*, selected papers of Ludwig Binswanger, translated and with a critical introduction to his existential psychoanalysis by Needleman, J., Basic Books, New York.

286

References 287

Bion, W. R. (1961) *Experiences in Groups*, Tavistock Publications, London.
Blum, L. H. (1972) *Reading Between the Lines: Doctor–Patient Communication*, International Universities Press, New York.
Boros, L. (1965) *The Moment of Truth: Mysterium Mortis*, Burns & Oates, London.
Bowlby, J. (1969) *Attachment and Loss: I, Attachment*, Hogarth Press, London.
British Medical Journal (1976a) Student counselling (leading article) **1**, 605
British Medical Journal (1976b) Today's dreams (leading article) **2**, 1523.
Buber, M. (1923) *I and Thou*, T. & T. Clark, Edinburgh (first British edition, 1937, T. & T. Clark, translated by Smith, R. G.).
Buber, M. (1947) *Between Man and Man*, Kegan Paul, Trench, Trübner & Co., London (Fontana Library, 1961, Collins, London, translated by Smith, R. G.).
Buber, M. (1957) Elements of the interhuman, *Psychiatry* **20**, 105–13.
Clark, D. H. (1964) *Administrative Therapy: The Role of the Doctor in the Therapeutic Community*, Tavistock Publications, London.
Clark-Kennedy, A. E. (1954) *Patients as People*, Faber & Faber, London.
Clark-Kennedy, A. E. and Bartley, C. W. (1960) *Clinical Medicine: The Modern Approach*, Pitman Medical, London.
Clinebell, H. J. (jr.) (1966) *Basic Types of Pastoral Counseling*, Abingdon Press, New York.
Coleman, J. C. (1969) The levels hypothesis: a re-examination and reorientation, *Journal of Projective Techniques and Personality Assessment* **33** (2) 118–22.
Coleman, J. C. (1970) The study of adolescent development using a sentence-completion method, *British Journal of Educational Psychology* **40** (1) 27–34.
Coleman, J. C. (1974) *Relationships in Adolescence*, Routledge and Kegan Paul, London.
Coleridge, S. T. (1884) *Lectures and Notes on Shakespeare and Other English Poets* (collected by Ashe, T.), George Bell & Sons, London.
Conrad, J. (1902) *Heart of Darkness*.
Conrad, J. (1903) *Typhoon*.
Cooke, D. (1959) *The Language of Music*, Oxford University Press, London.
Cooley, C. H. (1922) *Human Nature and the Social Order*, Charles Scribner's Sons, New York.
Council of Europe (1974) *Group and Community Work with the Offenders*, European Committee on Crime Problems, Council of Europe, Strasbourg.
Cox, M. (1973a) The group therapy interaction chronogram, *British Journal of Social Work* **3** (2) 243–56.
Cox, M. (1973b) Group psychotherapy as a redefining process, *International Journal of Group Psychotherapy* **XXIII** (4) 465–73.
Cox, M. (1974) The psychotherapist's anxiety: liability or asset?, *British Journal of Criminology* **14** (1) 1–17.
Cox, M. (1976) Group psychotherapy in a secure setting, *Proceedings of the Royal Society of Medicine* **69**, 215–20.
Cox, M. (1977 in preparation) Dynamic psychotherapy with sex-offenders, in *Sexual Deviation* (Rosen, I., editor), Oxford University Press, London.
Cox, M. (1978) *Coding the Therapeutic Process: Emblems of Encounter*, Pergamon Press, Oxford.
Crown, S. (editor) (1976) *Psychosexual Problems*, Academic Press, London.
Deri, S. (1968) Interpretation and language, in *Use of Interpretation in Treatment: Technique and Art* (Hammer, E. F., editor), Grune & Stratton, New York.
Dewald, P. A. (1969) *Psychotherapy: A Dynamic Approach*, 2nd edn., Blackwell Scientific Publications, Oxford.

Dickens, C. (1848) *Dombey and Son.*

Dyson, A. E. (1972) *Between Two Worlds: Aspects of Literary Form,* The Macmillan St Martin's Press, London.

Erikson, E. H. (1950) *Childhood and Society,* W. W. Norton, New York (revised edition (1964), Hogarth Press, London).

Erikson, E. H. (1959) *Young Man Luther,* Faber & Faber, London.

Farber, L. H. (1956) Martin Buber and psychiatry, *Psychiatry* **19,** 109–20.

Faulkner, W. (1930) *As I Lay Dying,* first published 1963, Penguin Books, London.

Federn, P. (1952) *Ego Psychology and the Psychoses,* Basic Books, New York.

Fisher, S. (1956) Plausibility and depth of interpretation, *Journal of Consulting Psychology* **20** (4) 249–56.

Foren, R. and Bailey, R. (1968) *Authority in Social Case-Work;* Pergamon Press, Oxford.

Foulkes, S. H. (1948) *Introduction to Group-Analytic Psychotherapy,* Heinemann, London.

Foulkes, S. H. (1964) *Therapeutic Group Analysis,* George Allen & Unwin, London.

Foulkes, S. H. (1975) *Group-Analytic Psychotherapy: Method and Principles,* Gordon & Breach, London.

Foulkes, S. H. and Anthony, E. J. (1957) *Group Psychotherapy: The Psychoanalytic Approach,* Penguin Books, London.

Fox, R. C. (1957) Training for uncertainty, in *The Student Physician* (Merton, R. K. *et al.,* editors), Oxford University Press, London (reprinted in *A Sociology of Medical Practice* (Cox, C. and Mead, A., editors), Collier–Macmillan, London, 1975).

Frank, J. D. (1961) *Persuasion and Healing: A Comparative Study of Psychotherapy,* Oxford University Press, London.

Freud, S. (1910) *The Future Prospects of Psycho-Analytic Therapy,* standard edition, 11, Hogarth Press, London.

Freud, S. (1927) *The Future of an Illusion,* standard edition, 21, Hogarth Press, London.

Freud, S. (1941) A disturbance of memory on the Acropolis, *International Journal of Psycho-Analysis* **22** (2) 93–101.

Frick, M. (1972) *All the Days of his Dying,* Allison & Busby, London.

Fromm-Reichmann, F. (1953) *Principles of Intensive Psychotherapy,* George Allen & Unwin, London.

Goffman, E. (1961) On the characteristics of total institutions: the inmate world in *The Prison: Studies in Institutional Organisation and Change* (Cressey, D. R., editor), Holt, Rinehart & Winston, London.

Goffman, E. (1963) *Stigma: Notes on the Management of Spoiled Identity,* Prentice-Hall, New Jersey.

Goffman, E. (1974) *Frame Analysis: An Essay on the Organisation of Experience,* Harvard University Press, Cambridge, Mass.

Gombrich, E. H. (1959) *Art and Illusion,* Phaidon Press, London.

Greenson, R. R. (1965) The working alliance and the transference neurosis, *Psychoanalytic Quarterly* **34,** 155–81.

Grinker, R. R. (1968) *The Borderline Syndrome: Behavioral Study of Ego Function,* Basic Books, New York.

Hamblin, D. (1974) *The Teacher and Counselling,* Blackwell, Oxford.

Harrison, R. (1974) *On What There Must Be,* Clarendon Press, Oxford.

Heaseman, K. (1969) *An Introduction to Pastoral Counselling,* Constable, London.

Heelan, P. (1971) The logic of framework transpositions, *International Philosophy*

Quarterly Fall issue 1971. Reprinted in *Language, Truth and Meaning* (1973) (McShane, P., editor). Gill and Macmillan, Dublin.

Hoch, P. and Polatin, P. (1949) Pseudoneurotic forms of schizophrenia, *Psychiatry Quarterly*, **23**, 248–76.

Hollis, F. (1964) *Casework: A Psychosocial Therapy.* Random House, New York.

Jacobs, R. L. (1958) *Understanding Harmony*, Oxford University Press, London.

Jones, M. (1968) *Social Psychiatry in Practice: The Idea of the Therapeutic Community*, Penguin Books, London.

Jourard, S. M. (1971) *The Transparent Self*, D. Vannestrand, New York.

Jung, C. G. (1954) *Psychology of the Transference. Collected Works*, vol. 16, Routledge and Kegan Paul, London.

Jung, C. G. (1965) *Memories. Dreams and Reflections.* Vintage Press, New York.

Jung, C. G. and Kerenyi, C. (1951) *Introduction to a Science of Mythology* (translated by Hull, R. F. C.), Routledge and Kegan Paul, London.

Kahn, J. H. (1972) Communication with children and parents, *British Medical Journal* **3**, 406–8.

Kelman, H. (1960) 'Kairos' and the therapeutic process, *Journal of Existential Psychiatry* **1** (2) 233–69.

Kermode, F. (1966) *The Sense of an Ending: Studies in the Theory of Fiction*, Oxford University Press, London.

Khan, M. M. R. (1974a) The finding and becoming of self, *The Privacy of the Self*, Hogarth Press, London.

Khan, M. M. R. (1974b) The role of illusion in the analytic space and process, *The Privacy of the Self*, Hogarth Press, London.

Kierkegaard, S. (1844) *The Concept of Dread* (translated by Lowrie, W., 1957), University Press, Princeton.

Kierkegaard, S. (1849) *The Sickness Unto Death* (translated by Lowrie, W., 1941), University Press, Princeton.

Klockars, C. B., jr. (1972) A theory of probation supervision, *Journal of Criminal Law, Criminology and Police Science* **63** (4) 550–7.

Kluckhorn, C. and Murray, H. A. (1949) Personality formation: the determinants, *Personality in Nature, Society and Culture*, Alfred A. Knopf, New York.

Kohut, H. (1959) Introspection, empathy and psychoanalysis, *Journal of American Psychoanalytic Association* **7**, 459–83.

Kreeger, L. C. (editor) (1975) *The Large Group: Dynamics and Therapy.* Constable, London.

Kris, E. (1952) *Psychoanalytic Explorations in Art*, International Universities Press, New York.

Laing, R. D. (1959) *The Divided Self*, Tavistock Publication, London.

Laing, R. D. (1976) *The Facts of Life*, Pantheon Books, New York.

Leibovich, M. (1975) An aspect of the psychotherapy of borderline personalities, *Psychotherapy and Psychosomatics* **25**, 53–7.

Lewis, C. S. (1955) *Surprised by Joy*, Geoffrey Bles, London.

Lewis, H. D. (1969) *The Elusive Mind*, First Series of Gifford Lectures 1966–8, George Allen & Unwin, London.

Macnab, F. A. (1965) *Estrangement and Relationship: Experience with Schizophrenics.* Tavistock Publications, London.

Macphail, D. S. and Cox, M. (1975) Dynamic psychotherapy with dangerous patients, *Psychotherapy and Psychosomatics* **25**, 13–19.

Maguire, U. (1975) The school counsellor as a therapist, *British Journal of Guidance and Counselling* **3**, (2) 160–71.

May, R. (1958) Contributions of existential psychotherapy, in *Existence: A New Dimension in Psychiatry and Psychology* (May, R., Angel, E. and Ellenberger, H. F., editors), Basic Books, New York.

Mayer, J. E. and Timms. N. (1970) *The Client Speaks*, Routledge and Kegan Paul, London.

Meeks. J. E. (1971) *The Fragile Alliance: An Orientation to the Out-patient Psychotherapy of the Adolescent*, Williams & Wilkins, Baltimore.

Merklin, L. and Little, R. B. (1967) Beginning psychiatry training syndrome, *American Journal of Psychiatry* **124** (2) 97–101.

Minuchin, S. (1974) *Families and Family Therapy*, Tavistock Publications, London.

Moltmann, J. (1967) *Theology of Hope*, SCM Press, London.

Moltmann, J. (1974) *The Crucified God*, SCM Press, London.

Muslin, H. L. and Schlessinger, N. (1971) Toward the teaching and learning of empathy, *Bulletin of the Menninger Clinic* **35** (4) 262–71.

Needleman. J. (1963) see Binswanger, L. (1963).

Nelson. M. C. (1968) Narcissistic and borderline states, in *Roles and Paradigms in Psychotherapy* (Nelson. M. C., ed.), Grune & Stratton. New York.

Parsloe. P. (1967) *The Work of the Probation and After-Care Officer*, Routledge and Kegan Paul, London.

Pascal. B. (1946) *Pensées of Pascal*, Peter Pauper Press. New York.

Pines, M. (1975a) *British Journal of Psychiatry* **127**, 302, reviewing *The Borderline Patient*, Wolberg, A. (*vide infra*).

Pines, M. (1975b) Borderline personality organisation, *Psychotherapy and Psychosomatics* **25**, 58–62.

Pitt, V. (1976) *Theology*, LXXIX, No. 667, 61, reviewing *Flesh of My Flesh*, Kroll, U. (1975) Dartman, Longman & Todd, London.

Raine, K. (1956) *Collected Poems*, Hamish Hamilton, London.

Ramsey, I. T. (1957) *Religious Language*, SCM Press, London.

Ramsey, I. T. (1964) *Models and Mystery*, Oxford University Press, London.

Ramsey, I. T. (1965) *Christian Discourse*, Riddell Memorial Lectures No. 35, Oxford University Press, London.

Rapoport, R. N. (1968) *Community as Doctor*, Tavistock Publications, London.

Raush, H. L., Sperber, Z., Rigler, D., Williams, J., Harway, N. I., Bordin, E. S., Dittmann, A. T. and Hays, W. L. (1956) A dimensional analysis of depth of interpretation, *Journal of Consulting Psychology* **20** (1) 43–8.

Reed. H. (1946) Naming of parts, in *Contemporary Verse* (1950) (Allott, K., editor). Penguin Books, London.

Richter, H. (1975) *The Family as Patient*, Souvenir Press, London.

Rogers, C. R. (1961) *On Becoming a Person: A Therapist's View of Psychotherapy*, Constable, London.

Rose, G. (1964) Creative imagination in terms of ego 'core' and boundaries, *International Journal of Psychoanalysis* **45**, 75–84.

Rosen, I. (1968) The treatment of sexual deviations, in *Proceedings of the Royal Society of Medicine* **61**, 793–9.

Rosen, I. (editor) (1977, in preparation) *Sexual Deviation*, Oxford University Press, London.

Rostand, E. (1953) *Cyrano de Bergerac* (translated by Hooker, B.), Heinemann Educational Books, George Allen & Unwin, London.

Roth, M. (1969) Seeking common ground in contemporary psychiatry, *Proceedings of the Royal Society of Medicine* **62**, 765–72.

Rothenberg, A. (1971) The process of Janusian thinking in creativity. *Archives of General Psychiatry* **24** (3) 195–205.

Rowe, W. W. (1968) *Dostoevsky: Child and Man in His Works*, New York University Press, New York.

Royal College of General Practitioners (1972). *The Future General Practitioner: Learning and Teaching*, British Medical Journal, London.

Rubinstein, D. and Alanen, Y. O. (editors) (1972) *Psychotherapy of Schizophrenia*, Proceedings of the Fourth International Symposium, Turku, Finland, August 1971, Excerpta Medica, Amsterdam.

Rutter, M. (1972) *Maternal Deprivation Reassessed*, Penguin Books, London.

Sandler, J., Dare, C. and Holder, A. (1973) *The Patient and the Analyst: The Basis of the Psychoanalytic Process*, George Allen & Unwin, London.

Sifneos, P. E. (1965) *Ascent from Chaos: A Psychosomatic Case Study*, Harvard University Press, Cambridge, Mass.

Siirala, A. (1964) *The Voice of Illness: A Study in Therapy and Prophecy*, Fortress Press, Philadelphia.

Siirala, M. (1963) Schizophrenia: a human situation, *American Journal of Psychoanalysis* **23** (1) 39–66.

Siirala, M. (1965) On some relations between thought and hope, *Acta Philosophica Fennica* **18**, 203–25.

Siirala, M. (1969) *Medicine in Metamorphosis: Speech, Presence and Integration*, Tavistock Publications, London.

Siirala, M. (1974) Personal communication, Helsinki.

Skynner, A. C. R. (1976) *One Flesh: Separate Persons. Principles of Family and Marital Psychotherapy*, Constable, London.

Small, L. (1971) *The Briefer Psychotherapies*, Brunner-Mazel, New York.

Smith, L. P. (1933) *On Reading Shakespeare*, Constable, London.

Sommer, R. (1969) *Personal Space: The Behavioral Basis of Design*, Prentice-Hall, New Jersey.

Spotnitz. H. (1957) The borderline schizophrenic in group psychotherapy: the importance of individualization *International Journal of Group Psychotherapy* VII. 155–74.

Spotnitz, H. (1969) *Modern Psychoanalysis of the Schizophrenic Patient: Theory of the Technique*, Grune & Stratton, New York.

Steiner, G. (1975) *After Babel: Aspects of Language and Translation*, Oxford University Press, London.

Stern, A. (1938) Borderline group of neuroses *Psychoanalytic Quarterly* **1**, 467–89.

Stieper, D. R. and Wiener, D. N. (1965) *Dimensions of Psychotherapy: An Experimental and Clinical Approach*, Aldine Publishing Co., Chicago.

Strupp, H. H. (1955) Psychotherapeutic technique, professional affiliation and experience level, *Journal of Consulting Psychology* **19**, 97–102.

Sullivan. H. S. (1940) *Conceptions of Modern Psychiatry*, William Alanson White Psychiatric Foundation (first published in Great Britain 1955), Tavistock Publications, London.

Thompson, S. and Kahn, J. H. (1970) *The Group Process as a Helping Technique*, Pergamon Press, Oxford.

Tillich, P. (1953) *The Courage To Be*, Nisbet, Welwyn, Herts.

Tolstoy, L. *Anna Karenina* (translated by Rosemary Edmonds) (1954), Penguin Books, London.

Tolstoy, L. *The Cossacks* and *The Death of Ivan Ilyich*, (translated by Rosemary Edmonds) (1960) Penguin Books, London.

Tournier, P. (1964) *The Meaning of Gifts*, SCM Press, London.

Truax, C. and Carkhuff, R. (1967) *Towards Effective Counseling and Psychotherapy*, Aldine Press, Chicago.

Tuovinen, M. (1973) *Crime as an Attempt at Intrapsychic Adaptation*, University of Oulu, Finland.

Venables, E. (1971) *Counselling*, National Marriage Guidance Council, London.

von Weizsäcker, V. (1956) *Pathosophie*, Vandenhoeck & Ruprecht, Gottingen.

Wallis, J. H. (1973) *Personal Counselling: An Introduction to Relationship Therapy*, George Allen & Unwin, London.

Williams, H. A. (1972) *True Resurrection*, Mitchell Beazley, London.

Williams, H. A. (1976) *Tensions: Necessary Conflicts in Life and Love*, Mitchell Beazley, London.

Winnicott, D. W. (1945) Primitive emotional development, *International Journal of Psycho-Analysis* **26**, 137–43.

Winnicott, D. W. (1960) String: a technique of communication, *Journal of Child Psychology and Psychiatry* **1**, 49–52.

Winnicott, D. W. (1963) Dependence in infant-care, in child-care, and in the psychoanalytic setting. *International Journal of Psycho-Analysis* **44**, 339–44.

Winnicott, D. W. (1965) *The Maturational Processes and the Facilitating Environment*, Hogarth Press, London.

Wolberg, A. R. (1973) *The Borderline Patient*, Intercontinental Medical Book Corporation, New York.

Zilboorg, G. (1967) *Psychoanalysis and Religion*, George Allen & Unwin, London.

Subject Index

Supplementary Literary Index